The Money Maker

By

Dan Sizemore

THE MONEY MAKER
A Network Marketing Adventure

By
Dan Sizemore

Copyright © 2012 by Dan Sizemore

All rights reserved. No part of this book may be reproduced in whole or in part, scanned, photocopied, recorded, distributed in any printed or electronic form, or reproduced in any manner whatsoever, or by any information storage and retrieval system now known or hereafter invented, without express written permission of the publisher, except in the case of brief quotations embodied in critical articles and reviews.

All of the characters in this book are fictitious, and any resemblance to actual persons, living or dead, is purely coincidental.

13-Digit ISBN: 978-0-9855078-0-0 First Edition paperback
Published by Dan Sizemore

www.dansizemore.com
www.themoneymakerbook.com

Acknowledgements

I would like to thank Sallie Bodie and Jane Braden for their words of encouragement during the writing process. You made me feel like I could succeed, and I thank both of you.

I want to thank my writing coach Diane O'Connell for her assistance and critical feedback. You were not afraid to tell it like it is.

I also want to thank Deborrah Hoag for her wonderful editing and support for my work as a writer.

A final thank you goes to my daughter, Rachel Sizemore, for her cover artwork and to Grant McManus for his skills and time in helping to get this book published.

Chapter 1

A loud banging on the front door kept Paul from killing himself. He stood on top of a table ready to put a noose around his neck. Sweat poured from his face as the loud banging continued. Paul was distracted just enough to decide to get rid of whoever was at his front door so he could proceed with his suicide. He hopped off the table to answer his door. He kicked away newspaper clippings strewn on the floor with job listings circled in red. Pizza boxes and empty beer bottles covered the island in the kitchen while months of bills lay unopened on the card table he used as a kitchen table. The banging became louder and louder as Paul approached the front door with a scowl on his face. He peered through his peephole and saw no one. Maybe they left, Paul told himself. He started to turn back when the banging came again like a gunshot.

Paul reached his clammy right hand to the doorknob and swung his front door open forcefully. Standing in front of him was a little black boy, no older than ten with bright eyes, grinning from ear to ear.

"Wanna buy some donuts?" the little boy asked excitedly.

"No, I'm busy," Paul said with a blank stare on his face.

"They're nice and hot," the boy added, hoping for a quick sale.

"Does your daddy know you're doing this?" asked Paul as a bead of sweat dripped from his nose. His graying hair stuck up in the middle like a mohawk, and he wore a ratty t-shirt with dirty gym shorts. He didn't care what he looked like when someone found his dead body. "Only five dollars a dozen," said the little boy as he held the hot donuts up for Paul to smell.

"I told you, I'm busy," said Paul gritting his teeth.

Undeterred, the little boy quickly ran to the house across the street. He saw two other little black boys running down the street with donut boxes in hand.

"Where the hell did they come from?" he thought to himself. Just then he saw a long black Buick creeping slowly down the street in front of his house. The car was stacked to the ceiling with boxes of donuts. "So there's the donut pimp," he mumbled to himself. A snappily dressed gray-haired black man stopped the car directly in front of Paul's house.

Carlos Ackman had tried more business ventures than he could ever recall. He kept his old black Buick running for well over 200,000 miles, but it always had a nice shiny coat of wax. Network marketing was his game, and the last company he was with went belly up along with his dreams. Carlos spotted Paul standing in his doorway and rolled his window down.

"Good mornin', sir. How are ya?" yelled Carlos to Paul. Carlos had no idea he was addressing a man about to kill himself.

Paul stood dead still not knowing if he should say anything. His suicide was not going well at all.

Carlos waited a few more seconds for Paul to respond. He noticed Paul's anguished face and sloppy appearance, but something darker was going on with this man. Carlos instinctively turned off his car and got out. He approached Paul and stuck out his hand.

"Carlos Ackman. How are ya today?" Carlos beamed. He had a natural warm smile and sparkling eyes that attracted people. Paul held out his hand for a weak handshake.

"Good Lord, your hands are cold!" said Carlos. "Are you okay?"

Paul was not about to dump his personal tragedies on a complete stranger. He shared his misfortunes only superficially with a few people.

"I'm fine," said Paul as he looked past Carlos.

"No, you ain't," said Carlos. "Somethin's not right with you. Your body language don't lie. What's your name?"

"Paul Cousins."

"Well, Paul I was just drivin' through the neighborhood with my grandson and two of his friends sellin' donuts. It's a great way to make a little extra money for me and the kids. These kids don't have much, but I'm teachin' 'em to get what you want, you've gotta work and work hard. Parents think discipline is for the army, but I'm telling ya the kids need it. Without it, they're lost!"

Paul felt the passion in Carlos's voice. The kids were still busy running from door to door. One came back with a fist full of cash.

"Need more donuts!" the little boy said excitedly as he handed Carlos his money.

"Go grab some boxes, son," said Carlos. The little boy pulled five boxes from the back of the Buick. He could barely see over the stack as he started running. One box slipped off, and the donuts spilled onto the street. Tears welled up in the boy's eyes as he knelt down to pick up the donuts.

"Don't let those profits go to waste," Carlos yelled. The boy cleaned off each donut as best he could and placed them carefully back in the box.

"That boy is gonna make it big one day. Successful people do what unsuccessful people won't. Discipline is the key, I'm tellin' ya. Now Paul, what seems to be so heavy on your mind?"

He was flabbergasted that one minute he was about to kill himself and the next a complete stranger was asking what was bothering him. He sensed there was a reason he was talking to Carlos. He struggled to speak and was hesitant to reveal his problem, but after a few awkward seconds, he spoke.

"Uh....I've got some major money problems, and I can't find a job."

"I'm sorry. Life does throw us some curve balls, doesn't it? But, no matter how low you think you've fallen, you should never ever give up. If you keep just a little bit of faith tucked someone in the corner of your brain, things can turn around. Man, look at me. The last business I was in tanked, but I decided I was not gonna let it ruin me. This donut sellin' is just one of my five businesses."

"You have five businesses?" asked Paul.

"Sho' do. But my main one's in international marketin'. I get paid from other people's work all over the world."

"What do you mean by international marketing?" asked Paul.

Carlos knew Paul had taken his bait. He always gave people just enough information so that they wanted to know more.

"Look, I don't have time to go over it now. I gotta take care of those kids. Why don't we get together for coffee tomorrow and talk about it a little more?"

"Okay," said Paul surprising himself.

"How about 10 a.m. at the Starbucks in the mall? And stop worryin' about money. I'll help you change how you're thinkin' about it. You're gonna like what I've got to show you."

Carlos handed Paul his business card. It read *Carlos Ackman, International Marketing Consultant* and a cell number. It sounded impressive enough to Paul. The kids finished up their donut sales and Carlos loaded them up. He waved goodbye to Paul from his shiny old Buick.

"See you tomorrow!" yelled Carlos as he pulled away, waving to Paul.

He waved back and stared at the card. International marketing seemed intriguing. He closed the door and walked back into his kitchen. The noose in his den hung from the ceiling waiting for him. Paul looked at the noose for several seconds and then back at Carlos's card. He had a strange feeling that he needed to meet with Carlos. He had always heard that the teacher will appear when the student is ready. He could always kill himself later.

Chapter 2

Paul arrived at Starbucks 15 minutes early for his appointment dressed in his nicest dark suit with a white shirt and red tie. It had been months since he had dressed up, and it actually made him feel better. He chose an empty table near the window, and after a few minutes, Paul spotted him walk in. Carlos smiled and waved at the employees like they were his best friends.

"Good morning, Mr. Ackman," said one of the servers behind the counter. Most customers' heads turned as though someone important had just walked in. Carlos waved back like he owned the place. His dark Armani suit added to his confident posture as he walked over to greet Paul. Carlos looked and walked like success.

"Good morning, Carlos," said Paul as he stood up to shake his hand.

"You certainly clean up well," said Carlos.

"Yeah, I wasn't at my best yesterday."

"Are you feelin' better today?" asked Carlos with the sincerity of a preacher.

"Absolutely. Thank you for your words of encouragement yesterday. You don't know how much it meant to me," said Paul, his voice quivering.

"You're welcome. Everybody needs a little help in their life sometimes. I was just there at the right time, I guess," said Carlos.

"You don't know how great your timing was," said Paul.

"Glad to help. Please sit down."

"I don't know anyone that has five businesses. All I want is one."

"What kinda business were you in?" asked Carlos.

"I was a paper salesman, but I got laid off. Then I went through a nasty divorce, and I still have legal bills to pay from that. I can't sell my house because it's under water, so it's been tough."

"I know, man. I got several friends in the same boat as you. I know what it's like to be broke. I was born in Mississippi the youngest of eight kids. My dad was a farmer, and my mother took care of all us kids. I wore hand-me-down clothes all through school. I was 20 before I wore a new set of clothes. I've had to fight and scratch for everythin' I've made. Nobody ever gave me nuthin'."

"Wow. You're a self-made man. But, I'm curious-what exactly is international marketing anyway?" asked Paul.

"I deal with a product that's marketed in six countries now and will soon be in twenty. I have associates sellin' this product now, and I get a little piece of everythin' they sell. That's the beauty of it. I get paid when other people work. If you wanna earn one hundred times what you are earnin' now in a regular job, you can't earn it by workin' one hundred times harder. It's impossible. With what I do, it's possible with one hundred other people. Basically, it's a lot of people doin' a little work, and we all get paid. And with your financial situation, this business could be just the thing to dig you out of your hole. In fact, the sky's the limit with this," said Carlos.

Paul leaned forward as he let what Carlos just said sink in.

"International marketing sounds good, but what exactly do you sell? This isn't one of those *things*, is it?"

"No, this ain't no Ponzi scheme. This is a legitimate product sold through word of mouth. A Ponzi scheme has no product. It's just money passin' hands until the whole thing falls apart. Then the last people in are left holding the bag. It's the oldest trick in the world."

"I've lost money in one before. They called it 'friends helping friends.' They should have named it 'friends screwing friends' because I lost $1,500 when it shut down. I swore I would never get involved in one of those again," said Paul.

"I understand. I've had friends lose money in those, too. The difference is I actually sell a product for a company called Bio Strength. Have you ever heard of 'em?"

"Nope."

"That's good," said Carlos. "That just shows what a ground floor opportunity this is. We have nowhere to go but up. Sales are now at 300 million, and we're experiencing unbelievable growth. I'm lookin' for a few key people who are serious about makin' money and makin' their dreams come true. Growin' up like I did, the only thing I had were dreams. I didn't even know what college was 'til the tenth grade. Nobody ever talked about it. I dreamed of havin' a business and a big garage to tinker around with cars. By the way, what kinda dreams did you have growin' up?"

Paul squinted and looked over Carlos's shoulder as he contemplated the question. He thought back to dreams he had not visited in years. Most of his dreams had involved living an easy, carefree life with no money worries.

"I really can't remember," said Paul with a bewildered look on his face.

"I'm sure you've had dreams before. You just stopped dreamin' like most adults do. The problems of everyday life stifle people's hopes and dreams too much. Come on, man. What have you always wanted?" asked Carlos smiling.

"Well, I always wanted a boat."

"What kind of boat?" Carlos asked.

"A 40-foot inboard Sea Ray with a captain's bridge."

"Wow, that's a yacht! What color is it?"

"White with red and blue pinstripes."

"That sounds fantastic," said Carlos. "Why do you want this yacht?"

"Because I love the water."

"Why do you love the water?"

"I love the feel of freedom when I'm on the water. I don't have a care in the world."

"When ya think about being on the water, how do ya feel?" asked Carlos.

"Pretty damn amazing, actually."

"Do you know that you can have that yacht or anything else you want? Just get into the feelin' of what it is you want. Then wait for the universe to bring it to you. Expect it to happen, act as if it has already happened to you. Then it will be yours," said Carlos confidently.

"That sounds kind of far-fetched."

"I ain't kiddin'. Whatever you want, you can have. But ya can't dwell on why you don't have it yet. Those thoughts send out bad vibes. You want the feel-good feelins'. Focusin' on the lack of anything only gets you more of the same…the lack of it. So get excited about where you're goin'. Expect it. Act as if you already have it…and just wait. It's yours, guaranteed. It may not always come in the way you expect it to, but it'll come."

Paul contemplated what Carlos had just said before responding.

"How do I get what I want then?" asked Paul. "What is it that you sell that can get me there?"

"There's a meetin' tomorrow night introducing people to the business. It's best that you learn about it there so you can see and hear it from other people besides me. How about I come pick you up at 6:30?"

"Sure, why not. I've got nothing to lose," said Paul. "But I'd still like to know what it is you sell."

"Bio Strength is in the health and wellness field, and here's a DVD that you can watch that tells you all about 'em. But the main thing I want you to think about until tomorrow night is those long lost dreams of yours. The most important part of this business is keepin' those dreams alive in front of you every day. Watch the DVD, and I'll see you tomorrow at 6:30. I remember where you live."

On the drive home, Paul imagined the ocean wind through his hair and the smell of the salty air while driving his yacht. Goosebumps rose on his arm as he dreamt of a beautiful blonde in a red bikini by his side on his boat. He docked his yacht in front of a brick mansion and walked while holding hands with the gorgeous woman. He opened the passenger door to a red Ferrari for her and hopped in the driver's seat without opening the door. Her hair flapped freely as he sped down his tree-lined driveway. He smiled in this blissful state he had put himself in. He had no clue what he was getting into, but at least he was not thinking about killing himself anymore.

Chapter 3

Bo Valentine flicked on his computer like he did every morning. A smug smile crept on his face as the sales numbers appeared on his screen. Thirty more distributors had signed up under him in the last week, and they all ordered Bio Strength products. He sipped his coffee and eased back in his reclining leather chair. He placed his hands on his protruding belly and basked in the glory of his upcoming commissions.

Bo made motivation a high priority in his organization. Turnover in Bio Strength approached 90 percent, but that was typical for a network marketing company. The phone rang in his office, and he checked his caller ID to see if he should answer. It was one of his successful downline distributors calling, so he quickly picked up the phone.

"Suzanne!" said Bo enthusiastically into the phone. "How's it going, honey?"

"I have had at least 10 people say they were coming to business previews that never came. I'm not making near as much money as I thought I would. Do you have any ideas on how I can get people to make a decision?"

"Absolutely. It all starts with your attitude. You have to walk and talk like a successful person even though things currently may not be going your way."

"How do I do that? You know, jobs have been hit hard here in Jacksonville, and people are watching their finances closely," said Suzanne.

"Sure, I know all of Florida has been hit hard in the recession," said Bo. But that is all the more reason why people need what we have. Not many jobs can offer financial freedom from the slavery of the paycheck. We can."

"Well, I'm not there yet," said Suzanne sarcastically. "A thousand dollars a month from Bio Strength won't pay my mortgage. I've still got stuff in my garage from the last network marketing company I was with. It's been two and a half years. When is this going to start paying off?" asked Suzanne.

"Hey, I know what you're saying. I've still got unsold water filters in my garage from my last gig. You've got to stay patient. I was patient, and look what's happened to me. I made it to the top in five years at Bio Strength. If I had quit after two and a half years, it would have been a huge mistake. Kitty and I are living the life of our dreams! And you can do it, too!"

"I heard you were separated."

"What?" said Bo. "No way. We are better than ever. Who told you that?"

"I heard it from a friend of mine. She said that's what you told her after you bought her a few drinks."

"That's ridiculous. Kitty is the love of my life. Now let's get back to your situation. I have a suggestion that will help your business explode. Do you want to hear it?"

"Of course."

"It's called *Fake it 'til you make it*," said Bo. "I only share this with my most successful downline, but it has worked for me like a charm in my 25 years in the business. I've made it to the top in my last three network marketing companies, so I know what I'm talking about."

"I kind of get what it means, but tell me more," said Suzanne.

"It means giving the appearance that you have succeeded before you actually have. Act as if you have achieved what you want now, and one way or another it will happen to you."

"That sounds like an insincere way of dealing with people to me," said Suzanne.

"It's not insincere at all," said Bo. "You are not lying to anyone. You simply are imagining yourself as already having achieved your goal. It puts you in a great frame of mind every day. Just put your dreams first and feel as if they have happened. Then everything will fall into place. You just don't know when."

"I guess I'll have to be a little more patient," said Suzanne. "*Fake it 'til I make it*, huh? Does that mean I can relax when I make it to the top?"

"Oh, not at all. It's just that your work changes to managing and motivating instead of recruiting all the time. Listen, I want you to imagine having already achieved your dreams. Let's talk again next month and see how you are doing. Trust me, you will see a big difference. Plus you'll have a blast imagining your success along the way!" said Bo.

"Okay. *Fake it 'til I make it* it is. Everyone looks up to you, so you must be doing something right. I'll give it a try."

"Good luck, Suzanne. I look forward to hearing from you next month. Take care."

Kitty tried to hang up the phone in the kitchen quietly. She listened to as many of Bo's phone calls as she could, and she rarely let him out of her sight. She followed him frequently to see who he was meeting with, and his car was easy to spot since it was a red Jaguar convertible with license plates that read *NO BOSS*. Kitty picked up the most recent Bio Strength magazine that featured their picture on the cover as a successful, happy, contented couple. She waltzed into Bo's office with the magazine in hand.

"Honey, did you see the Bio Strength magazine that came out yesterday? Isn't this a good picture of us?" asked Kitty sweetly.

"Yes, it is," said Bo feigning interest in the cover. "Sweetie, are you going to San Diego with me to the convention in a few months?"

"Of course. I wouldn't think of letting you go alone. That's an important event," said Kitty as she put on her one-carat diamond earrings.

Bo couldn't seem to shake Kitty anymore. She followed him wherever he went, and it was beginning to really bug him.

"Okay, great," mumbled Bo as he looked at his computer and forced a smile.

"I'm going to the store now. Do you need anything?" asked Kitty.

"No. Thanks for asking," he said as Kitty leaned over to kiss him on the cheek.

As soon as Kitty left, he picked up the phone to make another call.

"Hey, Sallie."

"Who is this?"

"It's Bo. Who did you think it was?"

"I haven't heard from you in six months. The last thing you said was that you were going to divorce your wife. Well…?"

"It's going to happen. The wheels are in motion, and I've already talked to my lawyer. The time is not right just yet. Listen, there's a convention in San Diego next month, and I'd like to see you."

"Sure, just bring your wife along and we'll make it a threesome," said Sallie sarcastically.

There was a moment of silence before Bo spoke again.

"My wife wouldn't go for that, but I like the way you think. Is there someone else you had in mind?"

"You're a bigger jerk than I thought. I saw you and your wife on the latest cover of the Bio Strength magazine looking like a happy couple. I don't want you to call me anymore. The article on you was a load of crap. All that talk of helping other people get what they want. You're only interested in one thing, and you ain't getting any more from me!" yelled Sallie as Bo held the phone away from his ear.

"But baby…," Bo interjected.

"Don't interrupt me, this is not a discussion. If you ever try to call me again, I'll write your wife a nice little note telling her about us."

"You wouldn't," said Bo nervously.

"Try me," snapped Sallie.

He heard the other end of the line go dead. He usually had an easy time impressing the women in his organization. Anyone at the Royal Diamond level was revered, and he was constantly asked how he had made it to the top. Sallie was not the only female conquest he had on his contact list.

Kitty called a private investigator named Rob Thigpen to do some snooping for her. She wanted to be ready when the time came for her to file for divorce. The more money Bo made now, the more she would get in a settlement later.

Rob Thigpen had been a private investigator for 23 years. His cases usually involved cheating spouses like Bo Valentine, and he was a successful investigator despite having a harelip and a lazy eye. Kitty arrived at Mr. Thigpen's office at the time when she told Bo that she was going to the store.

"Nice to meet you Mrs. Valentine," said Rob as he slowly enunciated his words. He avoided words starting with the letters "th" since he was unable to pronounce them. It was a cruel twist of fate that his last name was Thigpen. He often answered his phone by saying "Rob you-know-who."

Kitty had only spoken to his receptionist initially, so she was surprised to hear his speech impediment. She was also confused over which eye of his to focus on since his right eye wandered. She decided to focus on his left eye for now.

"Nice to meet you, too" said Kitty looking at his steady left eye.

"How can I help you?"

"I'm pretty certain my husband is cheating on me, but I need proof."

"Surprise, *anoder* cheating husband," Rob said wryly.

"I guess you do this all the time," said Kitty.

"Mrs. Valentine, I'm not surprised at what people do anymore. If you give me your husband's cell number, a picture of him and his license plate number, I'll get to work."

"I've already put together a packet of information for you on my husband," said Kitty as she handed Rob an envelope. "How much do you charge?"

"One hundred fifty per hour plus expenses. Are you aware of any trips he is planning to take soon?"

"He's going to San Diego to a convention, but I'm going with him. I usually don't let him out of my sight. Maybe now I can let you do some of the watching for me."

"I'll do my best. Usually your gut is right, but you need proof. My job isn't glamorous. I spend a lot of time in my Pontiac Firebird watching people. Just be patient and I'll get the evidence you need."

"I'm just so tired of being ignored. The money really doesn't matter anymore. I just…" said Kitty as her voice started to break.

"I just wanna feel loved. We lost it years ago, and we hung together for the kids," said Kitty with tears welling up in her eyes.

"I know it hurts. You're not alone. If I don't get him my name's not Rob-you- know-who."

Chapter 4

Paul peered out of his front window blinds and waited for Carlos. He paced back and forth and checked himself in the mirror one more time. He dressed in khaki pants and a blue golf shirt. The noose no longer hung from his ceiling, even though the stack of unpaid bills grew larger. He didn't even bother to open them anymore.

Carlos arrived at Paul's house promptly at 6:30. Carlos found that picking prospects up was much better than meeting them there. He had been stood up too many times over the years.

"Good evenin'," said Carlos as Paul got in the car.

"Thanks for picking me up. Where's the meeting tonight?" asked Paul.

"It's at a doctor's office not far from here," said Carlos.

"What's his name?"

"Dr. Roy Garfinkel. He's a general practitioner who's been around for years."

Dr. Garfinkel was a well-known and respected doctor in Jacksonville. He quickly scribbled a prescription for a kid with a stuffy nose and told the mother to call him if her son's symptoms worsened. Thankfully, this was his last appointment of the day. After they left, he quickly rushed to set up for the Bio Strength meeting that night. The room had enough space for about 30 metal folding chairs, and the walls were adorned with Bio Strength posters. He turned on some music and danced a little jig so his staff would not see him. The monotony of his work day made him anticipate tonight's meeting even more than usual. He saw Bio Strength as his way out of his humdrum life. Dr. Garfinkel had built a nice organization beneath him in Bio Strength mainly because of his credibility as a doctor.

Paul and Carlos arrived to the meeting early, and Carlos approached Dr. Garfinkel.

"Dr. Garfinkel," said Carlos, "I'd like you to meet my guest, Paul Cousins."

"Nice to meet you," said Paul as he nervously shook hands.

"Roy Garfinkel. Thanks for coming. You're in for a treat tonight."

"I can't wait to hear it," said Paul.

He showed Paul some of the Bio Strength products on the table and explained that the patent pending natural ingredients helped relieve joint pain.

"Not only does this lotion relieve pain and moisturize the skin, but it also increases your strength. The new line of nutritional meal replacement drinks has the same effect on the body," said Dr. Garfinkel.

"Before you try some of the products, let me do some muscle response testing. Stick your right arm out to the side." He stuck his right arm out. "Now you push your arm up against me as I apply pressure on your arm, okay? Let's start on three. Okay, 1…2…3…."

Dr. Garfinkel pushed down on his arm at his wrist, and Paul's arm went down easily.

"Why are you doing this?" asked Paul with a confused look.

"Just wait a minute." He reached on the display table for a bottle of lotion and rubbed a small dab on Paul's arm.

"Now, let's do the same thing again. On the count of three, I'll push down and you push up. Okay, 1…2…3…."

Dr. Garfinkel pushed down on his arm again. Paul's eyes bulged as he watched his arm stay as straight as a metal rod. Dr. Garfinkel tried again even harder, and his arm stayed straight.

"You must not be pushing down as hard. My arm didn't move."

"I pushed down even harder the second time. Let's try it again without the lotion." Carlos watched with amusement and leaned over and wiped the lotion off with a handi-wipe. "Okay, this time you will have no lotion on you. "1…2…3…resist." Dr. Garfinkel pushed down Paul's arm with ease.

"What kind of trick is this?" exclaimed Paul.

"It's no trick at all," replied Carlos calmly. "This is called applied kinesiology. Some people call it muscle response testin'. It can even be done with sublingual testin'. Try puttin' a piece of candy under your tongue while doin' the test. Refined sugar weakens the immune system, so your muscles will go weak. But if you put somethin' healthy under your tongue like a carrot, your muscles will test stronger."

The room filled up with around 30 people, and Dr. Garfinkel turned off the music and asked everyone to find a seat. Carlos and Paul sat front and center.

"Good evening and welcome to tonight's meeting," said Ronnie Brown. He smiled broadly and seemed to Paul a very enthusiastic introducer of Dr. Garfinkel. Ronnie had been in five different network marketing companies over the last 12 years, and he was sure that Bio Strength was the company to make him rich. His wife had become very jaded about his business ventures. She grew tired of him coming home every couple of years with another company that was going to be the next "big thing."

"I am pleased to see such a good turnout tonight," said Ronnie. "Our host tonight is none other than Dr. Roy Garfinkel. He has been a general practitioner for 14 years, and he is an avid user and promoter of all Bio Strength products. Please join me in welcoming Dr. Roy Garfinkel!"

Dr. Garfinkel always made sure that he was dressed in his white medical coat. It went a long way toward creating instant credibility when he spoke in front of groups. He was an excellent speaker and was good at establishing rapport. He earned approximately $2,500 per month from Bio Strength, and his goal was to eventually do Bio Strength full-time and drastically cut back on his practice hours.

"Thank you all for coming tonight. I've been using these Bio Strength products for years on my patients, and the results are nothing short of phenomenal. I had one patient who could barely get out of bed in the morning. Now he is running marathons. In fact, he is here tonight. Let's hear it straight from Mac Williams!"

Mac bolted up from his seat in the front row. He wore running sweats and shoes and had bundles of energy for a man in his mid-fifties.

"Bio Strength has changed my life," said Mac. "Before Dr. Garfinkel gave me this lotion and nutritional drinks, I was moving around like a cripple. I just recently qualified for the Boston marathon, and I owe it all to Dr. Garfinkel. I tell everyone I know about Bio Strength and what they've done for me. This stuff is just amazing! Thank you for changing my life," said Mac as he looked appreciatively at Dr. Garfinkel.

Mac turned to Dr. Garfinkel and clapped as the rest of the crowd rose up to join the applause. Dr. Garfinkel had never received a standing ovation before. He flashed a big smile as he reached to shake Mac's hand.

"If there are people you care about who are hurting, you owe it to them to tell them about Bio Strength," said Dr. Garfinkel. "Another benefit you may not know about is increased strength. Can I have a volunteer from the audience?"

Paul's arm shot straight up. He wanted to try again to test whether Carlos had played a trick on him. Paul stuck his arm out as Dr. Garfinkel instructed, and his arm went down easily when he pushed on it. Dr. Garfinkel gave Paul a sip from a Bio Strength nutritional drink. Paul stuck out his arm again for a retest of strength. His arm did not budge at all this time. Dr. Garfinkel's face turned red as he tried unsuccessfully to push Paul's arm down.

Several more audience members came up front to perform a strength test, and each had the same result as Paul. Paul could see that this was no placebo effect.

"Now behind every great product, there has to be a great business plan," said Dr. Garfinkel. "You can't buy these products in a store. They are marketed person to person. Isn't that the best way to buy anything? If you love your doctor, you'll recommend him. Well, this business is no different. All we do is tell enough people about it, and they tell their friends, and on it goes. How many of you guests have a negative opinion about network marketing?" All eight guests including Paul raised their hands.

"Direct selling is the cheapest way for a company to get its product to the consumer," said Dr. Garfinkel. "The traditional way of selling products is loaded with marketing costs from suppliers, advertisers, middlemen, and salespeople. What direct selling does is eliminate all of that. The company pays you to market its product. We take home the paycheck that would normally go to the middleman and advertisers. I'd like to introduce Joanne Griggs who will tell you about the compensation plan. Please help me welcome Joanne Griggs!"

Joanne was a 36-year-old tall blonde bombshell. Paul couldn't keep his eyes off her as she strutted confidently to the front of the room. She casually brushed her shoulder length hair off to the side as she turned to face the audience.

"Hi, I'm Joanne Griggs," said Joanne with a broad smile. "I've been involved with Bio Strength for a year now, and Dr. Garfinkel is my sponsor. My goal is to take my business all the way to Royal Diamond. That's the top level, and the average Royal Diamond makes over fifty grand a month. And some make much more. I don't know of any job where you can make that kind of continuous residual income for the rest of your life. My regular job is in the medical supply business, but I plan to quit that and do Bio Strength full-time when my Bio Strength income exceeds what I make in my job."

Paul sat up straight in his chair since he didn't want to miss a word Joanne said. He detected a slight New England accent in her voice. He tried to keep eye contact with her, but his eyes crept creeping down to check out her body. Paul liked her curves, and Carlos noticed Paul gawking at her. Carlos gave him a nudge and a knowing smile.

"This whole business is based on duplication," Joanne continued. "It really just takes a little effort from a large group of people. The growth is exponential when everyone produces. Let me ask you a question-if you had a choice of taking a million dollars right now *or* taking a penny and doubling it every day for 30 days, which would you take?"

A bald man in the back raised his hand. "Give me the million bucks now!"

"No, that would be a mistake," said Joanne. If you double a penny every day for 30 days, you will end up with over five and a half million dollars. That's what this business is like. The real money comes at the end where the law of exponential growth and duplication really takes off. You start as a general distributor and earn money when you sell products at retail. After you reach five thousand in one month in gross sales from yourself and your immediate group, you move up to the Bronze level," said Joanne as she pointed to a flip chart. The chart was arranged in a pyramid with the lower levels at the bottom and Royal Diamond at the top.

"I got to the Silver level in 30 days. Not everyone will do that, but you can if you are determined enough. I plan to become a Royal Diamond in three years. I also plan to make the San Diego trip this year. Bio Strength has the best qualifying trips and compensation plan of any other network marketing company. Believe me, I've looked at a lot of them."

Joanne turned the page on her flip chart revealing rows of numbers in columns. The figures showed income per month at each level, and the numbers for Royal Diamond were twenty-five times greater than for a Gold distributor.

"This represents a perfect model of what would happen with duplication. Of course, this illustration shows what would happen if every person reached his goals. That would be unique, but it does give you an idea of how quickly this can build up."

Joanne always read that to sell, you have to sell the sizzle. Never mind that the results on her chart would realistically never happen. Her job was to show what could happen in a perfect world. Joanne spoke so convincingly that no one questioned her, and Paul was leaning forward in his chair taking in her every word. He suddenly became aware of his body language and realized it showed how interested he was in what she was saying. He had read about body language before, but this was the first time he became consciously aware of his own. This awareness added to his feeling of excitement. His mind drifted for a moment as he began daydreaming…he pictured himself locked in an embrace with Joanne on a beach at sunset. He reached back to untie the strap on her red bikini. It fell to the sand at their feet, and they began a long, passionate kiss. Paul felt Carlos nudge him again.

Suddenly Paul realized everyone was looking at him. He felt like a third grader being caught daydreaming by his teacher. He realized he had been asked a question.

"I'm sorry, I was still thinking about that penny doubling every day. What did you ask me?" said Paul.

"Were you faking it?" Joanne asked again.

"Was I faking what?" Paul asked confused. Everyone giggled.

"The strength test," Joanne said with a smile.

"Oh, no, that was for real," said Paul as his face turned red.

"The strength test is commonly known as applied kinesiology," said Joanne. "It is used to determine how the body reacts to anything placed on it. The fact is your body does not lie. It knows what is good for you and what is not."

Paul was intrigued by this whole muscle testing stuff. It seemed like an old parlor trick, but it had really worked on him.

"Just to prove to you that this muscle testing is for real," continued Joanne, "I'll take another volunteer."

Most of the men in the room raised their hands, eager to get close to Joanne. Joanne pointed to an older gentleman sitting in the back.

"You sir, come on up here. I'll demonstrate how your body reacts and never lies, unlike most men."

"Not bitter at all, are ya honey," shot back the older man as he made his way to the front.

Joanne ignored his comeback. "Instead of using Bio Strength products, I'm going to do some sublingual testing with something else. I'm going to let you put some food in your mouth and muscle test you. That's what sublingual means. Let's start with a piece of candy. What did you say your name was?"

"Milo."

"Ok, Milo. Put this piece of candy under your tongue, and then I'll muscle test you." Milo put the hard candy under his tongue.

"Now, I'm going to push down on your arm while you push up. On the count of three, 1...2...3...resist."

Joanne pushed down and Milo's arm went down easily.

"See how sugar made his body weak? Now let's try something healthy. Sugar is an immune suppressor, so let's try a good food...say, a lima bean."

Milo's face turned pale. "Do we really have to use a lima bean?" Milo asked sheepishly.

"Yes, we do," said Joanne. You can spit the candy out into this trash can and take a sip of water." Joanne handed him a trash can and a bottle of water. Milo spit the candy out and took a sip of water.

"Now for the lima bean," said Joanne as she handed him a Baggie with a lima bean in it.

Milo's expression looked like he was holding a barf bag.

"Do I really have to use this?" Milo asked again.

"Yes, come on. It's not *that* bad. They're yummy."

Milo closed his eyes and placed the lima bean under his tongue. His face crunched up, and he looked like he was going to hurl.

"I'll test you quickly. I've never seen anybody vomit a lima bean before, goodness gracious."

Joanne pushed down on his arm. Unlike the test with the candy, Milo's arm held firm. Milo could not believe the difference in strength.

"Quite a difference, isn't it?" asked Joanne.

"Yes it is. Can I spit this out now?"

"Yes you can," said Joanne.

Milo ran over to the trash can and spit out the lima bean.

"Let's give Milo a hand for helping out!" The audience laughed and applauded for Milo as he went back to his seat.

"Why did you act so disgusted with the lima bean?" his friend sitting beside him asked.

Milo leaned over and whispered, "I *hate* lima beans. Always have. My mom made me eat them. I get sick to my stomach even looking at 'em, and that lady made me put one in my mouth. I never would've volunteered if I knew she was gonna make me put a damn lima bean in my mouth!"

"Bio Strength has the product and compensation plan to take you as far as you want to go," said Dr. Garfinkel as he stood beside Joanne. "As a physician, my income has declined severely over the years from insurance companies reducing payments. I needed a Plan B. What is *your* Plan B? What will happen to you if you're laid off tomorrow? Why not start building a business of your own now? One day, you'll be thankful you did. I'll stick around afterwards to answer any questions you may have. Please feel free to try the products yourself. Seeing is believing. Thank you all for coming."

The audience clapped and many started trying out the Bio Strength products themselves. Several tried their own versions of muscle testing.

"How do you get started in this?" Paul asked Carlos.

"Easy, man. Just $49 for your starter kit and then I'll help you with your first order after that. I keep an extra kit in my car so you can begin right away. Congratulations on a wise decision, partner!"

Paul smiled and shook hands with Carlos. Bio Strength gave him something to believe in, but the biggest reason for his attitude change was because of Carlos.

"Thanks for everything," Paul said looking Carlos squarely in the eye.

Carlos felt a warmness in Paul's hands he hadn't felt before. He sensed a shift in Paul and realized he had given Paul something he needed badly. For the first time in a long time, Paul had hope.

Chapter 5

Carlos had been around long enough to know when he had a motivated new distributor on his hands. Half would quit after six months, and only a handful were around after two years. Carlos believed that people with nothing have nothing to lose. He had no idea how low Paul had sunk when they met but had noticed the huge change in Paul's demeanor.

Paul stayed up until 3 a.m. going through his new distributor kit. The DVD he watched showed the lifestyle of several top Bio Strength Royal Diamond distributors. Paul finally fell asleep and dreamed of riding in his new boat on the open water. He slept soundly until his phone rang at 9:30 a.m.

"Good mornin', Paul. Carlos here. How's my future Royal Diamond distributor doin'?"

"Oh, I like the sound of that," said Paul rubbing his eyes.

"Did I wake you?"

"That's okay. I needed to get up anyway."

"Let me know when you want to place your first order," said Carlos. "I can help you with that."

"How much should I order?" asked Paul.

"Well, that depends on how fast you want to go. If you want to go slow, order small. If you want to build a business steadily, order more. But if you want to move quickly then order the maximum of $5,000. You've got to have product to demonstrate. So, how do you wanna do it?" asked Carlos.

"Let's do it fast."

"Okay, you'll need lots of product. Can you start with $5,000?"

"No problem."

"Are you sure?" asked Carlos. "You told me you didn't have any money."

"I've got a little rainy-day money," he said looking down at the floor. All he really had were maxed out credit cards.

"You should get the new distributor package because it gets you the most bang for your buck. It's a lot cheaper than orderin' product individually. Call me when your order comes in and we can start sellin'." Carlos liked for new distributors to buy the kits not only because they were cheaper but because he got a bonus whenever they were purchased.

Paul quickly clicked on the Bio Strength website and started ordering products. He felt strange spending $5,000 on a company he had heard of only a few days ago. He didn't even know if the products worked, but he took it on faith from the testimonials he heard. Paul figured that if he could sell everything he ordered at a profit, then he would recoup his investment. The first three credit cards Paul tried were rejected. He screamed at the screen in frustration and rummaged through his office drawer hunting for another card. He found a seldom-used Discover card and finally got his order to go through.

He closed his eyes and imagined riding in his new boat. Music thumped from the sound system as his red, white and blue yacht blasted through waves in the open water. When he opened his eyes, he saw goosebumps on his arm.

He quickly thumbed through the paper looking for some way to kickstart his Bio Strength business. He found an advertisement for a health fair the following weekend, and he signed up for a booth. He just prayed that his Bio Strength products would show up in time.

Two days later a UPS truck appeared at his home to unload his order. Paul was dumbfounded at how quickly his order showed up. The driver delivered 52 boxes, and he completely filled his living room with stacks six feet high. He was determined not to be another hapless network marketing loser with a garage full of unsold products years later. He remembered his parents still had leftover cleaning products 30 years later from a defunct network marketing company they were in.

Paul ripped open one of the boxes and pulled out a tube of moisturizing lotion. He sniffed the open tube and walked to the bathroom to wash his face and apply some lotion. It did feel silky smooth, but he couldn't do a strength test on himself. Paul needed to test someone who had no vested interest in Bio Strength, so he walked outside to see if he could spot one of his neighbors.

Paul knelt down to do some weeding. He had neglected his yard for months, and he pulled up a foot-tall weed by his mailbox. He looked up every minute or so to see if he spotted someone to do a strength test on. After several minutes of weeding, Paul noticed a car pull in the driveway five houses away. He didn't know this neighbor well, but he had waved to a woman in the yard there several times as he passed by. Paul thought this would be a good chance to make a new friend. He brushed the dirt off his knees and walked down to meet his neighbor. An attractive, tall, dark-haired woman was unloading groceries from her car when Paul walked up.

"Hello, I'm your neighbor Paul. I live right down the street," said Paul pointing in the direction of his house.

The woman appeared startled at the sound of Paul's voice and looked up anxiously. She relaxed when she recognized Paul.

"Hello, I've seen you before. I'm Heather. Nice to meet you. Sorry I can't shake your hand," said Heather as she cradled a large bag of groceries.

"Let me help you with those," said Paul as he reached into her trunk and pulled out two bags of groceries.

"Thanks, but you don't have to do that," said Heather as she turned to walk in the door from her garage into her kitchen. Paul followed her with two large bags.

"I don't mind at all," said Paul. "You must be shopping for a big family."

"Yeah, I've got three kids and we're on the go all the time. I took today off from work to take care of errands I can never seem to get to."

"What kind of work do you do?" asked Paul.

"I'm an auditor," said Heather. "What do you do?"

Paul hesitated before answering. He was unsure of what to say.

"I am an international marketing consultant," said Paul remembering Carlos's card.

"Oh, and what does an international marketing consultant do?"

"I work for a company called Bio Strength," said Paul.

"That's a new one. Bio Strength. What do they do?" asked Heather as she started putting groceries away.

Paul smiled inside. This was his big chance to start his business off, and Heather had set him up perfectly with her questions.

"Oh, I just happen to have some of our product on me," said Paul reaching into his pocket. "This lotion not only helps your skin look younger, but it makes you stronger," said Paul proudly.

"Really?" asked Heather. "How does it do that?"

"Let me show you," said Paul. "I can demonstrate this through some muscle response testing. It's pretty cool. Stick your arm out like this."

Heather stuck her arm out imitating Paul.

"Now I'm going to push down on your arm while you resist. On the count of three, resist. Okay, 1…2…3…resist," said Paul as he pushed Heather's arm down easily.

"See how easily your arm went down," said Paul.

"Yeah," said Heather not sure what to expect next.

"Now, I'll apply some Bio Strength lotion to your arm and try the test again."

Paul applied some lotion to Heather's arm and redid the strength test. Heather's arm stayed straight, as Paul's face turned red trying to push it down.

"You're not trying as hard," said Heather incredulously.

"I'm trying even harder than the first time," said Paul.

"That's unreal. How much is a tube of lotion?" asked Heather.

"Twenty dollars."

"Seems kind of expensive, but I'll try a tube," said Heather reaching for her purse.

"Let me go back to my house and get an unopened one for you. I'll be right back." Paul felt like running back to his house, but he didn't want to appear too eager to make a $20 sale. When he returned, Heather's teenage son had just come home from school and was talking to her in the kitchen.

"Hey, Mike, this is our neighbor Paul. He sells that crazy lotion I was telling you about. Do that strength test on my son," said Heather.

Paul did the strength test on Mike, and the kid was blown away.

"Wow, that's awesome. How does that stuff work?" Mike asked.

"It just does, that's all I know," said Paul.

"I'm calling up my friends over to try this out on them," said Mike. In five minutes the house was crawling with neighborhood teenagers all doing strength tests on each other. It didn't matter to Paul that they were doing them for fun. This was the beginning of the Paul Cousins business empire. The $20 in his pocket felt more like $20 million to Paul right now.

Paul called Carlos as soon as he got home.

"Carlos, hey. I just sold my first tube of lotion to a lady neighbor I just met!"

"That's great," said Carlos. "Is she interested in the business at all?"

"I didn't ask," said Paul. "I was so excited to make a sale that I didn't bring that up."

"That's okay," said Carlos. "Just follow up with her in a week or so and see how she's doin'."

"Okay. Man, she had all the neighborhood kids in the house doing strength testing. It was great."

"That's a good start, but your real money in this business comes from gettin' other people to sign up under you. You can sell product all day long, but it ain't gonna get you much money. I'd like you to speak with one of our upline about gettin' started in this business," said Carlos.

"What's an upline?" asked Paul.

"Your upline is me, then the person that recruited me, then the person that recruited him, and so on. It's like goin' up the chain of command. They all get paid based on what you do, so they have a vested interest in you. I'll get ya in with one of the big shots named Bo Valentine. He's a Royal Diamond distributor in our upline. I'll set up a three-way call with him. I'll shoot for this Friday."

"That's great," said Paul. "That'll be just in time before the health fair I signed up for."

"You signed up for a health fair?" asked Carlos.

"Yeah, it's at the convention center downtown. I've been to it before, and it's really packed with people."

"You know if you sign up late for those, they give you a crappy placement for your booth. Do you know where your booth will be?" asked Carlos.

"Not yet. I didn't think about where the booth would be," said Paul.

"I think I should be there with you for that. Next time check with me first before you go signin' up for something like that. You're an impulsive guy, I see."

"When I see something I want, I don't hesitate," said Paul. "Just sometimes I act a little too quickly."

"That's okay. You can always bounce things off me first. That's what I'm here for," said Carlos.

Paul spent the next several days performing strength tests on complete strangers. He carried a tube of lotion wherever he went and spent the rest of his time setting up a website and reviewing his starter kit. He nervously wrote down questions he wanted to ask Bo Valentine for the upcoming three-way call.

Carlos called Paul on Friday morning.

"You ready to speak to Bo Valentine?"

"Yeah. I've written some questions down," said Paul as he searched amongst piles of papers for his notes.

"Hold on," said Carlos. "I'll add Bo in to our call now."

Paul put the phone down and searched again for his questions. He pushed the unpaid bill pile off the desk and looked frantically in the desk drawers. After a minute Paul picked the phone back up to see if the three-way call had started. He never found his questions.

"Paul, are you there?" asked Carlos for the third time.

"Sorry, I was just looking through my notes," said Paul nervously.

"That's okay. Paul, I've got our upline Bo Valentine on the line with us. He's a Royal Diamond distributor right here in Jacksonville. Bo, we have on the line with us a new distributor who is all fired up and ready to start. Let me introduce you to Paul Cousins."

"Paul, how's it going? Carlos has told me a lot about you."

Paul's mind raced as tried to stay calm.

"Great. Just great," said Paul searching for something clever to say.

"Well, you've got a good sponsor in Carlos. I've known him for years, and he is great to work with. What question can I answer to help you get started?" asked Bo.

"What results have you seen with the products?" asked Paul. "I don't want to embarrass myself with a product that doesn't work as promised."

"Oh, probably the most memorable story was a lady in Georgia. Her face had been ravaged by the sun, and she had pockmarks and blemishes all over her face. She looked horrible, and her self-confidence was gone. Her husband left her, and she was at an all-time low. Then a friend told her about Bio Strength and what it did for her. She gave her a tube and instructed her to apply it twice a day. She did and you wouldn't believe how great she looks now," said Bo.

Carlos had heard this story many times before and could recite it almost word for word. If Bo found a good story, he kept telling it.

"I guess the market for Bio Strength is pretty huge," said Paul.

"The market is limitless. We're in six countries now, and we'll be in 20 countries within three years. Now is the time to get in. This is a ground floor opportunity," said Bo.

"What should I do to get my business started?" asked Paul excitedly.

"Go to San Diego for the North American convention," said Bo. "That's where you'll get the big picture. You see, this thing is bigger than you can imagine. This isn't some small-time business just in Jacksonville. We're going global."

"Okay, I'll go," said Paul with no thought to how he would pay for it.

"That's great. I'm going to let Carlos help you with specific product questions, but my job is to help you keep your eye on where this company is going. Baby Boomers want to stay looking young, and our products will help them do that. I also want to help you master a skill that is needed for every successful network marketer."

"What's that?" asked Paul.

"It's an idea called *Fake it 'til you make it*. It's all about acting as if you've already achieved the goals you want. Instead of waiting to achieve to appear successful, act *as if* you already have what you want. Then, somehow the universe will bring it to you. It's all about attitude."

"Carlos told me about this. Does it really work?" asked Paul.

"It worked for me, and it can work for you, too. Carlos has gotten you started on your dreams again, I hear. That's good. Now pretend you already have them. Get in that state of mind and expect it to happen to you. It's already yours. I'm telling you, this *really* works. You can have whatever it is you want. Both Carlos and I are always here to help you. Let me give you my cell number. It's 904-805-0208. Call me anytime. It may be a day or so before I get back to you, but I will," said Bo.

"I really appreciate your advice," said Paul. "I look forward to meeting you in San Diego."

"Me too. Okay, I've gotta do some honey-do's for the wife. Call me if you need me. Take care, Paul," said Bo.

"Goodbye," said Paul as Bo hung up.

"Man, he was awesome," said Paul to Carlos.

"Yeah, he has a great communication style, particularly with the ladies," said Carlos.

"I thought he was married," said Paul.

"He is. Oh, never mind. Hey, how about I pay for your flight to San Diego. I gotta free ticket on Southwest. Then you can share the room with me and split the cost. Does that sound good?" asked Carlos.

"That's great," said Paul. "I appreciate that. You've done so much for me. I don't know when I can pay you back. I can't thank you enough. Oh, by the way, I'll need some help at the health fair tomorrow. Do you have a banner and some brochures I can use?"

"Sho' do. Be glad to help."

"That's great. Maybe I'll recruit someone into the business tomorrow," said Paul.

"That usually doesn't happen, but I have sold some product at those before. I'll come over to your house at 7:30 a.m., and we can start loadin' up my truck," said Carlos.

The next morning Carlos arrived at Paul's house at 7:30 sharp, and Paul was ready to start loading boxes. They pulled up to the convention center in Carlos's truck at 8:15 for the 10 a.m. start. At the check-in desk a lady gave Paul a map of where their booth was located. Carlos grimaced as he saw a red circle drawn over their location on the map. They were located in the very back of the hall.

Paul and Carlos set up their Bio Strength banner and filled the table with products and brochures. Paul paced back and forth behind the table as people started coming into the room. Carlos pulled up a chair and sat down.

"Where is everybody?" asked Paul.

"They don't see us back here," said Carlos.

"It's been over an hour and we haven't talked to anyone," said Paul.

"You just have to be patient," said Carlos.

Finally a young woman made her way to their booth. Paul stood at attention and made himself taller.

"Good morning," said Paul. "Would you like to sample our nutritional drinks?"

"Sure. Do they taste good?" she asked.

"Yes, they do. And they also affect your body instantly. Here, let me show you with a strength test before you have a sip and then after you have one."

Paul performed the strength test and waited for her reaction.

"See how much stronger you are after having tried it?" Paul asked with a smile.

"Yeah, I guess. Thank you."

Paul's smile faded as she turned and walked away.

"I'm going to have to go find some people," said Paul. "This is ridiculous. This booth cost me $150, and no one is coming back here."

"Well, our booth location is not good," said Carlos. "If you are the last one to sign up, you get the worst booth. That's just the way it goes. Next time you do one of these, sign up early."

The health fair lasted until 5 p.m., but Paul was ready to leave at three. Carlos managed to keep him there until the end, and Paul packed up his products and slowly pushed the dolly.

"Hey, man, don't worry about today. You got stuck with a horrible booth. It ain't your fault. If you'd been at the front, you woulda been swamped with people. Let's chalk one up to experience and move on," said Carlos.

"I know. I just wanted a chance to talk to people. It was a frustrating day."

"Hey, we're going to San Diego in a few days. We're gonna have the time of our lives," said Carlos grinning. "This convention is going to blow your mind!"

Chapter 6

Paul and Carlos landed in San Diego and caught a cab to their hotel. Carlos had helped Paul forget the wasted day at the health fair. They decided to grab some lunch at a diner next door. Carlos recognized a tall, neatly dressed man in his 40s walk by.

"Bill Jennings," Carlos yelled out to him.

The man stopped and stared while trying to figure out who yelled his name.

"Carlos, buddy, how ya been?"

"Oh great, man. How long has it been since I saw you at the international convention? About two years?"

"Yeah, I think so. Hey, how's your check runnin' these days?"

"About $1,500 per month. I still have several businesses going 'til Bio Strength takes off. Then, I'll do this full-time. How's your check?"

"I'm doing just over $2,000. I'd hoped for more, but I've got some good prospects that I brought with me. I paid for their trip, and once they get the big picture, they'll be on board. My check should soar then. Listen, I gotta meet my team before the convention starts. We're all sitting together. It's been great seeing you, Carlos. Here's my card. Let's stay in touch."

Carlos took his card and handed him back one of his. A good network marketer always has a card handy. "Catch you later, Bill," said Carlos.

Paul listened closely to their conversation. He had never heard Carlos discuss his earnings before.

"That was kind of personal asking him how much his check was wasn't it?" Paul asked.

Carlos shot back, "Heck no, when you've been at this a while, you wanna know how everybody else is doing. I knew he was BSin' me. No way he's making over $2,000 a month. He might've made that one time, but I bet I'm making more than him. I've been at it a year more than he has. It doesn't make no difference anyhow, we'll all be sittin' pretty in a few years. Hell, you can make whatever you want at this. All you gotta do is just keep at it. Don't give up. Most people fail because they quit too soon."

Paul knew what Carlos made. Fifteen hundred was not enough to pay his rent, but it was better than what he was making now. A cute young hostess came to seat them.

"Your table is ready," she said to Paul and Carlos. Paul thought she was cute as a button, so he walked beside her to get to know her.

"What's your name?" asked Paul with a smile.

"Katelyn."

"Have you noticed all the people here for the convention?"

"Yeah, who are they with?"

"It's an international company called Bio Strength. It's a great way to supplement your income. Would you be interested in earning $2,000 extra dollars each month part-time?"

"Sure, who wouldn't," said Katelyn.

"Well, meet me at the entrance to the convention hall tonight at 7:30. You'll get to hear all about it. Here's my card with my cell number."

"Thanks, I'll check it out."

Carlos beamed with pride at his initiative.

"You're not wastin' any time are you?" Carlos asked.

"Heck no. I may as well start now. Who knows, she could make us both rich!"

Paul was unaware of the biggest mistake he was making as a new network marketer. Not only was he too eager, he had not qualified his prospect at all. He knew nothing about her. He was just prospecting for whoever showed up in front of him. Carlos knew this, but he didn't want to discourage him either.

Paul and Carlos finished dinner and headed to the convention center. Paul was excited to meet his first prospect.

"Go ahead, Carlos. I'm going to wait at the entrance for Katelyn."

"Don't wait too long. You don't want to miss the show."

Carlos knew the girl wouldn't show, but he had to let Paul find out on his own. Qualifying prospects was the most important skill that Paul hadn't yet begun to master.

The convention center buzzed with anticipation. A huge roar erupted as the lights went out. The song "What a Feeling" blared from the sound system. The crowd came to its feet and clapped along. It was as if the Beatles had been resurrected for a reunion concert.

"Hello, San Diego," the moderator bellowed out into the microphone. "Welcome to the North American conference of the fastest growing direct sales company in the world, Bio Strength!"

Paul could hear the cheers outside the door. He waited about 10 minutes after the convention had started, but he could not stand to miss any more. He found his way in to Carlos's seat.

"What did I miss?" Paul yelled.

"Just the introduction of the distributor of the year," said Carlos.

"Where's your prospect?"

"She didn't show. I couldn't wait any longer."

"That's okay. You're better off in here," said Carlos.

The speaker was talking about how Bio Strength had changed his life. "I was up to my neck in credit card debt. My marriage was on the rocks until a friend introduced us to Bio Strength. My wife and I were skeptical at first, but after those monthly checks started coming in, we were sold. I know in my heart that if we can make it, so can you. We want to meet all of you on the road to financial freedom!"

The crowd rose to its feet in a roar of approval. Carlos and Paul joined in the applause. The energy was infectious, and "What a Feeling" blared through the speakers as the next speaker came up.

"Hi, I'm Peter Mancini from Cleveland. I'd like to tell you how Bio Strength changed my life. For years I had arthritis so bad I had to roll out of bed in the morning and crawl to the bathroom. Then a friend of mine loaned me some of his Bio Strength cream. I had no idea if it would work or not, but I figured, oh why not, can't hurt nothing. Well, the first day I rolled out of bed and walked to the bathroom. It didn't hit me' til the next day when it happened again. I realized my pain was gone! Just like that! The pain went away, so I forgot about it. Then I remembered how it used to hurt so much. I can't believe the difference Bio Strength has made for me. I have my life back. Heck, I can even play golf now. I gotta tee-time Sunday. Who wants to join me?"

The crowd cheered wildly for Peter. A succession of people gave testimonials about how Bio Strength had changed their lives. Each person seemed convincing and sincere. Some talked about how the money had changed their lives for the better. The speakers that got the most attention were the ones that tugged at your heart.

A mother walked to the front of the stage holding the hand of a cute little seven-year old girl wearing a yellow shirt, black patent-leather shoes and blonde hair tied in a ponytail.

"Hi, my name is Tracy Mullins, and this is my daughter Annie. Annie had suffered for two years with stiff joints and had trouble breathing. It is heartbreaking to see your child suffer. All you want is to see your child have a happy, normal childhood like other kids. Well, she couldn't play with them since her legs always hurt and her coughing spells were so bad sometimes. I was already using Bio Strength, so I figured if it could help me, it might help her. Well, lo and behold, after a week or so of rubbing Bio Strength on her legs and chest before she went to bed, she stopped complaining about her legs. Then she stopped coughing. She started playing with the other kids on the street." Tears welled up in Tracy's eyes.

"This product has made such a difference in Annie's life. I've got my little girl back!" The crowd gave them a standing ovation. Tears were flowing everywhere. Paul felt a huge lump in his throat.

"And that's not all," said Tracy. "I don't know if it's a coincidence or not, but Annie has grown two inches since we've used Bio Strength. She has always been short, and now she's catching up to other kids. I can't explain it, but I don't care. We *love* Bio Strength!"

Carlos explained to Paul that Bio Strength always told its distributors to never make medical claims. Specific medical conditions were never to be mentioned by name. You could legally say things like increased energy, strength, or easing discomfort. The word "pain" is a medical term, so its use was strictly forbidden. Every person giving a testimonial was coached on what they could and could not say. The FDA watched closely to see if medical claims were ever made.

Paul had never felt so much energy and emotion in one place in his life. Even in his childhood church, there was none of this kind of enthusiasm. This had the feel of an old-time gospel hour.

"Our next speaker is a gold distributor from Jacksonville, Florida. She's going to tell us how she achieved her success in Bio Strength. Let's hear it for Joanne Griggs!"

Joanne was dressed in a stylish black pantsuit. Her long blonde hair was curled and bounced as she strode to the lectern. The spotlight on Joanne glistened off her long blonde hair. Paul and Carlos were giddy seeing one of their own on stage.

"Hi, I'm Joanne Griggs. When I was first introduced to Bio Strength by Dr. Garfinkel, I immediately saw the income potential. I was in sales and was tired of limits put on how much I could make. But with Bio Strength, there is no limit! There really isn't. How many jobs do you see where the earnings potential is unlimited? None."

"I approach this as a business with prospects first. I'm looking for leaders who want to run their own business. If you simply tell enough people about what you have, someone great is going to join you." Joanne had a habit of brushing her hair away from her face when she talked.

"Anthony Robbins said all of us can live the life of our dreams. I don't apologize to anyone about getting into Bio Strength for the money. I just lay it out there for people to see. Some see it, some don't. But no one is going to stop me from my dreams. I'm going to get there with Bio Strength," said Joanne with her voice rising. "Don't you want it, too?" she yelled to the crowd.

The crowd roared and came to its feet. Paul and Carlos high-fived each other. The music began and everyone danced in the aisles. It was a full-fledged party. When the music died down, Joanne grabbed the microphone.

"We hope you enjoyed the program tonight. There's a full day tomorrow of fantastic breakout sessions. Have a great night!"

Bo Valentine was seated in the second row on the floor. All the bigwigs got to sit together up close. Bo had planned to meet a woman backstage during the program who was a Bio Strength wannabe and looked at him with childlike adoration. That was just the way he liked it.

Bo kissed Kitty goodbye and told her he was needed backstage to plan the next day's session. Several rows back sat Melanie Waters, a successful distributor from Portland. She had a fling with him several years ago, but he dumped her for another woman in Portland. Bo had violated one of his own rules---never date more than one woman from the same town.

Melanie's eyes glared at Bo as he strode past her. He walked with a pompous Donald Trump attitude that she always hated.

Another pair of eyes caught sight of Bo. Kim Davis had been in Bio Strength for three years, and Bo was in her upline. He had sponsored her and convinced her she could make money. She had some initial success, since Bo fed her some leads and helped her. He pulled his usual tricks with her and got her excited about a life of financial freedom, so she approached all her friends and family and managed to alienate most of them. Bo had a brief fling with her until he dumped her for someone he found more attractive. He stopped returning her calls and pretended that he hardly knew her. She almost dropped out of Bio Strength several times, but she decided to come to the national conference anyway.

Kim thought she might see Bo, but she didn't know how she would feel about it. She knew she had to confront him. He was a creep to end things the way he did. What burned her up more was his pretending not to remember her.

Kim got up from her seat and followed Bo backstage. The crowd was still dancing to the music as Bo found his way down a hallway backstage. His assistant was waiting for him at the door to a dressing room while the starry-eyed wannabe was inside. There seemed to be an endless supply of women admirers, and Bo was all too willing to oblige them. He loved playing a god.

Bo slipped into the room and shut the door behind him. Just as the door closed, Melanie and Kim bumped into each other as they burst around the corner.

"I'm sorry. Are you okay?" asked Melanie.

"I think so," said Kim. "Do I know you?"

"I don't think so. I'm Melanie Waters. I was just going back to speak to Bo Valentine."

"So am I. Hi, I'm Kim Davis. How do you know him?"

"He got me into Bio Strength and made me think I was gonna get rich," said Melanie.

"Funny, he told me the same thing."

"He also told me he was divorcing his wife, but that never happened."

"Same here. Seems like he tells the same story to a lot of people. Why don't we both go talk to him?"

"Alright. I'm a little nervous. Who's that guy standing in front of the door?" asked Kim.

"I don't know, but let's go find out."

Melanie and Kim approached a small, thin young man smoking a cigarette.

"May I help you?" he asked as he casually leaned against the door.

"Yes, please. We want to speak to Bo."

"I'm sorry. He's in a meeting right now," he said as he eyed the ladies suspiciously.

"Is he in there?" Melanie asked, gesturing toward the door.

"And who exactly *are* you?" he said sarcastically.

"We're both old friends. Oh, is that Tony Robbins?" said Melanie as she pointed behind him.

Just as he turned to look, Melanie grabbed the door handle and pushed as hard as she could. To her surprise the door was unlocked, and the young man fell backwards into the room with Melanie on top of him. Bo and a young lady were lying on a sofa half- naked when the door swung wide open.

"What's going on?" screamed Bo as Melanie picked herself off the floor. She grabbed a bra strewn on the floor and handed it casually to the young lady on the couch.

"Here, you might need this, sweetie."

Bo scrambled to find his pants while the young woman turned around to put on her bra.

"Melanie? What are you doing here?" asked Bo as he put his belt on.

"I might ask the same question to her. I think Kitty would love to hear about this."

"You wouldn't."

"Yes, I would. And by the way, do you remember Kim Davis?"

"Of course I do."

"Oh, now you remember me? Do you also recall how things ended?" snarled Kim.

"Yes, I'm sorry. Listen, I would appreciate it if you didn't mention this to anyone," said Bo as he buttoned his shirt.

"It's gonna cost ya," said Melanie.

"Tim, could you get my checkbook and take care of these ladies?"

"Sure, boss," said Tim as he casually pulled out a checkbook from his rear pocket. "How much do you want me to write it for?"

"I'll give each of you ladies a thousand dollars if you leave this convention and don't come back. Deal?"

Melanie and Kim exchanged a quick glance and smiled.

"Deal," said Melanie.

"Great. Tim, could you escort these ladies out the back of the arena and give them each a check?"

"My pleasure, boss. This way ladies," said Tim as he led them down the hallway to the back door of the convention hall.

"If you step out that door right over there, I'll hand you your checks."

"Oh, we're not falling for that," said Kim. "Give us the checks first, and then we'll leave."

"I didn't want to have to do this, but you leave me no choice," said Tim as he pulled out his two way radio.

"Security backstage, *now!*"

"You're not gonna have us thrown out of here," said Melanie as two beefy security guards quickly walked towards them.

"I'm sorry to have to do this. Guys, could you see these ladies make it safely outside?"

"We'll still get our checks, right?" asked Kim.

"I'll mail them to you. Take them out, *now.*"

Each security guard grabbed Melanie and Kim and led them out of the door to the parking lot.

"Hey, easy on those arms, Sasquatch. That hurts!" yelled Melanie.

The guards let go and turned around to go back inside. They left Melanie and Kim alone in a dimly lit section of the parking lot.

"I can't believe he screwed us over again. I'm not finished with Bo," said Melanie.

"Neither am I," said Kim. "Hey, it's kinda creepy in this parking lot. Let's get outta here."

Just then a large rat rustled around in a trash bin nearby.

"What was that?" whispered Melanie as she grabbed hold of Kim's arm.

"I'm not sure, but I'm not waiting around to find out," said Kim as the two of them walked briskly from the back of the lot. They found their way to a small Italian restaurant across the street and sat at a table in the back and ordered a bottle of wine.

"I feel horrible for Bo's wife," said Melanie as she sipped her wine. "Do you think she knows anything about us or the other women?"

"I don't know, but I'm glad to know I'm not alone. I really thought he loved me."

"I thought he loved me, too. Ya know what they say, though," said Melanie.

"What's that?"

"What goes around comes around."

Chapter 7

Paul and Carlos woke up at 7 a.m. to the alarm clock. It had been hard to go to sleep after the opening night of the convention since they were both so wired up from the celebration. They had stayed up until 2 a.m. talking to fellow distributors from around the country. It was amazing to Paul the many different walks of life people came from in Bio Strength. Most were in their 40s and 50s. Their common thread was a need to be part of something exciting that was bigger than them. The monotony of making a living was numbing their souls little by little, and most of them were just plain bored. Paul had almost killed himself from depression, but the energy he got from the Bio Strength crowd was intoxicating. He had longed for years to have something to be excited about. Bio Strength gave him the outlet he needed to dream again.

Carlos had signed both of them up for the same classes. He had learned the importance of supporting your downline and the team concept. No one needed to do this business alone.

"We got a long day ahead of us. Lots to learn. Let's go grab some breakfast," said Carlos.

"Let me take a quick shower," said Paul.

"Hurry it up. Some of the classes fill up quickly. Ya got to get there early to get a seat."

Bio Strength had lined up an array of doctors to sit on a panel to answer questions. The sight of a doctor in a white coat gave an unquestioned stamp of validity to Bio Strength. Distributors were much more apt to believe in something doctors used. Every doctor who signed on had established a solid downline, mainly from recommending to patients and speaking at Bio Strength meetings. Many were approaching six-figure incomes with Bio Strength after being involved for less than two years.

Dr. Garfinkel was the speaker for the first session of the day, and Paul and Carlos got there early for a good seat. The room quickly became standing room only. Just as the meeting was about to start, a tall, attractive blonde strutted into the room. It was hard to miss Joanne Griggs. Every guy's head turned and followed her into the room. Seeing there were no seats, she turned to the back of the room. Carlos elbowed Paul in the ribs hard.

"Give her your seat, dummy."

Paul came out of his trance and quickly jumped up to offer his seat to Joanne.

"Why, thank you so much," said Joanne with a big smile.

"My pleasure," said Paul blushing.

Paul headed to the back wall, proud of his chivalry. Carlos was more than happy to sit beside Joanne. That was his ulterior motive anyway.

"Thank you so much for coming," Dr. Garfinkel began. My name is Roy Garfinkel, and I am a general practitioner in Jacksonville, Florida. Before I talk about the Bio Strength products, I have to tell you about the business opportunity. For years now I've watched my income drop due to insurance companies slashing reimbursements and cutting corners everywhere. I quickly decided I needed a Plan B if I was to make money. Everyone should have a back-up plan for making money. You never know if your job will be terminated. Look at all the downsizing companies have done. I needed something to fall back on, but it had to be a product I believed in."

"A physician friend of mine told me about the success he had using Bio Strength. I deal with patients and their pain. Most of them are pretty desperate when they come to me, so they'll try anything. I had one patient with a frozen shoulder so bad he couldn't lift his arm up but a few inches. He was an avid tennis player, but he had to give it up. I gave him some Bio Strength to try, and the results were phenomenal! After one week of using Bio Strength cream on his shoulder, he was back to playing tennis again. No pain pill can give you these results that fast and with no side effects. That patient signed up to be a distributor and already is at the Silver rank. What better way for someone to start a business than when they already have used it and are a big believer in it?"

The audience hung on every word Dr. Garfinkel said. Many were taking notes. The 45-minute session flew by for Paul. Carlos had heard Dr. Garfinkel speak a dozen times, so he pretended to be listening. He was mostly interested in checking out the plunging cleavage Joanne was showing off next to him.

"Does anyone have any questions?" Dr. Garfinkel asked.

Instantly twenty hands went up in the audience, and Dr. Garfinkel recognized a lady in the front row for her question.

"You've had a great deal of success, it seems, because you're a doctor and have instant credibility and a steady stream of patients who are in pain. We don't have that, and I want to know how us ordinary folks can make it since we're not doctors!"

"Good question," said Dr. Garfinkel. "You definitely don't have to be a doctor to make it in this business. In fact, I believe it can be a liability. When I talk about Bio Strength, I'm putting my credibility on the line. Other physicians are clearly skeptical of something they've never heard of before, so I have to be careful what I say. All you have to do is let the product do the talking for you. Anyway you don't have to be a doctor to share Bio Strength. Most of the top distributors aren't doctors. Most doctors don't have the time to think about another business. It's only when they see their incomes shrink that they start to look for alternative streams of income. Did that answer your question?"

"Yes, thank you Dr. Garfinkel."

After a few more questions the session ended and Paul and Carlos were off to their next class. The rest of the day was filled with everything from more sessions with medical panels to product-oriented classes filled with testimonials. Paul took notes furiously and became more and more excited. He could not wait to go home and start his business. He knew somehow he was going to make it big with Bio Strength.

Carlos could see the fire in Paul's eyes. He knew that bringing him on this trip was the right thing to do. All he had to do was turn him loose.

"After classes are over, let's get a quick bite to eat before the closin' ceremonies tonight," said Carlos.

"Sure," said Paul. "What's on tap for the closing ceremony? Do you know who's speaking?" Paul was speaking very quickly and with an animation that he hadn't felt in years. Finally had had something to be excited about, and he hadn't even made a dime yet.

I'm not sure who's speakin'," said Carlos, "but I'm sure they'll send us outta here with a bang!"

Carlos could not get over how excited Paul was. He didn't dare tell him how the initial enthusiasm wears off within a month after one of these conventions. He remembered one distributor who was so excited after a convention that he called every one of his relatives about his new business. He ended up bugging his extended family so much that they no longer took his calls.

Carlos had been in the business long enough to see how reality set in quickly with new distributors. He felt that telling Paul how hard it was would be like telling newlyweds how quickly the honeymoon ends only to be replaced by stress, kids, money worries, infidelity, and divorce. He knew that even with his help, Paul would have to navigate the next stage on his own.

Chapter 8

"Good evening Bio Strength people! How ya feelin' tonight?" said Bo Valentine as the crowd roared their approval. Paul and Carlos sat in the seventh row on the floor in the middle of the madness. Melanie and Kim sat stone faced in a back row and shot death rays from their eyes at him.

"How did ya'll like the breakout sessions today?" asked Bo again as the crowd cheered. They were like putty in the hands of an evangelical preacher.

"Awwwright, that's great! But you ain't heard nothin' til you've heard our next speaker. He's here to tell us about his inspirational climb up Mt. Everest. Please welcome Nate Williams!"

Neither Paul nor Carlos had heard of Nate Williams before. Nate was six feet tall with black curly hair. He appeared to be in his early 30s, and he approached the lectern confidently with a big smile.

"Good evening San Diego!" yelled Nate. I know most of you don't know me, but I'm Nate Williams. Now I don't know much about Bio Strength, but Bo asked me to come talk to you about goals, dreams and finding inspiration in your life."

"I never thought in a million years I'd be standing in front of thousands of people talking about climbing Mt. Everest. I also never thought I'd have testicular cancer at age 28, but I did. But I'm here to tell you that no matter where you come from, no matter what's happened to you in the past, your life is an open book from here on out. The pages are blank, and you can decide what you want written on them."

Paul and Carlos leaned forward in their seats to listen. Nate had captured the audience's attention.

"When I was 28, I was diagnosed with testicular cancer, and they had to remove one of my testicles. A cancer diagnosis is always scary, but getting it in your 20s is a shock. I began to think of all the things I wanted to do in my life because I really had drifted and had no real direction. I always knew where the next party was, though. I started thinking how I wanted my life to be. What did I really want out of life? I made a conscious decision to pursue my dreams. I had always wanted to climb Mt. Everest, so I promised myself after I got well, I would do it."

"I figured you could still climb Everest with one testicle. A friend told me I had really big balls to climb Everest. I told him no, not anymore. Just *one big one*." Paul and Carlos almost fell out of their seats on that line. The crowd loved it.

"I put together a team for the expedition, but then I realized you needed money…lots of it to climb Everest. I became a professional beggar. I asked everyone I knew to help me, but it just wasn't enough."

"I had already started getting in shape. I began running and lifting weights, and soon I was running 10 miles a day. While I was running, I came up with the idea of making a documentary of my climb. I looked for sponsors to help me get started, but I realized that actually climbing Everest would be easier than finding a sponsor for some unknown guy who had never been on any kind of expedition and had never done a documentary. I had no experience whatsoever, but what I really had was enthusiasm. I couldn't stop thinking about what it would feel like to be at the summit of Mt. Everest. The view I had in my dreams was breathtaking. I felt such a sense of peace standing on top of the world. The icy peaks and blue sky stretched on forever, and I was complete."

"Don't ever let the excuse 'I'm new at this,' or 'I've never done this before' stop you from your goals and dreams. If you really want them bad enough, you can achieve them. It's like walking down a path. I once went running in a beautiful, green wooded trail, and I came to a fork in the path. The left side was straight and wide open while the right side was dense, curvy and filled with ditches and tree roots. I decided to take the path less traveled. One trip walking through the woods does not make a path, but if you walk it many times, a real path forms. It's the same with your dreams. Keep dreaming it…keep walking down that path, and you *can* make your dreams a reality."

"I finally found a sponsor who really felt sorry for me, I think. He actually told me to buy life insurance before I went because he didn't think I'd make it back. He had that much confidence in me. I put together a six-man team with two cameramen. The second cameraman was a backup in case the first one died, we all joked. As we gathered our equipment together at the base, I had to find a local Sherpa to guide us. Believe me, it's critical to have a good Sherpa. Here is a picture of our group the day before we started." A large screen behind the stage flashed the picture Nate described.

"That's our Sherpa right there," Nate said pointing a long stick at the screen. "We couldn't pronounce his name, so we decided to call him Shermie. He was so cool and didn't care what we called him as long as we paid him. Shermie had climbed Everest 12 times and almost died twice. He got frostbite so bad he lost a toe on each foot. We came up with another nickname for Shermie. We called him Octopus since he only had eight toes. I don't think he liked that nickname very much."

"Here's a picture of us with Everest in the background. Did you know there are still bodies frozen in the snow on the mountain? You pass them on your way up. There are dozens of corpses frozen on the slopes of Everest. I stopped and paid my respects whenever I came upon a body. I said the same little prayer each time that went something like, 'Dear Lord, please commit this person's soul to the Mt. Everest in heaven. My dream is to climb to the summit, and I need you here with me. Thank you for all you have blessed me with, and bless the dead here before me. Amen.'"

"At 29,000 feet, the thin air makes each step difficult. Breathing is almost impossible without oxygen. Humans weren't made to survive in those conditions. If one of those white-out blizzards comes up, all you can see is the hand in front of your face. You think you've felt cold before? There's cold, then there's cold as hell, and then there's Everest cold. When that wind blows off the mountain, wind chills reach minus-60 degrees. Here's a picture of us about half-way up. As you can see, ice is forming on our beards. You have to be vigilant with your extremities. Frostbite can happen so quickly. None of wanted to have octopus feet."

"On the morning of our final ascent, we were within 200 feet of the summit, but a monster storm developed. We had to make a decision on whether we would risk it all to get to the summit or turn back. I said a little prayer asking for guidance on what to do. We had worked so hard for months putting this expedition together, and it seemed so cruel to have to turn back now. But what good does it do anyone to die on a mountain when you have a choice to live? I had given everything I had. My muscles were aching, and my feet were frozen. I suspected I would lose several toes. I'm not a quitter, but I made a decision to live that day. I would come back to the summit another day. We headed back down the mountain. It was tough, but we made the right decision."

"Just because you are descending the mountain doesn't mean you're out of danger. In fact, most deaths on climbs like this occur on the descent. Two of our group made a dangerous fall into a crevice, and if not for Shermie having rescued them, they would be frozen blocks of ice up there now."

"I made my second attempt at Everest the next year. My first sponsor backed out, but he was glad I made it back alive. He couldn't bear the thought of financing another attempt at dying, so he backed out. He said the guilt would've been too much for him to bear if I died because he financed another trip. I understood his decision, but I had to go begging again. We put together a different team this time and mapped out our strategy. I was so confident in our team's ability. I knew we would make it up to the summit this time. The unknown variable is always the weather, but it was unbelievably cooperative for the first four days of the climb. We were making record time. Here's a picture of us making snow angels with Shermie. You know he lives in the snow and had never made a snow angel before. He made his first with us. Isn't he a cute little Sherpa?" asked Nate as the audience laughed at the picture of Shermie doing a snow angel.

"The weather started to turn as we made camp the night before our final ascent. The forecast was for a huge storm the next day. When we woke, the conditions were horrendous. Any attempt to take the summit was pure suicide. Even Shermie didn't want to try it. I couldn't believe I was going to be denied two times on my attempt to climb Mt. Everest. I was beginning to wonder if I would ever get a chance again. Our hearts were heavy as we started our descent. The temperature was minus 28, and the wind felt like it was slicing through our bodies. One of our crew got severe frostbite and lost several toes. Each of us was beyond exhaustion. We made it back safely, but I questioned whether I wanted to try it again. I couldn't take a third failed attempt. Maybe it was time for me to move on to my next dream." Nate's voice was filled with emotion as he continued to speak. Paul and Carlos sat on the edge of their seats to listen.

"But something happened a year later," Nate said with tears welling up. "Show the picture, please." There was a momentary pause. "Here I am on the summit of Mt. Everest!" The screen showed a triumphant Nate standing on the summit of the tallest mountain in the world. His arm was around Shermie as they beamed with pride. The crowd erupted and gave a thunderous spontaneous standing ovation. Paul felt a lump in his throat as he stood and applauded.

Nate paused and took in the ovation as he turned and gazed at the picture.

"I get chills when I look at this picture. I was literally on top of the world. The sky was the most beautiful blue I have ever seen, and it was surreal standing there. I had made it. I had dreamed this dream a thousand times, and it finally came true. I thought of a verse from Hebrews that I read every night for the three years it took me to climb Everest. It says, *"Faith is the assurance of things hoped for, the conviction of things not seen."* I was so sure that I would stand on top of Everest. I anticipated that moment in my thoughts every day for years. I vividly imagined myself on top of that mountain."

"Each of you can do the same. What are your dreams? At what age did we stop dreaming? Don't wait until you get sick like me to chase them. You've got one life, so go live it to the fullest. Your life is an open book, so go fill in the pages. Remember that verse *"Faith is the assurance of things hoped for, the conviction of things not seen."* Imagine your dream. Taste it. See it. *Feeeel* it. Now go live it. It's yours if you want it bad enough. God bless you. Thank you."

Paul and Carlos stood with the rest of the crowd for a two-minute ovation for Nate Smith. His speech was more motivating than anything Paul had ever heard. He was ready to take on the world.

Chapter 9

Paul talked non-stop on the flight back to Jacksonville. He did three strength tests on people while waiting in line at the terminal. Carlos had given him a small tube of Bio Strength, and Paul was putting it to use. He handed out at least ten business cards. On the plane he dreamed of the house he would buy. It would be a large brick Georgian- style mansion on a hill with a pool. His red Ferrari was parked in front, and a beautiful blonde woman in a red bikini stepped out of his pool. The water glistened off her rock- hard body.

"Paul," said Carlos while shaking him. "Paul, we're landing."

Paul was blissful as he dreamed about his future life, so it took him a few seconds to realize he was dreaming.

"I'm sorry. I was in a beautiful dream," said Paul.

"Oh, yeah?" said Carlos. What was it about?"

"Oh, just a beautiful house, a gorgeous woman and a red Ferrari."

"Sounds good to me," said Carlos. "How'd it feel to have all that?"

"Awesome, of course," said Paul.

"Good, here's how to make it come into your life. Think about your dream scenario now. Do you feel it?" asked Carlos.

Paul closed his eyes for a moment. "Yeah," he said.

"No, do you really *feeeeel* it? Imagine you've got what you desire *right no*w. Then tell me how you feel."

A broad smile crept onto Paul's face. Carlos watched for that smile. It was then that he knew Paul was feeling right.

"Now you've got it! Keep that feelin' going. Act as if you have it now, and you know what, the universe will bring it to you. It has to happen. It may not always happen the way you think it will. But it'll come. It's a natural law."

"You mean, all I gotta do is get into that feeling place I wanna be in, imagine I already have it, act as if I have it now, and boom it's mine?" asked Paul.

"That's right," Carlos replied.

"How come everybody doesn't do it?"

"Not everyone knows about it. And if they did, they might try for a little while and then give up. Somethin' happens, life gets in the way, and they lose their enthusiasm and their dreams. They go back to the same old rut as before and wonder why they're not happy," said Carlos.

"I'm not going to let that happen," said Paul. "You just watch me. I used to be in sales, and I know tons of people. I'm going straight to the top."

Carlos had been around long enough to predict who would burn out and who would make it. Paul seemed very committed, but he would wait and see what happened in a month. He witnessed too many that came back all psyched up like Paul only to quit when the first relative they call rebuffed them.

Carlos and Paul headed towards the baggage claim. Paul handed a business card to the man beside him with whom he had struck up a conversation. He even managed to do a strength test on him before the bags rolled out. Carlos rolled his eyes in disbelief. He did not want to dampen Paul's enthusiasm, so he just watched as Paul grabbed his bag from the carousel.

"Thanks for giving this opportunity to me. I needed something to believe in."

"It's been my pleasure," said Carlos. "You've come a long way from when I first met ya. Let's talk before the next Bio Strength preview."

Paul stepped outside to call a cab, and the Florida humidity enveloped him. He hailed a taxi and hopped in.

"Where to?" asked the driver.

"Fruit Cove," said Paul. It would be a forty-five minute drive home from the airport, so Paul struck up a conversation with the driver.

"What's your name," said Paul.

"George."

"How do you like being a cab driver?"

"Oh, it's okay. It suits me for now."

"Ever wish you had more money?"

"Of course. Who doesn't?"

"Well, I've just come from a national convention of a company called Bio Strength. Ever heard of 'em?"

"No."

Paul started enthusiastically telling George about the company and how amazing the products were. He had a captive audience, so there was nothing for George to do but sit there and listen. As they neared Paul's home, Paul finally stopped and asked a question.

"Why don't I drop by this week and show it to you? Which day is better, Tuesday or Wednesday?"

"Wednesday would be okay," George said half-heartedly.

"Alright, let me get your address." Paul pulled out his notebook.

"102 Airport Road."

"What's better, days or nights?"

"Evenings are better."

"Ok, how about Wed. at 7 p.m.?"

"That's fine."

"How much do I owe you?"

"Forty dollars."

Paul handed him a fifty-dollar bill. It was money Paul couldn't afford, but he wanted to give the impression of success. Besides, George was his first prospect.

"Keep the change," said Paul.

"Thanks!"

"I'll see you Wednesday at 7 p.m."

Paul walked to his front door and passed the stacked boxes of Bio Strength products. He sat down and made a list of everyone he knew just like his Bio Strength manual told him to do. He thought he would have no problem selling his inventory at a profit and then adding lots of distributors to his downline.

That night he dreamt of driving a red Ferrari up to a beautiful brick house with a pool overlooking a river. A beautiful blonde was there to greet him at the door. Paul was so certain of his success at Bio Strength he could taste it. He was beginning to create the world he wanted to live in with his thoughts. He remembered Carlos had told him to begin with the end in mind. Finally, he drifted asleep in dreams of his perfect world.

Paul woke up at 9:30 a.m. to a car alarm going off in front of his house, and he could not believe he had slept so late. Paul felt an intense sense of urgency to get his business going. All he had at this point for his business was a living room full of boxes and a large credit card bill.

The Bio Strength manual said to start by contacting your "warm market" consisting of family and friends. There was a page with 100 lines for your warm-market contacts. Paul started writing down names and phone numbers and came up with 150. He had plenty of contacts from his previous sales jobs.

He sat down for breakfast with a bowl of corn flakes and sniffed the milk before pouring it on his cereal. It smelled sour, but he didn't think a week past the expiration date was too bad. Paul started calling the first twenty names on his warm-market list. He invited each to attend a preview of Bio Strength at Dr.Garfinkel's office on Thursday night. The calls took longer than he expected because he had to go through the social formalities of catching up with people that he had hadn't spoken to in a while. Paul felt awkward inviting old friends to a business meeting about a company they knew nothing about. No one had heard of Bio Strength, and they felt no compelling reason to jump into a company that Paul had been involved with for only a few weeks. Everyone seemed to have plans for Thursday night. Paul decided to quit for the day and try again tomorrow. He focused his thoughts on his dreams again and started feeling better.

Paul told himself that the first day was an aberration and that the next day would be different. He made 37 calls and left 25 messages. His actual conversations with his warm market resulted in nine "no's" and three "maybes" to his invitation to the preview.

Paul took the "maybes" as a yes. It didn't occur to him that some people were too polite to say no because they didn't want to openly disappoint a friend.

Paul called Carlos to tell him what he was up to. "Carlos, this is Paul."

"What's goin' on, my future Royal Diamond?" asked Carlos.

"I've made my 100-name list and have called about half of them already. I don't have a firm yes yet about coming to the preview."

"What are you sayin' to 'em in your calls?"

"That I've gotten into a new business with a company called Bio Strength, and then I invite them to a preview of the company on Thursday."

"I would suggest findin' out which ones have an interest in lookin' at a business. You could start somethin' like, 'Have you ever thought of starting your own business?' You need to ask a few more questions before you invite them to a meeting. Just because they're your warm market doesn't mean they're automatically gonna be interested in comin' to a meetin'."

"Oh, you've got a point there," said Paul. "Also, I left 25 messages yesterday, and no one has called me back yet."

"What are you sayin' in your message?" asked Carlos.

"I invite them to a preview of a new business I'm involved with, and I give them the time, date and place for the preview. That way they have the information already, and I don't have to call them back," Paul said.

"Paul, I'm impressed with your initiative in making so many calls. I'd like to suggest never leavin' an invitation to a preview in your message. These people don't know squat about Bio Strength, and your warm list needs to be treated warmly. Leavin' a message about a business preview they know nothin' about is very impersonal. Does that make sense?"

"Yeah, boy I've really screwed up my start haven't I?"

"That's okay, there's a learnin' curve with everything. You're gonna do great. All it takes is one or two good people to drive your business. You just gotta keep lookin'."

Paul was disappointed in the lack of response to his invitation, but he was grateful that Carlos told him what he was doing wrong. At least he had an appointment Wednesday night. The cab driver named George seemed very friendly and interested. He woke up on Wednesday ready to go out and tell the world about Bio Strength. He knocked over one of the stacks of Bio Strength boxes in his living room when he walked to the kitchen. He realized he needed to get some of his money back by selling his inventory, so he got ready for his appointment that night. He printed up some pages from the Bio Strength website, and he placed an order for some Bio Strength pamphlets. He had to have some professional pamphlets to be taken seriously.

He had forgotten to get George's phone number, so he couldn't call to confirm the appointment. All he had was an address and a weak commitment for an appointment that night at seven. Paul set his GPS for 102 Airport Road. He was not too familiar with that part of town except for passing it on the way to the airport. He drove down a busy section full of check cashing businesses, bars, and tattoo parlors. An old black man on the side of the road turned up a brown bag for a swig of beer. Paul came to a red light and stopped. A man with an Atlanta Braves baseball cap stood in the median with a sign that read, *"homeless need money for food."* The man caught Paul looking at him, and Paul quickly averted his glance and locked his doors.

His GPS told him to turn right on Airport Road. Paul came upon rows and rows of small cinderblock houses with cars parked in the front yard. Many were vacant and had overgrown yards. Paul thought about turning around, but he was committed to keeping his appointment. He arrived at 102 Airport Road, and it looked like all the other houses but worse. The front door was hanging on by one hinge. A large tree branch that had fallen hung on the top of the roof. It was dark inside the house, and Paul was glad it was still light outside.

Paul walked briskly up to the front door. He had a briefcase and a bottle of Bio Strength ready for a muscle testing demonstration. He tried the doorbell, but it did not work. He rapped on the door three times, waited a minute and tried again. Still there was no response, and it did not appear anyone was home. He peered through the window glass and saw an old television with a single chair in the living room.

He raised his hand up to knock a third time when he heard a low growl behind him. He turned slowly around to see a huge fierce looking German shepherd glaring at him from the end of the sidewalk. This dog looked hungry, and he did not want to be chewed up. His mind raced as he plotted what to do. He had always read that dogs can sense fear, so he tried his best to appear calm. He knew if he made a run for it, he would never make it back to his car. The German shepherd started barking ferociously and inched closer to Paul.

Paul remembered seeing a trampoline beside the house next door. It had one of those tall protective nets around it to keep people from falling off. If he could make it there, he might be stuck on it, but at least he would be safe.

He avoided facing the dog or making eye contact as he remembered that facing a dog head-on is confrontational. He took a few slow baby steps towards the trampoline and then made a lightning fast dash toward it. He never saw the dog, but he heard it come tearing after him. Paul ditched his briefcase and Bio Strength bottle and ran for his life. As he neared the trampoline the German shepherd was right at his heels. The Shepherd started to take a chomp at Paul's ankle when Paul made a leaping dive onto the trampoline. Paul's adrenaline helped him fly through an opening in the netting and land in the middle of the trampoline. The shepherd jumped up and missed the opening in the netting where Paul had slipped through. The dog's nose buried deep into the net and sprung it back to the ground. Paul quickly moved toward the opening in the net and reattached the Velcro together. The shepherd got back on its feet and barked menacingly at Paul. The dog must have thought he couldn't get on the trampoline after the first try, so he decided he was going to guard the net to make sure Paul couldn't escape.

Paul's heart was thumping through his chest. He started jumping on the middle of the trampoline to keep his distance. He thought if the shepherd got on the trampoline, he would try to bounce the dog around with a big rebound bounce.

Next door Mrs. Gail Jones was sitting down for dinner. She was a retired postal worker who had bought the trampoline for her grandchildren to jump on. As she sat down, she thought she heard a dog barking outside.

Mrs. Jones saw something out of the corner of her eye through her kitchen window. She kept her gaze out of the window and saw the head of a middle aged white man bounce up and then disappear. A few seconds later the head popped up again. She bolted to the front door to see if it was a Peeping Tom.

She stood on her front porch in amazement as she watched Paul jumping up and down and talking to the dog. "Good boy, good boy, why don't you go home now," she heard Paul say.

Mrs. Jones belted out, "Excuse me, can I help you?"

Paul was never so glad to hear someone's voice.

"Yes, please. This dog chased me up here after I knocked on George's door. Could you please call him off?"

She called out to the dog.

"Max, go on home or I'll wup your hide. Go on!"

Max turned and ran away with his tail between his legs. Mrs. Jones had swatted him with a broom too many times for him to hang around.

Paul watched Max run across the street. He couldn't believe such a ferocious dog could be such a wimp at the sight of an old black woman.

"Thank you," said Paul. "How did you do that?"

"He was just playin' with you. He's like a little puppy."

"Oh, really," said Paul. He pointed to the holes in his pants from the dog bite.

"If he was just playing, then I'm bleeding," Paul said pointing to his pants.

"Well, if I were a dog and saw a stranger bouncing on a trampoline, I'd bite you too. Who were you here to see anyway?"

"George. Do you know where he is?"

"No, I don't," said Mrs. Jones as she put her hands on her hips and swayed her head back and forth. "I don't poke my nose in my neighbor's whereabouts. I just keep to myself and keep my doors locked. I was just sitting down for dinner when I saw your head bop up and down like a Mexican jumping bean."

Paul figured now was a good time to leave. "Thank you for helping me. I think I'll go home now."

"That's a good idea. You better make it quick 'cause I'm hungry and when I go back inside, ol' Max will come back."

"Good night ma'am. Paul hopped off the trampoline and picked up his briefcase. He handed the Bio Strength bottle to Mrs. Jones. "This is for your trouble. It's great for your skin and for wrinkles."

"You sayin' I got wrinkles?" said Mrs. Jones raising the pitch of her voice.

"No, of course not. But if you did...."

She interrupted him. "Max, come here boy, I've got a treat for you."

With those words, Paul ran to his car and was gone. His first appointment was a disaster. He got stood up, almost eaten by a vicious dog and sassed at by a little old lady. He needed a mental attitude adjustment, so he popped in a motivational CD he bought at the Bio Strength convention. The speaker said that most people quit too soon and that perseverance was the key. Paul listened intently as he drove, and he began to feel better. He slipped into his dreamlike state of his future. Think and create it, he repeated over and over. *Act as if I've already achieved my dreams.* Paul was not about to give up. He called Carlos who laughed hard after hearing his story.

"Lesson number one, Paul, is *always* confirm your appointment. You've learned a valuable lesson. Besides, you gotta learn to laugh at yourself. I woulda given anythin' to see you bouncin' on that trampoline!" Carlos laughed.

"Okay, I've learned something. I've learned how fast I can run with a German shepherd chasing me! For the next month Paul worked harder than he ever had in his life. He had gone through his warm-market list. His results were only about $650 in product sales. His friends felt sorry for him and bought product when they were not interested in looking at Paul's "business." Several friends were really put off that Paul called them to sell them something. Paul felt weird about it too, but he was willing to do anything to succeed.

Paul attended the weekly preview of Bio Strength held at Dr. Garfinkel's office. He kept an eye out during the preview for his invited guests that never came. Many said they would try to come, but they never showed up. Carlos had told him to go pick up people and bring them to the meeting, but Paul never had any luck with that angle.

Paul had $397 in his checking account and had maxed out his credit card. Bio Strength so far had cost him almost $7,000 from the cost of the convention to buying product, supplies, cards, books, and motivational CDs. Bio Strength was big into its distributors having the right "attitude" toward their business. Before you could really succeed, you needed to have the right mindset.

Paul bought into the mindset adjustment big time. He listened to CDs in his car and at home constantly. His world became Bio Strength, and every person he met was a potential Diamond distributor in his mind. A CD that Paul really liked had a speaker who compared finding the right person to digging for diamonds. It said you can dig for years and not find anything. Most people would quit too soon. But if you keep picking away with your ax, you will see just the top of what you're looking for. Dig a little deeper, and you've got a huge diamond under the surface. The speaker encouraged all Bio Strength distributors to keep picking away with an ax to find the right person. Most downlines had one or two people that really made most of the money for the sponsor. The message was to just keep looking for that diamond in the rough.

Paul received a pre-foreclosure letter from his bank and tossed the letter on top of his other unpaid bills. He needed to eat, so he rationed every dollar he had left. He told himself that many millionaires had once been broke, so why couldn't he be that once-broke future millionaire? Paul read about the actor Jim Carrey and how poor he was growing up. Carrey used to find ways to cheer his sick mother up by making funny faces at her to make her laugh. He was determined that he would not be poor as an adult like he was as a child. He began to imagine a better life, and he wrote a check to himself for one million dollars dated five years in the future. Within five years, he was able to write multiple million-dollar checks.

Paul liked the Jim Carrey success story so much that he pulled out his checkbook with $397 in it and wrote himself a check for one million dollars. It felt weird and wonderful to stroke a check for a million. He dated it a year in the future. Why wait five years to live your dream, thought Paul.

He kept listening to motivational CDs and reading about the network marketing business. Despite his current miserable financial shape, Paul was quite upbeat. He got a call from a friend who had bought a bottle of Bio Strength. He had great results with his arthritis in his hands, and he wanted to sign up to buy Bio Strength at wholesale prices. Paul was ecstatic to get his first distributor signed up. He called Carlos to tell him what happened. He was like a little kid who hit his first home run. Paul helped his friend sign up, and the next day Paul looked at his website to look at his new downline of one person. Each day Paul looked at his website to see if his friend had ordered anything yet. Finally, after a week he saw a glimmer of what every distributor longed to see…residual income. He had earned a whopping $12 in overrides on the order. But to him it may as well have been a million dollars.

Several more weeks passed, and Paul had managed to only sell a few cases of Bio Strength. Collection agencies left threatening voicemails about late payments. He tried listening to motivational CDs, but it was not helping him. He needed to talk to Carlos, so they met at the Starbucks where they first got together.

"Carlos, I'm really struggling with this business. I'm in over seven grand now and have almost nothing to show. I've tried everything. Even listening to motivational stuff is getting old. What should I do?"

Carlos had heard these same lines for years from new recruits. Paul was going though the typical buyer's remorse phase. Carlos had to be careful not to lose him now.

"Paul, you are doin' everythin' right and workin' hard. If this were easy then everybody would be doin' it. Anybody can do this business, but it's not for everybody. All it takes is the right person, and you just gotta keep looking. You can't quit now. You never know when the right person will come along. There's an old sayin' that the teacher will arrive when the student is ready. There's someone out there waitin' for you to tell them what you've got. They just haven't met you yet."

"I'm not quitting. I just need to see some positive results. It's hard to keep motivated with only some vague picture of future success."

"Vague?" asked Carlos curiously. "Is that what it is to you? Paul, you gotta refocus and make this real to you now. I'm gonna loan you a book called *Excuse Me, Your Life is Waiting* by Lynn Grabhorn. It'll help you get to the feelin' place you need to be at. Without the right feelin's, you send out negative vibes, and that's what you'll attract back to you. Like attracts like, so be very careful what you think and how you feel. Ever notice how complainers like to hang out with other complainers? They like to wallow together in their misery. You know, birds of a feather flock together."

Paul held the book in his hands. *Excuse Me, Your Life is Waiting*-what kind of name is that for a book?"

"A damn good one. Just read it. I'm gonna go so you can start reading it now. Call me when you're done, and we'll talk about it some more," said Carlos.

"Okay, said Paul sheepishly. He felt like he had just been scolded by his father. "I'll read it."

Carlos always had several copies of the book ready. He used it as a motivational tool for distributors when they needed it most.

Carlos left Paul at the table. He moved to a corner table so he could have some privacy. He was embarrassed to be seen reading a book with such a weird title. Self-help books were not supposed to be read in public, Paul thought. He used to make fun of people who read them. He had met many Bio Strength distributors that had every self-help and motivational book written. They could tell you everything about attitude adjustments and motivation, but none of them had made a dime in network marketing. Somehow their knowledge had not translated into success for them, but they felt good about themselves for trying.

The book talked about the astonishing power of feelings and how everything you bring into your life flows from how you are feeling. Paul had been stuck in negative thoughts about why his business was so bad. He was worried how he was going to pay his bills. The book said we create our lives by our feelings and not by thoughts. That was something different. Paul closed his eyes and thought of what he wanted. Same old nice house, car, pool, and beautiful blonde. Not much change there, he thought. He went a little deeper and imagined he already had all of those things and how that would make him feel. He felt the wind blowing his hair as he drove his red Ferrari. His stately brick mansion had a circular driveway. He parked his car out front and walked up the front stairs. A beautiful blonde had just gotten out of the pool in back and was drying off in the kitchen. He walked in the kitchen and she said, "Ya wanna go skinny dipping?"

Paul had a huge smile on his face. The couple at the next table was watching Paul's expressions and started giggling at him. His eyes were closed, and he had a look of pure ecstasy on his face. Paul opened his eyes to see the couple staring at him.

"Excuse me, what is that you're reading?" asked the woman.

"*Excuse Me, Your Life is Waiting*," said Paul.

"Guess you'd recommend it," the woman said.

Paul jumped up. "Sure. But I've got to go now, 'cause you know, my life is waiting."

Paul burst out of the Starbucks like it was the last day of school before summer vacation. He was on top of the world, and he was going to share his positive vibrations with everyone he met.

Paul headed to Melito's Restaurant for lunch. A line of a dozen or so people stood outside the door. He had eaten there hundreds of times, and he always felt like it was a second home. It was a cozy place with a long mahogany bar. Paul had known the owner Mike Melito for a long time. Mike was a gregarious Italian in his early 50s who knew everyone in his restaurant. If you sat too long in your booth when there were people waiting, he would yell out, "Hey, can I get a percentage of that deal?" It was his not so subtle way of getting you to leave so others waiting could sit down.

Mike had a penchant for hiring beautiful young waitresses. Several had side modeling jobs, and Mike could take his pick among them for his new flavor of the month. He had never married, and he felt no reason to. He was having too much fun. Melito's was an institution, and Mike was the kind of guy everybody wanted to be around.

Paul stepped into the usual Melito's madness. The only seat left was one at the bar, and Paul made his way to the barstool. Mike was busy glad-handing everyone. A pretty young bartender approached Paul.

"Whatcha havin' to drink?"

"Iced tea, please." Paul did not want to go for a beer now. He didn't want to spoil his positive vibes with soul-numbing alcohol. Paul watched Mike work the crowd. He was so smooth and natural. He was confident but not cocky, and people were drawn to his charisma. Mike walked by and recognized Paul.

"Hey, Paul, how have you been? Haven't seen you in a while."

"I've been great. I'm keeping busy with my new business," said Paul calmly.

"What is it? Weren't you selling paper?"

"Once upon a time, but this thing is ready to take off. We're exporting product in six countries now and four more by the end of the year," said Paul confidently.

Mike still didn't know what Paul was talking about, and Paul had drawn his interest successfully.

"What's the product?" asked Mike.

"It's called Bio Strength. It helps all kinds of joint pain. Here, I've got a little sample here. Paul pulled out a small tube of Bio Strength lotion. "Got any hurting joints?" asked Paul.

"Yeah, my shoulder is killing me. Look, I can't lift my arms up past my ear. I have to get someone to reach stuff high up on a shelf for me."

"Try some of this on it," said Paul. Mike grabbed the tube and rubbed a dab of lotion over each shoulder.

"Hey, I've got to catch the register. Thanks, I'll talk to you in a minute." Mike washed his hands off and smiled at the customer waiting to pay his bill. Mike was a continuous ball of energy and motion.

Paul ordered his hamburger and watched Mike work the room. He knew every person in the place. Local politicians liked to come there and be seen. Mike had run it for 24 years. Paul watched the flat screen television tuned to ESPN as the restaurant hummed with activity and conversation. Mike had to be making a killing with the restaurant, thought Paul. It ran so smoothly that Mike took several months off during the year.

Paul ate his burger and watched Mike in action some more. If he could somehow get Mike in his business, he would have it made. Paul wanted to talk to him some more, but Mike was too busy. Paul was content to watch the waitresses work their magic. Many guys came there just to flirt with them. The young ladies ate it up because they knew it translated into big tips. Paul had finished his burger and handed over the last dollars out of his wallet for his lunch. Somehow Paul didn't worry about money at this moment. Paul glanced over at Mike and saw him reach up with his right arm and grab a wine bottle off a shelf. Mike didn't even notice what he had done. Paul caught his attention on the way out.

"Hey Mike, try raising your right arm up for me." Mike raised his right arm up easily over his head. A look of utter disbelief crossed Mike's face. He hadn't been able to lift his arm up like that in five years.

"Paul, what the hell did you put on me?" asked Mike incredulously.

"Bio Strength lotion."

"What's in it?" asked Mike.

"I'm not really sure, but it's all natural ingredients," said Paul confidently.

"I haven't been able to do this at all for five years." Mike started swinging his right arm around like a windmill. "Hey everybody! Look at me!" yelled Mike. "Paul Cousins just put some kinda arthritis lotion on my shoulder, and I'm able to raise my arms up over my head for the first time in five years! This is unbelievable! Ya gotta see this stuff. I'm cured!"

All the lunch goers at Melito's erupted into applause for Mike. One customer said, "Here, try some on my hands. I've got arthritis bad." Paul started splashing Bio Strength on any hand or limb that was thrust at him. He even did a few strength tests on people. They were amazed at how strong they became with Bio Strength on. Paul had a ready-made audience, and he was taking advantage of it. Mike was constantly raising his arms over his head in disbelief.

"Look at this, som' bitch. I can fly like an eagle. Whooooo...." Mike hopped up on the bar and started flapping his arms like a bird. "Hey Laura, put on the Steve Miller song "Fly Like an Eagle" for me. A waitress walked to the stereo and put on the Steve Miller song for Mike. The whole restaurant became a karaoke bar with Mike leading the way on top of the bar. "Fly like an eagle let my spirit carry me...."

Paul sat back and let this scene sink in for a moment. Just a few hours ago he was depressed and almost ready to quit Bio Strength. Then Carlos gives him a book to read, he applied what he learned, and it worked like a charm. He still thought perhaps this was just luck, but he was not going to question how it happened.

Paul sold 15 bottles of Bio Strength at the restaurant that day. After all of the hubbub died down, Mike sat down with Paul to talk about what just happened.

"Paul, I don't know what's in this Bio Strength stuff, but I don't care. You don't know how fantastic my shoulder feels now. This can't be a placebo effect because I wasn't expecting anything to happen. There's a fortune to be made with this stuff, and I want in. How is your business going?"

Paul was trying his best to contain his excitement. He wanted Mike to think that this always happened when he put Bio Strength on people.

"I'm doing great," said Paul. He told himself he was not lying. *Fake it 'til you make it,* he thought.

"This stuff is fantastic," said Mike. "My shoulder has never felt better. This is a great way to supplement what I do in the restaurant. I'm doing fine financially, but the restaurant business really wears on you after 20 years. I've put in some serious hours here. I'd love to take some more time off, man. I'll sell this stuff from behind my bar. How much can I order at one time?"

Paul couldn't believe his ears. He had hit the mother load. "Five thousand dollars," said Paul.

"Well, let's do it now. Show me what to order," said Mike.

"Where's your computer?" asked Paul trying to stay cool.

"It's back here in my office."

Paul sat down and registered Mike as a new consultant. He had never signed anyone up before, so he had to bluff his way through it. Paul explained the compensation system and how each level paid more as you moved up in rank.

"Once you reach Royal Diamond level, you get paid on six levels below you. It's the ultimate in residual earnings. That's my goal-Royal Diamond," said Paul.

"Well, that's my goal, too," said Mike. He held his hand up for a high five.

"This Thursday at 7 p.m. there's a Bio Strength preview at Dr. Garfinkel's office. It'll be a great way for you to learn about the company and meet other distributors."

"Dr. Garfinkel's into this? I don't believe it," said Mike. "I've known him for years. He's always been into some different stuff financially, like race horses and capital venture stuff. He's all about the money, man. Everything he touches turns to gold. Man, I can't wait to tell him I'm in this. It'll kill him that I signed up under you instead of him. What's his level anyway?"

"He's a Gold distributor," said Paul.

"I wanna pass him and piss him off. He's so damn competitive. Last time I played golf with him, I bet him $100 I could beat him with all irons and no woods or driver. I beat him by five strokes, and he was steamed," laughed Mike.

"I didn't know he was like that."

"Hell, yeah. He's a horrible sport. Watch his face when I start making more money than him! He'll look like he bit into a lemon."

Paul stood up to leave. He felt if he stayed any longer, he might say something stupid and Mike would change his mind.

"Hey, I've gotta run. I've got some product to deliver. I'll see you at Dr. Garfinkel's office. How about if I pick you up?"

"Oh, no. I'll be there."

"Great! I'll see you then."

Paul shook hands with Mike and walked out to his car. He restrained himself from doing a little jig on his way out the door. When he got in his car, he let out a gut wrenching yell.

Yeahhhhhh!!!" Paul screamed. He pumped his fists like Tiger Woods sinking a long putt for a win. He slipped in a Van Halen CD, and the opening chords of "Jump" blared from the stereo. Paul could feel the energy coursing through his veins. He turned the volume up so loud that the rear windows shook. Paul sang in unison when David Lee Roth sang, "You might as well...*jump!*" Paul started bouncing up and down in the car to the beat. He was on top of the world right now. He pulled out his cell phone to call Carlos.

"Carlos baby, what's happenen?" shouted Paul.

Carlos had to hold the phone away from his ear because the music was so loud.

"Paul? Hey, can you turn the music down?"

Paul turned Van Halen down. "Hey, you know Mike Melito from Melito's Restaurant?"

"Of course. Everybody knows Mike Melito," said Carlos.

"Well, he's my second downline!" Paul said excitedly.

"You're kiddin', man!" exclaimed Carlos.

"Hell no. He's already ordered $5,000 of product. He's going to sell Bio Strength from his restaurant. I gave him lotion to put on his shoulders, and he had the fastest product experience I have ever seen. He could lift his arms above his shoulders for the first time in five years. Then he started dancing on the bar, and people were lining up to buy Bio Strength. It was surreal. I've got to thank you for giving me that book. I got into that place of feeling I wanted, and things turned around. It worked like magic."

"That's fantastic. It doesn't always happen that fast, but you certainly put out the right vibes, and your energy connected with his. I told you how important your attitude is. Now you *really* understand!"

"You bet I do. I'm gonna work on it every day. You watch my business take off."

"I'm with you every step of the way," said Carlos. Carlos knew that Paul had hit the jackpot by signing up a person like Mike Melito.

Over the next several months, Mike Melito sold case after case of Bio Strength lotion and nutritional drinks from his restaurant. He signed up 47 people in his downline.

Melito's was the perfect place to be a hub for Bio Strength. It was always packed, and Mike was telling everyone about his life changing product experience. Many customers had similar results and told their friends. It was a cycle that kept repeating itself, and it showed network marketing skeptics the power of many people doing a little to earn a lot. Bo Valentine called this leveraging the efforts of others to achieve your dreams.

  Paul received his first override check in the mail, and he had no idea how much it was going to be. He was several months behind on his mortgage, and his credit card was maxed out. He shook with excitement as he tore open the envelope. Paul could not believe his eyes when he gazed at the number. He stared at it for several seconds to let it sink in. Six thousand. Two hundred. Forty-seven dollars. Paul jumped up and down like a lottery winner. This was just the first month. If his growth kept going this fast, his checks would soon be over twelve thousand a month. Paul sank to his knees and screamed joyfully at his newfound success. He couldn't believe how fast this was happening. He pulled out *Excuse Me, Your Life is Waiting* to read up on how to handle success. It said to keep the good vibrations going and to continue the flow of money into your life, you had to give back. It seemed that hoarding money was not the right way to operate in the energy universe. Paul realized that he needed to give in order to keep on receiving. He had never had much money to give, and he always felt like he had to pay his bills first. There never seemed to be anything left for charity.

  Paul decided he would pay part of his credit card balance. To follow the book's advice, he decided on a charity he had read about in the paper called Builders Care. They fixed up homes for people who couldn't afford to do it on their own. Paul drove to their office the next day to deliver a check for $1,000.

  The Builders Care office was a small one-story brick home just outside downtown Jacksonville. Paul walked into the office and found a pleasant lady receptionist who appeared to be in her late 50s.

  "May I help you?" the receptionist asked politely.
  "Yes, I'd like to make a donation."

"Fantastic! Oh, bless you, my dear. And what is your name?"

"Paul Cousins."

"Paul, I'm Suzanne Leach. Very nice to meet you. Would you like to see some examples of where your money will go?"

"Yes, absolutely," said Paul.

"I'm not too busy now. There's a house just around the corner that we are doing some work in now. Why don't you ride with me to see our work first hand?"

"I'd be glad to," said Paul. He could not get over how friendly Suzanne was.

Suzanne drove Paul less than a mile away to an older neighborhood filled with homes in various states of disrepair. She stopped in front of a house with blue tarp on the roof. It was a small cinderblock house with a rusted gas grill in front. Two broken Wal-Mart plastic chairs sat on either side of the grill. At least ten workers scurried in and out of the house. All of them had a purposeful look on their faces.

"Those are our volunteers. They all contribute their time to help fix up these properties. This old home is all this lady has, and she couldn't afford to fix her roof. Let's go see how far they've gotten today," said Suzanne.

Paul and Suzanne walked to the front door. Every volunteer called out to Suzanne by name.

"Suzanne! How ya doin'. You're not dressed to work on a roof!" called out a volunteer kneeling on the roof.

"I'm up there with ya in spirit, honey. I'd break my neck climbing on a roof. Can we look inside?"

"Sure, go ahead."

Paul and Suzanne walked into a dark, musty living room. A frail elderly black lady sat in an antique wingback chair with plastic covering it. Her eyes got as wide as saucers when she saw Suzanne come in.

"Miss Ellie, how ya doin' honey?" Suzanne asked. Ellie grabbed her cane to stand up to give her a big hug.

"I'm doin' fine, but I don't know what I would have done without Builders Care," said Ellie as she started to cry. "My roof had been leaking for years, but I just couldn't afford to fix it. Then everything was gettin' mildew and my asthma got worse. I didn't know what I was gonna do. And then you called to tell me you were gonna fix it for me. That was the best phone call I ever had. Ya'll are a bunch of angels, that's what you are. Thank you so much!"

Paul watched as Suzanne and Ellie held their embrace for a minute. All the workers inside stopped and watched as the two ladies held on to each other like long lost sisters. Paul felt a lump forming in his throat. He looked around at the buckled, mildewed floors. Sunlight beamed through a gaping three-foot hole in the roof.

Suzanne introduced Paul to Ellie. "Miss Ellie, here is a man who walked into our office today and wanted to give to Builders Care. This is Paul Cousins."

"Nice to meet you," said Paul putting out his arm for a handshake.

"Put down that arm, you deserve a big hug," said Ellie as she gave Paul a warm hug. Paul hadn't hugged a woman since his divorce, and he never expected his first hug post-divorce would be from a sweet, old lady named Ellie. Paul felt more love in this Bio Strength hug than any in his life.

"We love helping people like you, Miss Ellie," said Suzanne. "We'll also sand these floors down and get them looking like new. It's not going to rain today is it?"

"Nah, we'll be fine," said a volunteer as he removed a moldy chair.

"And what do you do for a livin' Paul?" asked Ellie.

Paul was not prepared for this question. How did he respond without sounding like a snake oil salesman? He remembered practicing this answer with Carlos.

"I help people improve their health and eliminate joint pain. I then show them how to make a good living sharing the product with others," said Paul. There was a moment of silence as Suzanne and Ellie took in what Paul just said.

"What type of product is it?" asked Suzanne.

"It's an all-natural nutritional drink and a body lotion called Bio Strength."

"Well, I've got nothin' but aches and pains. Do you have any I can try?" asked Ellie.

Luckily Paul had a tube of Bio Strength in his jacket and pulled it out. "Sure, where does it hurt?"

"Where does it not hurt?" said Ellie laughing. "I'll try a little on my hands. My arthritis is pretty bad today."

Paul squirted some lotion in Ellie's outreached palm. He noticed how bent her wrinkled fingers were from arthritis. Ellie rubbed the lotion gently over her hands.

"Can I try some on my shoulder?" asked Suzanne. "It's been bothering me for years."

"Sure," said Paul. "Is it your right shoulder?"

"Yeah, I used to play tennis, but I can't anymore." Paul plopped a dab in Suzanne's palm, and she slowly rubbed her aching shoulder under her sleeve.

Most of the volunteers had various aches and pains, and Paul was passing the lotion around to each of them. The tube was empty when Paul finally got it back. Carlos had taught him to never be without product or a business card, and he would be proud of his student right now. Paul watched the volunteers all happily going about their duties. He smiled when he overheard one person say how his arthritis pain in his elbow felt better already from the lotion. He could not believe Ellie had lived with a hole in her roof for so long. People were removing buckets and a large trash can she had put down to catch the water. They were each filled to the top, and they had to dip buckets into the trash can to empty them some before they attempted to remove them. Paul had been used to having nothing since his divorce, but at least he had a roof over his head. Seeing this reminded him to be grateful for everything he had. He knew there was always someone worse off than you no matter how bad you had it. His life was on the upswing now anyway.

"Paul, I should probably get back to the office. Ellie, call me when this is all finished. I want to see how nice it looks."

"I can't wait," said Ellie. "But the best thing will be to get a nice visit from you. I get so doggone lonely sometimes. My kids moved away, and this house is way too quiet. Will you please come for a visit?"

"I'd love to," said Suzanne. She leaned over to hug Ellie goodbye. After giving another big hug, Suzanne stepped back and rubbed her right shoulder.

"Paul, my shoulder didn't hurt at all when I hugged Ellie. The first time I hugged her, it really hurt."

Ellie piped in, "You know, my hands feel a little looser already. What's in that stuff?"

Paul had seen this same kind of thing happen at Melito's. But this time he was not as surprised as before.

Ellie continued to move her fingers around. "You know, I think they are feelin' better every minute. You said you show people how to make money at this. Social security doesn't go very far. Is this something a little old lady like me could do?"

"You sure could. Why don't I come pick you up this Thursday for a preview of the company? You'll hear from a local doctor who'll tell how Bio Strength has positively affected his life and his patients."

"Yeah, I'll come. I can't afford to buy anything yet, but I'd like hear about it."

"Great, I'll pick you up at seven."

"Wonderful," said Ellie.

Paul took down phone numbers from several volunteers who were interested in trying out the lotion for themselves or friends and family. Paul had walked into another gold mine.

Suzanne drove Paul back to Builders Care. "Oh, I almost forgot to give you the check. Here you go."

Suzanne was overwhelmed with his generosity. "A thousand dollars. That's fantastic! This will go a long way to helping people stay in their homes. How about I see to it that it gets applied to Ellie's house?"

"Absolutely. She deserves it," said Paul.

"Thank you so much," said Suzanne as she pulled up to Builders Care. "It has been a pleasure meeting you. You are a wonderful, generous man!"

"Believe me, the pleasure was all mine."

Paul got out of Suzanne's car and headed home. His mind was racing over what had just happened. He could not believe how a book had affected his life so dramatically. Paul made a commitment to himself that he would donate each month to Builders Care when he received his override check. He had made more contacts for himself, and the beautiful thing about it was that he was not really trying to. Paul had been approached over the years by obnoxious, overbearing network marketers who were in it for themselves. Paul saw himself as a generous network marketing guru who had more than enough money to give to charities. The problem was deciding who to give it to. Paul pictured himself handing out checks for thousands of dollars to charities all over Jacksonville. He felt more, so much more from giving than from getting.

Chapter 10

Paul attended every Thursday night Bio Strength preview, and he was proud to now have Ellie in his downline. She couldn't afford to buy much, but she always gave inspirational talks at the previews. She always told people how Bio Strength helped her arthritic hands feel better.

Paul watched his monthly checks grow quickly. After three months his check was over $14,000. He made sure to give to Builders Care each month. Carlos was reaping the benefits of Paul's success as well. He made about the same amount of money as Paul during those months. He had never made money like this in all his years of network marketing, and he refused to buy anything for himself except a nice bottle of wine to celebrate.

Bio Strength sales were growing rapidly worldwide. Seven more countries were set to come online by the end of the year. Paul and Carlos set up their websites and started recruiting people from all over the world. Paul used every trick in the book to get people to his site. He tied in with other companies through affiliate marketing and got referred by other health-related sites. Every week several dozen people bought product and two or three became a distributor.

Paul decided to focus on the Bio Strength products more than the business side when talking to prospects. Paul and Carlos had heated discussions on which strategy to use.

"Carlos, people want to try the product before they jump into the business. If they try it first, then they are sold on Bio Strength and the decision to become a distributor is easy."

"That's not how you came into the business," said Carlos. "You were lookin' for somethin' to do, and I was the right person at the right time. All I did was ask you some questions to get you thinkin' about your dreams again. The perfect candidate is someone who's bored. They're lookin' for somethin' to do, and it costs almost nothin' to join. If you find the right person like I did with you, they can take you to the top."

"That's what I did with Mike Melito. He had an incredible experience with it. Now he's the one who will push me to the top. Bo always said it is one or two people who make 80 percent of your income. Mike's downline is doing that now."

"Listen, man. That did work for you. I can't argue with that. Just realize that there are some people out there who are lookin' for somethin'. I suggest you put out ads that talk about a business opportunity marketin' revolutionary healthcare products worldwide," said Carlos.

"I can do that. But my main focus will still be on the product."

"That's fine. Hey, I just got wind of some new products comin' out soon. This will be a big boost in money right away."

"Doesn't it take time to get the word out about new products?"

"Heck no," said Carlos. "You gotta remember that the real customers for our products ain't the general public. They're the distributors themselves. They're the ones who drive most of the sales. You'll never make it in network marketin' tryin' to sell bottles of this stuff door to door. It's not set up that way. The money is in getting' other people to join you and earn money off what they buy. There are always huge incentives for distributors to buy value packs of the new product when it's introduced. I bet we see a 40 percent boost in our income the next month after a new product introduction. I've been through enough of 'em to predict that."

"I always knew the money was in building a downline, but I didn't really understand that the customers for Bio Strength are really the distributors. I should have known that because I had a living room full of product when I first started."

"Right. There are incentives paid to the sponsor whenever one of these value packs is sold. Remember, there ain't no advertisin' fees in our business. Retail products have huge costs with middlemen, shipping and advertisin'. We got none of that, so the distributors share in all the profit. It's a *beautiful* marketin' concept. It's just gotten a bad rep in the past by a few unscrupulous people," said Carlos.

"What is the new product being introduced?" asked Paul.

"I don't know. But they always bring out the big guns to introduce it. I'm sure it'll do well. I did hear they'll be introducin' a new way to market Bio Strength through a giftin' program."

"What do you mean by gifting?" asked Paul.

"Giftin' means you do exactly that. You give product away with no expectation of payment," said Carlos.

"What the hell kind of business model is that?" asked Paul incredulously.

"A damn good one. Let me tell you why. Your downline will buy into this because who doesn't wanna get free stuff? And the distributor gets to look like such a generous soul giving stuff away out of the goodness of his heart. But the real advantage is the volume of product bought. These product introductions generate huge volumes in themselves. But addin' a giftin' program is ingenious. We'll make a killin' off this. You've gotta convince your downline to be there for the kickoff. They'll buy whatever is introduced. The company is puttin' a lotta energy into this new product rollout."

"The part about us making money is great, but I still don't understand why anybody would want to give product away," said Paul.

"The idea is to get people to try the product, and then they'll sign up and buy product themselves to gift it to someone else. The circle keeps on goin'," said Carlos.

"What happens when people stop gifting?" asked Paul. "Then the whole thing falls down."

"That ain't gonna happen. Besides, people will still sell some product at retail. Distributors will keep buyin' product for themselves. This giftin' gets the product into as many people's hands as possible very quickly. You watch what happens," said Carlos.

"I feel kind of funny about this gifting stuff. I'm not too sure I like it, but I'll see how it goes," said Paul.

"Trust me, you'll like it. You'll like it even more after next month's paycheck."

"Ya know, maybe I should gift some to Miss Ellie. She can't afford to give product away."

"Good idea. Maybe she'll recruit somebody," said Carlos.

Paul picked up his phone and called Ellie.

"Hello."

"Miss Ellie. This is Paul. How are you?"

"Oh, Paul. I'm doin' just fine. Every mornin' I wake up is a great day."

"Listen, I want to tell you about a new program Bio Strength is coming out with soon. It's called a gifting program where you give product away to people for them to use."

"Oh, I can't afford to give anythin' away. I can barely buy any for myself."

"That's why I'm calling. I'm going to buy a few gifting packs for you to give away to your friends. It'll be my treat."

"Well I'll be. You don't hafta do that."

"I know I don't, but I want to."

"That's great. I got several friends who would love the lotion for their arthritis."

"Just come to the new product introduction and you'll see how it all works."

"I wouldn't miss it for the world. Thank you so much."

"You're welcome. I'll be in touch about the rollout for the gifting program. You take care, now."

"Goodbye."

Meanwhile, Bo Valentine was preparing for the big introduction of new Bio Strength products. His assistant told him about the two angry ladies looking for him, so he suggested to Bo that he lay low for a while. Bo took his advice and became as good as an altar boy. Little did he know Kitty was still using the private detective to help her snoop on him.

Kitty saw him writing notes and talking to the Bio Strength executives about some new product offering. She knew a new product always meant more commissions, so she was immediately curious about what it was. After all, she wanted Bo to be making as much money as possible when she divorced him.

"What is the new product coming out, honey?" Kitty asked sweetly.

"Sunscreen. It doesn't have all the harmful chemicals that most other sunscreens have. We're introducing it along with a new gifting program. Basically, you can buy packages of product of five hundred, a thousand or fifteen hundred dollars to gift to people. The more you buy, the less it costs per bottle of sunscreen. It's going to be huge, especially here in Florida with all the skin cancer," said Bo.

"Wow, that sounds great. When is the rollout happening?"

"This Saturday. We're expecting over three hundred people. We rented a large room at the Marriot in Ponte Vedra."

"That's great. I'd like to be there to help set up." She knew Bo would try anything to get away from her, so she didn't give him a chance to escape.

"Thanks, but I think we've got it covered."

Paul and Carlos continued working on their Internet sites. It was becoming increasingly clear that signing up a prospect online was much easier than face to face prospecting. When people made an inquiry online, they were usually somewhat interested. After trying Bio Strength and seeing the results, many signed up. It was a huge effort and waste of time to call people up and get them to come to a meeting. People didn't seem to have time anymore for meetings at night, particularly for a network marketing company. Paul still prospected, but the computer was going to be his real moneymaker down the road. He bought pop-up ads that said "*If you have pain, click here.*" If prospects responded, they were linked to Paul's Bio Strength website. Paul and Carlos put out signs on telephone poles around town advertising a home-based business with executive pay. They both got several calls a day from their signs.

Mike Melito did no advertising or online prospecting. All he did was display Bio Strength in his store and rake in the money.

Paul wished he had a natural market like Mike, but it didn't really matter. Mike was having a ball selling it out of his restaurant.

Paul, Carlos and Mike rode to the new product rollout together. Upbeat music filled the air as Bo was onstage making last minute adjustments to the program. Dr. Garfinkel and Joanne Griggs were presenters with Bo Valentine as the featured speaker. Paul, Carlos, and Mike sat in the third row. They were all pleased to see that Joanne was wearing a short red skirt and high heels. The room was jam-packed and brimming with excitement. A display table was beside the lectern with a tablecloth over the new product.

"Good morning, Bio Strength distributors!" yelled Joanne into the microphone.

"Good morning!" the crowd of over three hundred raucous distributors yelled back.

"You're in for a treat this morning. We will be introducing our new product line today, and I've seen it, and you're gonna love it!"

The crowd whooped and hollered like they were at a football game. Only at a network marketing product rollout could people get so excited over something they knew nothing about. Most people had heard of Mike Melito's success and were jealous. The typical distributor always wondered why they didn't have the same success. Most didn't know it was Paul who was Mike's sponsor.

"Before we go further," said Joanne, "I'd like to introduce you to a rising star right here in Jacksonville. He has really made a big impact the last few months, and he has just reached the Platinum level. I'd like to ask Paul Cousins to stand up now and be recognized."

Paul was stunned. He had no idea he was going to be recognized, much less that he had advanced to Platinum. The crowd erupted in applause and Carlos turned to Paul and said, "Stand up, boy. They're clappin' for you!"

Paul felt his face turn beet red. He slowly rose and turned to wave at the crowd. He had craved recognition like this his whole life, but it had been years since he'd had any.

"Great job, Paul. Congratulations!" said Joanne. "Another rising star is someone most of you probably already know. He owns a restaurant that is an institution around here. Paul Cousins sponsored this man just a few short months ago, and it is amazing how far he has come. Let's hear it for Mike Melito!"

Mike stood and flashed his million dollar smile to the crowd. Everyone cheered and applauded Mike heartily except Dr. Garfinkel. He gave a few half-hearted claps and stopped. Dr. Garfinkel did not like the way Mike was marketing Bio Strength out of his restaurant. He felt it was a cheesy way to sell, and selling Bio Strength from a doctor's office gave it much more credibility. He also did not like the limelight being taken from him. He felt Mike was just a flash in the pan and would fizzle out soon enough.

"Keep up the good work, Mike. You're on your way to a Royal Diamond!" said Joanne. "Now I'd like to bring up Dr. Roy Garfinkel. He has been a general practitioner for over 20 years and is a Gold distributor. He is a great believer in Bio Strength products, and we are lucky to have him on our team. Please help me welcome Dr. Roy Garfinkel!"

"Thank you, Joanne. You all are going to love this new product launch. Bio Strength is constantly researching the best new technologies and ingredients to place in their products, and today is no exception. Every home in America will want to have what we are introducing today. Not only will we improve people's health with this product, but each of you will make more money! Now that's a real win-win!" Paul, Carlos, and Mike all stood up with the rest of the crowd. They were as eager as everyone else to see what was being introduced.

"Are you ready to see what the new product is?" Dr. Garfinkel yelled.

"*Yes!!!*" the crowd roared.

Dr. Garfinkel reached over and pulled the cover off the display table.

"Introducing the most innovative sunscreen in the world! The new BioStrength Body Block sunscreens!" said Dr. Garfinkel excitedly.

Every head craned up and around to get a good look. It was like no one had seen a bottle of sunscreen before. Dr. Garfinkel grabbed a bottle and said to the crowd, "Who would like to do a strength test with me?" Mike Melito raised his hand even though he knew Dr. Garfinkel would never call on him. A pretty young distributor in the front row raised her hand, and Dr. Garfinkel motioned to her to come up to the stage.

"He always goes for the pretty ones," said Carlos to Paul.

Dr. Garfinkel rubbed a small amount of the sunscreen on the young lady and performed the usual strength test on her arms. She became much stronger after the application of the new sunscreen. The crowd cheered, and Dr. Garfinkel thanked the young lady for volunteering.

"Ladies and gentlemen, not only do you get the same benefits as Bio Strength lotion, but you get to help people save their skin from the damaging effects of the sun. Here in Florida the incidence of skin cancer is one of the highest in the nation. You can help reverse this trend by selling this sunscreen. It incorporates far-infrared energy with the introduction of microscopic ceramic particles. These particles act as a temperature stabilizer to keep you cooler in the sun. It offers an SPF of 50. It protects, moisturizes, and keeps you cool in the heat. Folks, no one offers a sunscreen like this. You have cutting-edge technology here, and we can help prevent skin cancer. And you make money while helping people. What a win-win! Good luck!"

"Thank you Dr. Garfinkel," said Joanne. "We are so lucky to have a physician who not only understands the health benefits of Bio Strength products but also knows how to run a successful business. Let's hear it for Dr. Roy Garfinkel!"

Bo stood up to applaud Dr. Garfinkel with the rest of the crowd, and he drew a big breath knowing he was next to speak.

He had rehearsed his speech dozens of times, and he knew how important product launches were to his business. This was a ripe opportunity to whip the legions into a frenzy. He was gonna kill 'em.

"And now, I'd like to introduce our keynote speaker. Bo Valentine is a Royal Diamond distributor right here in Jacksonville. He has been with Bio Strength for five years, and with his inspirational leadership, he can take each and every one of you to the top. Bo is introducing the newest Bio Strength marketing program that will boost your business to the next level. I am proud to introduce my upline and mentor, Bo Valentine!"

The crowd rose enthusiastically to their feet to applaud Bo. He gave a big hug to Joanne as she walked back to her seat. Kitty's face turned red with rage since she suspected he was having an affair with her. Kitty thought Bo was having an affair with everybody.

"Good evening, Bio Strength distributors!" yelled Bo. "I am so happy to see so many motivated people here today. Dr. Garfinkel explained the new sunscreen line that is unmatched in the market. You have been given the best products to market, no question."

"But even the best products can fail without the best marketing plan. And I am here to show you how you can market these products to many more people and make more money than you ever thought possible."

"Are you ready to make some money, Jacksonville?" said Bo excitedly.

"*Yesss!!!*" the crowd roared.

"Well, here is how you do it."

Bo paused for a few seconds to build anticipation. The crowd waited anxiously for his next words.

"Are you ready? Okay, here it is. You are going to give as much of these products away as you can for people to try as their free sample. Who in here likes free stuff?"

Everyone in the audience raised their hand.

"Of course you do. If you offered me something free, I'd take it too. We call this our gifting program. All Bio Strength products will be offered in gifting economy packs so you can have plenty on hand to share with people. All you have to do is give it away. Then, once people have tried Bio Strength products, most people will buy them at retail or become a distributor and pay wholesale. The amount you spend on these gifting economy packs will pale in comparison to what you make in the long run. The bottom line is how many people you can get these products to. The more people that see results, the more sales you make."

"Distributors will see a huge increase in their monthly volumes right away. This is truly a win-win. Bio Strength has made success available to each of you. The question is, what are you going to do next? Will you take advantage of this?"

"I want each of you to have the same success that Kitty and I have had the good fortune to have. I get asked all the time, 'How did you do it?' My answer is always the same. I kept my dream in front of me no matter how bad things were going. 'Cause once you get lost in the daily details of living, your dream gets crowded out. Life gets in the way so easily. So cut out some pictures of what it is you really want and plaster them all around your house. Put them on the mirror in the bathroom so you see them when you first wake up. Tape a picture to the dashboard of your car. Say your affirmations daily. *Never* allow the negative to seep into your vocabulary."

"If someone asks you how your business is going, always say 'fantastic' even if things are not going so well. Do you think they would believe in you and Bio Strength if you said how horrible things were going? Of course not. Be careful what you say. Words are powerful things."

"I've had people come to me and say, 'Bo, that is lying to people. I could never tell someone things are fantastic if they are really not.' I say to them that you are not lying. You are projecting how you want your business to be, and you are doing everything in your power to make it as you see it. You are acting *as if* you have already achieved success. If you have already achieved success in your mind, how can you be lying?"

"Most people believe in things beyond themselves. All religions are based on the belief in a higher power. There is power in belief. Just ask any doctor about the placebo effect. It is scientifically proven that if you believe a pill is good for you, your body will respond to it positively, even if it is a sugar pill. So never question the validity of the power of belief. In our business, belief is everything."

"I believe with all my heart that this is the right company with the right products at the right time. Bio Strength is going to be a household name soon. How many of you want to be a part of this? I am all in. Let's go to work on making your dreams come true. God bless you. Thank you."

Paul felt like he had just heard a sermon from a Baptist preacher, and he was inspired like never before. The audience gave Bo a standing ovation as he hugged Kitty. This was about everyday people believing in something beyond themselves. Paul believed that Bio Strength was everything he had looked for in his life. The paychecks he was getting were real. This was no dream.

Joanne took center stage again. "What an inspiration you are to all of us, Bo. We are so grateful to have you here in Jacksonville. We have an important announcement for you all to hear today. The company has selected its new distributor of the year. And the winner is right here in this room today. Ladies and gentleman, please welcome to the stage our new Distributor of the Year award winner, Paul Cousins!"

Paul was stunned. Carlos and Mike were going crazy, and they started pushing him to the stage.

"Come on up here, Paul," said Joanne. "We have something for you." Paul finally inched his way to the stage. Everyone slapped him on the back as he made his way. He felt like he had just won the nomination for President of the United States. Joanne greeted him with a big smile and hug on the stage.

"Congratulations, Paul. You earned every bit of this award." Joanne handed him a plaque. "Go ahead, Paul. We all want to hear how you did it."

"I am speechless for the first time in my life," Paul said while staring glowingly at his Distributor of the Year plaque. "I…I am grateful to my sponsor Carlos Ackman for introducing Bio Strength to me when I needed it most. He made me dream again. I had always wanted to buy nice things. And I will one day with the business I am building. But there is one lady who has really taught me the most about what life is all about. She has very few material things, yet she is the happiest person I know. She has a sparkle in her eyes and a zest for life. I'd like to dedicate this award to my fellow team member, Miss Ellie Washington. Where are you, Ellie?"

Ellie was seated in the back row and stood up to speak.

"Ya'll will get gray hair waiting for me to walk up there, so don't even try," Ellie shouted out with energy. "Paul, you've embarrassed me enough. Don't pay no mind to him. That man's crazy. Just keep doin' what you're doin, and everything will be alright. That's my motto. I'm gonna sit down now cause my back is killing me."

The audience laughed and gave her a standing ovation. Paul had never been so proud of someone in his life. Bio Strength was proving to be everything he wanted it to be.

Chapter 11

The gifting program was working like a charm. Paul saw his checks double in the next three months, and he met with a real estate agent to look at houses. Carlos, meanwhile, used his money to pay off old bills. Even though he was optimistic about Bio Strength, the only thing Carlos spent money on was a new fishing pole.

Bio Strength sales worldwide were taking off. The gifting program was generating huge volumes as Bo had predicted. Any distributor at the top of the pyramid was making a killing while all the newbies were running around giving product away for free. Everyone at the bottom looked up the pyramid and wished they were at the top. A lucky few would make it, and the rest were dreamers. Paul was convinced he was going to the top. He could see it, feel it taste it. He applied what he learned in *Excuse Me, Your Life is Waiting* every day. He listened to "Jump" by Van Halen when he felt his energy level getting low. The song had a weird magic over him. He could tell when he was really energized by the song when the hairs on his arm stood straight up.

The sudden popularity of Bio Strength caught the watchful eyes of the FDA. While Bio Strength was careful to never make medical claims with their products, the FDA did occasionally check the legitimacy of products. A few dozen people had complained of unusual side effects from using Bio Strength products.

Ernie Zimmerman had worked as a fraud investigator for the FDA for twenty-four years. His boss asked him to test some of Bio Strength's products to verify the contents on the label. Ernie groaned when he heard of another network marketing company's products he was asked to check out. He hated seeing innocent people taken advantage of by being conned into buying snake oil products. It reminded him of magic elixirs sold a hundred years ago promising to cure almost anything. Most were simply booze with fancy names.

Ernie was 55 years old and bored stiff with his job. He had been passed over several times for promotions, so his motivation had vanished a long time ago. As bored as he was with his job, his home life made his job seem exhilarating. He stayed at work late surfing the Internet so his wife wouldn't nag at him for so long. She fussed at him for working too much, and when he came home around seven, she never had dinner ready. Most nights she would stick him with the kids on the way out the door to go play bunko with the ladies in the neighborhood. His life sucked, but he saw no way out. Divorce was not an option. He had married at age 45 since he had taken care of his elderly parents before they died. He was definitely a Jewish momma's boy. He wore thick, round glasses and had still had jet black hair. Most of his male relatives were bald, but somehow he was spared the male pattern baldness gene. His wife Marlo was more interested in getting her hair colored and playing cards with her friends than in her marriage. Ernie felt trapped, but he knew he had made his bed and had to lie in it. He had decided to endure his marriage like the Brits endured the Blitzkrieg.

Needing a test sample of Bio Strength products, Ernie looked up the location of business previews on the company website. He found a location for a preview at a Dr. Garfinkel's office in Jacksonville. He started a background search on Dr. Garfinkel and found no complaints against his medical license. His credit was squeaky clean as well. Ernie usually could smell a rat quickly with these background checks, but everything was good so far with this doctor. Ernie knew bad people were attracted like flies to crooked companies.

Bio Strength was current on all their state and federal taxes and appeared to be in solid financial shape. Ernie needed to be a mole at a meeting and see if Bio Strength reps made any medical claims. He had heard one of the juice company distributors actually say that their product cured cancer. Making medical claims was a sure way to get in trouble with the FDA. Ernie planned to buy some Bio Strength product for testing to make sure what was claimed to be the ingredients actually were. He found that many nutritional supplement companies claimed main ingredients that were often found only in trace amounts or not at all. Ernie knew that only a handful of nutritional companies incorporate pharmaceutical standards in the making of their supplements. This process insures that over 99 percent of the ingredients listed are actually in the bottle.

Ernie looked forward to the Bio Strength business preview. It was a chance for him to get away from his wife and kids for the evening. Ernie knew Marlo would chew him out for coming home late again, so he asked his boss Joe Martini to call her for him.

"Please Joe," said Ernie. "Just tell her how important this project is. If she hears it from me, she'll never believe me."

Joe reluctantly agreed to call Marlo. Ernie was his best investigator, and he was eager to get the process started. He had heard Ernie arguing with Marlo before on the phone.

"Okay, but you sure are a spineless son of a bitch. I'll put on the speaker phone for you." Ernie nervously dialed his home number for Joe. He was so glad he was not going to be alone on this call.

Marlo was having a bad day at home. The baby was crying, the two-year-old had a dirty diaper and the dog was barking and had peed on the foyer carpet again. The only thing she looked forward to all day was getting out of the house when Ernie got home. She never thought raising kids would be this hard, and she felt Ernie did his best to avoid helping her at home. She heard the phone ring during the mayhem and looked at the caller ID. She saw it was Ernie's work number, and her blood pressure spiked. "He's calling to say he's going to be late again," she mumbled to herself as she reached for the phone.

"You working late again?" she screamed into the phone. "You need to come home right now. Ray won't stop crying, Amy needs a diaper change and *your* damn dog peed in the house again. Just listen to *this*!" Marlo held the phone up for Ernie to hear the disaster unfolding.

Joe was not prepared for this spew of venom emanating from the phone. Ernie held his head in his hands. Joe heard a dog barking relentlessly, and now both kids were crying hysterically.

"*Are you still there?*" Marlo screamed.

Joe gathered his wits about him. "Uh, Marlo. This is Ernie's boss, Joe. There's this important job I'm sending Ernie on, and he will be a little late getting home tonight. He said you would understand."

Marlo was not fazed at all that someone else had heard the way she spoke to Ernie.

"Is he there with you, Joe?" Marlo asked.

Ernie looked up at Joe with desperate eyes and shook his head back and forth quickly to say no. Joe knew this was a good time to cover for Ernie.

"He's in another meeting now, but he wanted to make sure you knew he would be late. He will call you as soon as he is on the way home. This is the beginning of an investigation for us, and he said he was sure you would understand."

"Well, you tell my husband that he needs to let me know when he's gonna be late. I'm pulling my hair out at home, and I could damn sure use his help."

"I'll be sure to tell him. Have a nice night," said Joe as he quickly hung up. "Wow, Ernie I feel pretty good about my wife right now. Marlo was like a psycho."

"She *is* a psycho," said Ernie. "I don't know how much longer I can take it. Guess I'm sleeping on the sofa tonight."

"You better get going now so you're not too late getting home," said Joe.

"It doesn't matter, really. She's already mad. Maybe this Bio Strength meeting will have some food there. I'm starved. She never fixes dinner. I've gained ten pounds this year from eating out so damn much."

"Good luck with Bio Strength," said Joe. "Don't forget to get as many samples as you can."

Ernie trudged out to the parking lot and plugged the address for Dr. Garfinkel's office into his GPS. He felt his pocket to make sure his miniature recorder was there because he liked to record meetings to verify what was said. He wanted none of the he-said-she-said stuff if a lawsuit emerged.

The Bio Strength meeting had already started when Ernie walked in. Dr. Garfinkel was talking about the products when Ernie slipped quietly into a seat in the back. He reached into his pocket to turn on his recorder. Ernie liked to come late so he wouldn't have to interact too much with people.

Ernie watched with amusement as several guests were subjected to some strength tests with Bio Strength products. He was very skeptical of these sudden increases in strength people were having. Surely it was some kind of trick, he thought to himself. He had seen so many false claims in his years of investigations. Ernie was as jaded about network marketing companies as insurance adjusters are about personal injury attorneys.

The next strength test subject caught Ernie's eyes. She was an elegantly dressed tall blonde with voluptuous curves. Her tight fitting red blouse exposed her cantaloupe breasts. She moved with poise in front of the room, and she raised her silky arm up for a strength test. Ernie couldn't take his eyes off her. She was the most beautiful woman he had ever seen.

"How about one more strength test from someone new?" asked Joanne as she scanned the room. She spotted Ernie in the back row.

"You sir, are you a first-time visitor?" asked Joanne.

Ernie wasn't sure she was talking to him. He felt like a day dreaming student suddenly called on by the teacher and nervously pointed at himself to make sure he was the one being asked.

"Yes, you sir, the good looking guy with black hair," said Joanne smiling. "Would you like to come up for a strength test?"

Ernie blushed profusely. He just wanted to be a fly on the wall, but now he was being asked to interact with the most gorgeous woman he had ever seen. Ernie stood and approached Joanne as everyone applauded.

Carlos leaned over to Paul and whispered "Who is that guy? Is he new?"

"I've never seen him before," said Paul.

"Hey, Mike. You know this guy?"

"Nah," said Mike Melito. "Don't get your hopes up to sign him up. Joanne nabs all guy visitors. Especially the ones with puppy dog eyes like this one."

"Hi, what's your name?" asked Joanne still smiling.

"Ernie Zimmerman," said Ernie before he realized he had said his name in front of a group from a company he was investigating. Ernie was so distracted by Joanne that he forgot to use his cover name. He thought he had blown the investigation before it had started.

"Ernie, you've seen what we are doing here. I'm going to test some Bio Strength product on you to see how your body responds. Let's do a baseline test first. Just hold your arm out like this and I'll push down as you resist. Okay, ready…1…2…3…resist."

Ernie looked into Joanne's eyes as she pushed down on his arm. He felt electricity flow from her soft hands into him as he struggled to keep his arm in the air. He was turning beet red resisting her and grunted as she pushed down.

"Ernie, this is not a strength contest here. I know you are a really strong guy, but all I'm doing is trying to see how your arm bounces back after I push down. And, avoid looking me in the eyes since that seems to affect the results. It's been shown that looking someone in the eyes makes them stronger, so we want the test to be neutral."

"I'm sorry," said Ernie nervously. "I've never done this before."

"It's alright, just resist me a little."

"Joanne, *nobody* can resist you!" yelled out Mike Melito as the audience laughed.

"Aw, shut up, Mike. Just leave and go sell some cheeseburgers." Joanne was used to the ribbing. No one could embarrass her. She was on a mission, and no one was going to stop her. Joanne did another baseline test on Ernie and grabbed a bottle of Bio Strength lotion to apply to his arm.

"Remember how far your arm went down when I pushed on it? Let's see how you do this time with some Bio Strength lotion on you," said Joanne as she rubbed a small dab of lotion on Ernie's wrist. Ernie was enthralled to have this beautiful woman rubbing lotion on him. This was the most attention he had had from any woman in six months.

"Okay, on three, I want you to resist. 1…2…3 resist!"

Joanne pushed down while Ernie tried to avert his gaze from Joanne's beautiful blue eyes. He didn't want to screw up the testing again. Ernie was amazed that his arm hardly moved at all as she pushed.

"You must not have been pushing as hard that time," Ernie said incredulously.

"Actually, I was pushing harder. Your body reacted well to the Bio Strength. You should be using this lotion every day. Men should be taking care of their skin just as much as women do. I don't understand why you guys let your skin dry out like you do. Even if you don't want to use the lotion, you can always drink the Bio Strength antioxidant. It has the same effects on your body as the lotion. Your body knows what's good for you."

"And I know what's good for *your* body," Mike said as he stood up and high-fived the guy beside him.

"Did you ever finish ninth grade, Mike?" said Joanne sarcastically with her hands on her hips. She was growing tired of Mike's incessant comments from the gallery. He did this every week, and she was going to put a stop to it. He had also tried to hit on her at every opportunity. She was way out of his league, but he didn't care.

"Let's give Ernie a round of applause!" she said as Ernie sheepishly made his way back to his seat. Ernie managed a half-hearted wave and wished he was a wallflower again. He was not used to this sort of attention, but he did love looking at Joanne and wished his wife was like her.

The preview finished up and Ernie walked up to the display table to take a look at the samples. Joanne saw him and approached like a lion hungry for a meal.

"So Ernie, how did you hear about Bio Strength?" asked Joanne.

Ernie's mind raced as he tried to think of something. All those years of experience in the field investigating were thrown out the window in front of a pair of boobs. His brain was kaput, and he tried to act cool and not to stare at her breasts.

"I heard about it from some friends who used the products," said Ernie nervously.

"Who was it? Maybe I know 'em," said Joanne.

Ernie felt like he was being interrogated by the Gestapo. His mind raced to think of something…anything to say.

"Uh, you wouldn't know them, they're from Rhode Island." Ernie picked the smallest state he could think of.

"What part of Rhode Island?" asked Joanne.

"Providence," said Ernie.

"Oh, I grew up there! I know a lot of people there. Would you know…."

" Hi, I'm Paul," said Paul sticking his hand out towards Ernie. Ernie had never been so glad to be interrupted.

"Are you a guest of someone?" asked Paul. Joanne could sense that her potential new recruit was being scouted as well. The hunt was on.

"Yes, he's my guest," said Joanne.

"Oh, how do you know each other?" Paul asked.

"We know some of the same people from Providence," said Joanne.

"That's great. I'm sure Joanne will make a great sponsor if you join. Are you interested in becoming a distributor?"

"Perhaps. This is all a little new to me."

"Well, it was nice to meet you. Thanks for coming."

Paul walked away in defeat since he knew he was no match for Joanne's charms.

"So which product did your friends use?" asked Joanne. "Was it the lotion or the antioxidant drink?"

"It was the lotion," said Ernie. They had arthritis real bad, and the lotion really helped them."

"That's great," said Joanne. "That happens all the time. In the future I see these products being the first thing doctors recommend instead of prescription drugs. The side effects from all prescription drugs are horrible. Did you know that adverse reaction to properly prescribed prescription drugs is the fourth leading cause of death in this country? Where is the outrage? Our doctors are killing us, and nobody cares!"

Joanne paused for a second before continuing. "I'm sorry to get so worked up over this, but my mother suffered horribly from rheumatoid arthritis for years before she died. Her quality of life was zero. I just wish Bio Strength had been around for her. It would have made such a difference in her life. That's why I'm so committed to bringing Bio Strength to as many people as I can. That's my mission."

Ernie was impressed by the sincerity in Joanne's voice. He was surprised she did not mention money as her main motivation. There weren't many network marketers he had met who did not mention the words *financial freedom*. It was refreshing to hear this, and Ernie wanted to hear more. Joanne knew that tugging on someone's heart was always more effective than spewing facts.

"My back has been bothering me for a while," said Ernie. "Could I buy a few of these bottles tonight to give them a try? I've also got a few friends who could use some of this."

"Absolutely, you can buy whatever you want. I might have some in my car. Why don't you come out with me and see what I've got." Joanne's car was loaded with every imaginable product she could stuff in her trunk. Her garage was stuffed to the ceiling with Bio Strength products, and she always wanted to have something to give right away. Besides, she preferred to sell her own inventory rather than something out of Dr. Garfinkel's office.

Joanne opened the back of her silver Mercedes convertible. It was jammed with Bio Strength boxes.

"I'll just take one of everything right now," said Ernie. "How much do I owe you?"

"Eighty-four dollars," said Joanne. She knew the prices off the top of her head. "This will save you shipping."

Ernie pulled out his checkbook. "Who do I make the check to?"

"Joanne Griggs. Hey, are you hungry? Why don't we get a bite to eat and I can tell you a little more about how these products work and how to use them? That would be really helpful to you," said Joanne with a smile.

Ernie hesitated before answering. He knew he was already in for it when he got home, so what would another 30 minutes late mean anyway? Besides, how often was he asked out to dinner by a blonde bombshell?

"Sure," said Ernie trying to remain calm. "Where do you wanna go?"

"There's a great sub shop called Firehouse Subs not far away. I recommend the Hook and Ladder. I'm addicted to those subs."

"Sounds good to me," said Ernie as he got into his car. "I'll follow you."

Paul, Carlos, and Mike watched from the parking lot as Joanne and Ernie left.

"Man, it just ain't fair," said Mike. "She gets all the new guys."

"Guys, she is just using her god-given abilities. She could be just a flash in the pan. All sizzle but no substance," said Carlos.

"Sizzle sells. But I'm gonna make it anyway. Screw her," said Paul.

"You'd like to," said Mike.

"Do you ever think about anything but sex?" asked Carlos.

Mike thought about it for a minute. "Yeah. Sex, drugs, and rock n' roll. In that order. At least I'm not faking it like most people here. What you see is what you get."

"You can't keep that stuff up much longer," said Carlos. "You ain't twenty anymore. When are you gonna grow up?"

"Never," said Mike. "I like my life simple."

Ernie's cell phone rang as he followed Joanne to Firehouse Subs, and he could see it was his wife calling. He quickly threw his cell phone into the glove box and slammed it shut. He pulled into the parking lot behind her with his heart racing with excitement. It was all in the line of work. He would become a mole in Bio Strength, and Joanne would be his point of contact. So what if his contact was the most beautiful woman he had ever seen? That was just icing on the cake. He had to remind himself that he was starting an investigation.

Joanne emerged from her Mercedes, and the wind caught her blonde hair and blew it away from her face. Ernie saw her standing there by her car, and he suddenly felt time stand still. A sharp chill went down his spine. "What is happening to me?" he thought. "It's just a sub sandwich. I'm not cheating," he reminded himself. Ernie opened the door for her.

"Thank you. I'm not used to that."

"Oh, I'm sure you are. You must have guys fighting to open the door for you."

"Not really. I think most men are turned off by a successful business woman," said Joanne as she placed an order for both of them.

"I'm not," said Ernie. "I think it's great. Although having children can sometimes keep women from advancing their careers. Do you have children?"

"No, I've never married. I guess I just haven't met the right one yet. All the good ones are taken," said Joanne as she grabbed her sandwich. "Let's grab a table in the back. Wait 'til you try this Hook and Ladder. You'll be hooked forever like me."

The sub shop was long and narrow with murals of firefighters in action all over the walls. Little kids ran around with plastic fire hats on.

"This restaurant was actually started by two Jacksonville firemen. Now they have over 400 restaurants on the East Coast. It's amazing what you can achieve when you have a vision," said

Joanne. "So tell me about yourself. What kind of work do you do?"

Ernie was not used to answering questions like this during an investigation. He usually stayed very much in the background. He felt more at home in front of a computer.

"I do some contract work for the Navy. Tech support, that kind of thing." Ernie knew the Jax Naval Base was huge, so it would be a good cover for him.

"Are you happy with your job?" asked Joanne.

No one had asked Ernie that question in years. "It's okay. I should have gotten a promotion years ago, but I was passed over. That kinda killed my motivation. I'm just putting in time until I reach 30 years. I only have six years left."

"Just okay, huh. That's too bad. You should love your work. You should be passionate about it. Then it doesn't feel like work. What would you really like to do if you could?"

Ernie thought for a moment. It had been so long since he had dreamed about anything that he couldn't come up with an answer.

"I'm ashamed to say I really don't know."

"Nothing at all? Aw, come on. There has to be something that gets your juices going. You can tell me."

Ernie felt like he was talking to a therapist he had known for 20 years. He felt strangely comfortable with Joanne.

"Well, there is one thing I've always wanted to do, but I never seem to have the time to do it."

"What is it?" asked Joanne leaning forward in her seat. Ernie caught a view of her cleavage when she leaned forward. He tried his best to look her in the eye.

"I've always wanted to write a book about my experiences in the Navy. I traveled the world and saw come crazy things. I enlisted right after college because I wasn't sure what I wanted to do. You wouldn't believe some of the things we did. It was so long ago that much of it is not classified anymore."

"Why don't you do it then?"

"My job keeps me so busy, and then I get home and get stuck with the kids while my wife goes out. There's no way I can chase the kids around and write a book. I'll get to it one of these days when the kids are older."

"One of these days? That usually means never. That's just an excuse for not doing anything. What are you waiting for? The perfect time? There is no such thing as the perfect time. The only thing you have is right now, and right now you are simply biding time just to get through to some future date. What happens when you get to your 30 years? Something else will crop up, and you'll have a new excuse. Just start writing your book a page at a time. If you write a page a day, you'll have your book done in a year. That's doable, isn't it?" asked Joanne convincingly.

"I guess it is, but my wife wouldn't let me do anything that took away from the kids. She is mad as hell at me tonight for not coming home after work. I'm sure she was planning on playing bunko. There's no way she would let me write a book. It'll just have to wait."

"That's sad. There's no reason to put your life completely on hold. We aren't guaranteed tomorrow, ya know. That's why I have such a sense of urgency about my Bio Strength business. I don't want to have to work like a dog my whole life and then have nothing to show for it. I *love* what I'm doing. It's not like work at all. What better thing can you do for someone else than to make them feel better? And the money is phenomenal. Honestly, that is what attracted me to this business in the first place. I was looking for something but didn't know what. A friend showed me this, and it just hit me- *bam!* This is a business model that you can't beat. Of course, you have to have the products to back it up. I've seen some remarkable product experiences with Bio Strength products. I'm riding this wave to the top, and I'm looking for some people to take with me."

Ernie contemplated what Joanne had just said. He was not impulsive by nature, and he liked to analyze things several different ways. That drove his wife crazy since she felt he never could make a decision.

"How do you know this company will take you to the top? You seem awful sure of yourself. Many of these multi-level companies come out of nowhere only to never be heard from again. Aren't you afraid of becoming another statistic in a failed business?"

"I can't live my live in fear. If people were afraid to try anything new, we never would have walked on the moon. The first astronauts were blasted into space in a tiny two-seat capsule on top of an intercontinental ballistic missile. You think they weren't afraid? That didn't stop them. So all I'm doing is running a business. My life doesn't depend on it. If it fails, so be it, but I'll make it one way or another. Ya know, I don't tell many people this, but I grew up in a trailer park. As a kid I spent many hours reading, and as a teenager I loved motivational books, especially Tony Robbins. He inspired me more than anyone. I was desperate to get out of that trailer park. I swore to myself that I would make it out."

"I'm glad you found something you enjoy," said Ernie. "I hope you make it to the top. What do you do now?"

I sell medical supplies, but I'm getting ready to turn in my notice. My Bio Strength check has almost equaled my salary. I promised myself I would quit my job when I made more money with Bio Strength. I'm almost there, and I can't wait to see the look on my boss's face when I quit! Some people quit their jobs to do this full-time, but that's dumb. You should always make sure you can make it before you quit your job."

"My wife would never let me do anything like you're doing. She thinks all network marketing companies are nothing but pyramid schemes. No offense to you, but I tend to agree with her on that. I haven't seen many people make a dime at it. I know an accountant that does personal returns, and in 20 years of doing people's taxes he has seen only a handful record a profit on their multi-level marketing business. It's only profitable for the lucky few at the top."

"Wanna see my last check from Bio Strength?" said Joanne defiantly. "I have a stub in my glove box in my car. Come on out to my car and I'll show you," said Joanne as she stood up to leave.

"I didn't mean to offend you. I believe you!" said Ernie as he wolfed down the last bite of his sandwich. "By the way, that sub was delicious."

Joanne was waiting at the door for Ernie to follow her. She didn't like it when people didn't believe her success. She walked quickly to her car and started fumbling through the glove box. She retrieved a stub from her last month's commission from Bio Strength.

"See this?" she said to Ernie as she thrust it into his hands.

Ernie stared at the stub and read the amount out loud.

"Seven thousand, eight hundred fifty six dollars," said Ernie. "Not bad."

Joanne grabbed the stub back. "It's doubled in the last two months since the start of the gifting program. It'll probably double again this year."

"That's fantastic! Seeing is believing. By the way, I really should be going now. My wife is going to kill me for being so late."

"What's wrong with her, anyway? Don't you ever have any fun anymore?"

"No, actually tonight is the most fun I've had in a long time. I'm just holding on to marriage for the kids," said Ernie.

"Why stay miserable?" said Joanne. "I'm glad I never married. I've seen way too many friends in terrible marriages. It's just not worth it. I don't think I'll ever get married. I'm too focused on my business right now for a relationship."

Ernie suddenly felt he didn't want to go home just yet. A strange spontaneity crept over him.

"Hey, can we take a quick ride in your car with the top down before I go?"

"Sure, it's a great night for a drive." She opened the passenger door for him and hopped in. The top went down with the push of a button.

"Buckle up, here we go!" said Joanne as she peeled out of the parking lot. Ernie was a very conservative driver, and he gripped onto the handle of her car as though his life depended on it. She turned on the satellite radio to her favorite station.

"Satellite radio is the only way to go," said Joanne. "I never listen to FM radio anymore. It's a dinosaur. Do you have satellite radio?"

"No," said Ernie. I usually listen to NPR."

"NPR, huh? Sounds exciting. Oh, one of my favorite songs ever is playing," said Joanne as she cranked up the Fleetwood Mac song "You Make Loving Fun." Joanne took the exit for the interstate at 60 mph as she sang her heart out. Ernie relaxed a little as she came out of the turn like an Indy racecar driver. He glanced over at her and saw a beautiful woman with blonde hair flapping in the wind singing to her favorite song with not a care in the world. His reality would hit him in the face soon, but he was soaking this moment in. The pulsing beat of the song and the exhilarating speed at which Joanne was driving made Ernie's heart race. He was not used to feeling such adrenaline.

"Don't you love it?" screamed Joanne over the music.

"Yes, I do," said Ernie.

"I can usually talk my way out of tickets," said Joanne.

"Gee, that's surprising," said Ernie sarcastically.

"I just hike my skirt up a little and flirt. Most just give me a warning." Joanne took the interstate exit and revved her engine to take the turn. "Most people brake on turns, but you should actually accelerate to hold the car better around the turn."

The force of the hard turn pushed Ernie closer to Joanne. He felt her hair whip him in the face and smelled her rose-scented perfume. Her skirt was hiked up just enough for him to check out her long, muscular legs. He had always been a legs man. Ernie had never had a joyride like this in his life. Was he dreaming? When would he wake up? He remembered hearing his wife bitch over the phone, and he was supposed to be going on a company investigation. How did he end up in a convertible screaming down the road with a beautiful woman?

"Here's Firehouse Subs again" said Joanne as she pulled up beside Ernie's car.

"That was a blast!" said Ernie. He felt just like a kid getting off the roller coaster for the first time.

"My pleasure," said Joanne. "And be sure to let me know how the products work out for you. If they work, think about joining me in business. I'd love to have you as a partner. Certainly your wife would like seeing some more money come in every month. That makes sense, doesn't it?" Joanne liked to ask that question after an obvious statement. It led her prospect to where she wanted them to go.

"I'm very flattered," said Ernie. "Let me use the products and talk to my wife and see what happens. You never know."

"Here's my card. You call me if you have any questions," said Joanne with her million-dollar smile.

"Sure thing," said Ernie. He stared at the card as Joanne waved goodbye. She left skid marks in the parking lot as she pulled away in her convertible. Ernie watched her drive away in the night with her long hair rustling in the wind.

Ernie was prepared for the worst when he got home. He didn't even bother listening to his voicemail since he knew Marlo would be yelling at him. He walked into his dark house around 10 p.m. The house was silent, and it appeared that everyone was asleep. "So far, so good," thought Ernie. He reached for the bedroom door only to find it locked. He would be sleeping on the sofa tonight. He was used to it, so he went through his routine of checking on the kids before heading to the living room sofa. Both kids were sound asleep. Ernie felt a wave of gratitude for his kids since they were the only thing that kept him going. He would deal with Marlo in the morning. Maybe he would miss her if he got up early enough for work.

Ernie prepared the sofa for the night. It was way too soft which was why his back hurt him so much. He closed his eyes and dreamed of a joyride in a convertible with a beautiful woman. Ernie could not stop thinking about Joanne, and this would be his little secret from Marlo. He wondered if he should call Joanne tomorrow. *No, that's too soon. I'll wait a few days. I don't want her to think I'm too anxious.*

Ernie tossed and turned for several hours. He hadn't dreamt about anyone like this since he was a teenager in puppy love. It was a good feeling, and he wanted more. The investigation would take a back seat for a little while.

Chapter 12

Paul looked in the real estate section of the paper for the house of his dreams. He had a picture in his mind of what he was looking for. He wanted a big brick house on the river adorned with white columns. He saw a beautiful pool in the backyard surrounded by huge oak trees. He loved the oak trees with Spanish moss hanging from them. They formed a peaceful shade and gave him a quiet sense of contentment.

Carlos had warned Paul not to increase his standard of living so quickly, but Paul felt he had waited long enough. He pumped himself up listening to Van Halen music while picturing his house. He wanted a dance floor with lights to throw parties. "Dance the Night Away" by Van Halen was a favorite one that Paul played, dreaming of his own personal dance floor. He knew the house was out there. He just had to go find it. Paul was riding an emotional high, and he was going to act while his intentions were matching his emotions. He was making a cool 22,000 a month, so he could afford to buy the house of his dreams. He was now debt free.

Paul turned the page, and a picture of a home jumped out at him. It was in the Mandarin section of town and was advertised as a short sale. It was just what he was looking for-brick home, white columns on the front, a pool, on the river. He dialed the number for the real estate agent.

"Yes, do you have the listing for the short sale on Mandarin Road still available?" asked Paul.

The agent, Betty Tisdale, had been in the business for over 20 years. She had never seen so many big houses for sale going at such discounts. Times were hard in the real estate market, and it had hit particularly hard in Jacksonville. Prices had run up way too fast in the previous six to seven years. Betty knew it was a buyer's market.

"Yes, I do," answered Betty. It's listed at $950,000. It sold five years ago for $1.2 million, so it's a great buy. Would you like to look at it?"

"Yes, I would," said Paul. "How about today?"

Betty could tell she had an eager buyer on her hands. "I'll move some things around to meet you. How is two o'clock?" asked Betty.

"That's great. See you then."

"Hold on. I never got your name," said Betty.

"Oh, sorry. Paul Cousins. I'll see you at two."

Paul hung up and called Mike even though they had had a few arguments lately. "Hey, Mike. It's Paul. I think I found my dream house on the river. Wanna come take a look at it with me?" He knew Carlos would not approve, so he didn't bother to call him.

"Sure, man. What time?" asked Mike.

"Two o'clock. I'll come pick you up at the restaurant at 1:30. You're gonna love it. It's a party pad on the river with a pool."

"Awright. I'm there," said Mike. Mike was always in favor of any friend who had a great place to party. "Can I bring along my new girlfriend?" asked Mike.

"Sure, I don't care. Is she one of your flavor-of-the-month bimbo waitresses?" asked Paul.

"We've been very serious for the last two days. I think I'm in love Paul."

"You fall in love every two weeks," said Paul.

"This one is different. She has a brain. She finished high school and everything."

"Okay, I believe you. I'll see you at 1:30."

Paul never bothered to get pre-qualified for a home purchase. He was running completely on an emotional high. He hopped in his car and popped in some Van Halen for inspiration. Mike and his girlfriend were waiting in the parking lot. They each had a beer in a plastic cup in their hands. She was wearing white shorts and a small, tight fitting blue shirt that exposed her pierced bellybutton. She was a tall brunette with muscular legs, and Paul was hoping she was legal.

"Thanks for coming, Mike," said Paul as he pulled up beside them. They hopped in the back seat.

"Can't wait to see it. Hey, this is my girlfriend Chastity. Chastity, this is Paul Cousins."

Paul couldn't resist commenting on her name. "Chastity, is that really your name or is it a nickname? The only woman I've ever met with that name was in a strip club."

"Yes, it really is. I've heard jokes my whole life about it, so I'm used to it. You can call me Chas if you want."

"I'm going to give her a belt for her birthday with her name etched on the buckle," said Mike.

"Very funny, Mike." Hey Chas, are you working for Mike?"

 "Yes. I'm having a ball. Mike's a blast to work for."

"I'm sure."

"How much are they asking for this house?" asked Mike.

"Nine hundred fifty thousand," said Paul nonchalantly.

Mike spit beer out all over the back of Paul's head. "Nine hundred fifty thousand? You mean fifty grand short of a million? You're kiddin' me, right? Of course, you have a pre-qualification letter from a lender stating that they would loan you money for this big of a house, right?"

Paul searched for a tissue to wipe the beer off his neck. "Well, not exactly."

"What do you mean, *not exactly*?" asked Mike. "You either do or you don't. Only a moron would go looking for a million dollar house without getting pre-qualified."

"Well, at least I'm not the moron who got busted for buying pot from the sheriff's seventeen-year-old daughter," said Paul.

"You've been busted before?" asked Chas.

"It was a long time ago, babe. The sheriff had it out for me, anyway. He didn't like the fact that I was dating his daughter," said Mike.

"It was either a drug bust or a statutory rape charge," said Paul. "Mike took the drug bust and promised never to see the sheriff's daughter again."

"Hey, no one is supposed to know that, you asshole," yelled Mike. "Why don't I dish out some dirt on you, mister altar boy?"

Betty Tisdale was waiting on the sidewalk of her riverfront listing to meet Paul when she saw a car weaving dangerously in the road down the street. A man and a young woman in the back seat were screaming hysterically at the driver. The car screeched to a halt in front of her, and Betty could hear them yelling loudly at each other. Every other word was a curse word. She was horrified and pulled out her cell phone to call 911.

Paul jumped out of the car and straightened out his hair and shirt to look presentable. He walked ahead of Mike and Chas to greet Betty. Betty was hoping this was not her two o'clock showing.

"Hi. I'm Paul Cousins. I called you about looking at the house."

Betty's heart sank to her stomach. She had moved several appointments around to meet a maniac driver with a man and his scantily clad daughter in the back seat. She smelled beer on Paul and almost walked back to her car, but she learned long ago to never discount anyone as a prospect too quickly. Some of her biggest sales were to people who dressed like slobs. Maybe Paul would turn out okay. His money was green, too, she rationalized. She put her cell phone away.

"Nice to meet you, Paul," said Betty. "Are these people with you, too?"

"Not really. They're friends of a friend. They just wanted to tag along. I'll ask them to leave if you want me to," said Paul.

"That's alright," said Betty. "Just keep an eye on them so they don't steal anything. That fella looks a little shifty. Well, what do you think of the outside?"

Paul turned his gaze towards the house. It had a long driveway lined with 100 year-old oak trees covered in Spanish moss. The front porch had two huge white columns supporting a second porch above, and the eighty-year-old house was a two-story, all brick mansion.

"This lot is two acres and backs up to the St. Johns River. The pool is unscreened and has solar panels. It's got a detached three-car garage which was added in 1980. It's a bargain at nine hundred fifty thousand," said Betty. Paul could not believe how beautiful it was. It matched everything that he had dreamt of for years. He wanted it without even looking on the inside.

Betty had her back to Paul when she heard the words she loved to hear from a prospect, "I'll take it."

Betty was surprised to hear Paul make a decision so quickly.

"Don't you want to look at the inside, Mr. Cousins?" asked Betty.

"I said *I'll* take it," spoke Mike confidently.

Paul jerked his head around to face Mike. "What do you mean, *you'll* take it? I brought you here to help *me* buy it. You're not serious, are you?" asked Paul incredulously.

"I'm dead serious," said Mike. "Hi, I'm Mike Melito, and…."

Betty interrupted Mike with, "Are you *the* Mike Melito from the restaurant?"

"The one and only."

"I've taken clients there for years and love your food. I just want to thank you for running Melito's for so long. It's an institution here in town. I thought you looked familiar. Now which of you wants to buy this house?" asked Betty.

"*I do!*" both of them said simultaneously.

"Look Ms….I'm sorry, I did not get your name," said Mike.

"Tisdale, Betty Tisdale."

"Betty, I am the only qualified buyer here. Mr. Cousins thinks he can buy this house, but he is hallucinating if he thinks the bank will lend him money. I've got 20 years of proven income and the assets to back it up. Paul's got nothing but a recent lucky streak. Just go ahead and ask him if he's been pre-qualified," said Mike.

Betty was not used to having two people fighting over a house like this. She turned to Paul and asked, "Is it true that you have not been pre-qualified, Mr. Cousins?"

"Yes, but I've got the income now to buy it, and I can prove it. The bank can give a record of all my deposits, and Bio Strength can show my monthly checks," said Paul desperately. He couldn't believe Mike was trying to buy his dream home out from under him.

"Listen," said Betty, "Why don't I let you two work this out before I show the house. I'll just hang around a few minutes, and you let me know what you decide."

"Absolutely, Betty," said Mike. "We'll have this straightened out in a jiffy."

Paul put his arm around Mike like they were old pals and said, "Let's talk about this around back, old buddy."

"Sure, Paul. I'm sure we can come to some sort of agreement."

The back of the house had a large pool, sculptured garden, boat dock, and a gorgeous view of the river. As they turned the corner of the house, Paul grabbed hold of Mike's ear and started pulling it hard. Mike screamed as Paul pulled him by the ear toward the pool.

"What the hell are you doing?!" yelled Mike. "That really hurts!"

"Oh yeah? Well I'll show you something that hurts twice as much if you think you're gonna buy this house out from under me."

"Let go of my ear!" yelled Mike. "I can't talk with you pulling on it."

"Just say *Uncle* and I'll quit," said Paul.

"Does Uncle mean that you'll quit pulling on my ear or Uncle I give up on the house?" asked Mike wincing in pain. Chastity heard Mike screaming and came around to investigate. Betty told herself she would give them five minutes to figure it out before she left. She had other appointments that didn't involve drunk belligerent men.

"Both! Uncle means both," yelled Paul. "I didn't invite you here to snake this house from me. It's *mine*, so give it up."

Mike couldn't stand the pain any longer.

"*Okay, Uncle*! You win," said Mike.

Paul released his grip on Mike's ear. Chastity was furious with Paul.

"You better not touch him again or I'll take you down," said Chastity. "I'm a black belt."

"Is that right?" said Paul sarcastically. "Mike told me that the only belt you've ever worn was a chastity belt because you've been open for business since you were thirteen."

"Don't you talk to Chas that way!" yelled Mike.

"What's she gonna do to me? She ain't no black belt. What else have…."

Paul did not have a chance to finish speaking as Chastity gave him a karate kick to his head. Paul stumbled back away from Mike. Paul's legs were wobbly as he put up his hands for a fight.

"Okay, little girl. Show me what you've got."

"Paul, I wouldn't mess with her. I'm serious," said Mike.

Chastity walked up to Paul. Betty heard the commotion from the front yard and peered around a tree to see what was going on.

"I can't hit a girl first, so you have to throw the first punch," said Paul.

"You think I won't do it, don't you?" said Chastity.

"You don't have the guts to," said Paul.

Chastity relaxed her stance. "Yeah, you're right. I couldn't hit an old fart like you without reason," said Chastity.

"Told ya she was chicken," said Paul turning to Mike.

"You already gave me a reason to by insulting me and hurting my boyfriend."

Chastity laid three quick punches to Paul's stomach before he could prepare for the impact. Chastity then did a roundhouse kick to finish off Paul. The kick landed in his chest and catapulted Paul into the pool.

Betty gasped as she saw the fight unfold. She pulled out her cell phone and called 911.

Mike and Chastity walked up to the edge of the pool to wait for Paul to come out. Paul's body started floating lifelessly to the bottom of the pool.

"He looks dead," said Mike anxiously.

"I used to be a lifeguard," said Chastity as she dove in after him. She grabbed him from behind and pulled him to the surface. Mike helped her pull Paul over to the edge of the pool. Paul's limp body felt like an anchor as they pulled him out.

"Is he breathing?" asked Mike nervously.

Chastity checked for signs of breathing.

"Barely. I'll have to perform CPR." Chastity leaned over Paul to blow air into his lungs. Betty panicked as she waited for the police to show up. She couldn't believe she just witnessed a murder at a house showing.

Chastity continued to blow air and check for a pulse. As she started a second round of CPR, she felt Paul's tongue enter her mouth. Paul was French kissing her. Chastity got a look of disgust on her face, but before she could pull away, Paul grabbed her by the shirt and tossed her into the pool. Chastity couldn't believe Paul had just duped her into giving him CPR.

"*Aaagghhh*! I can't believe he kissed me," said Chastity as she kicked and splashed in the pool.

"Did he really kiss you, Chas?" asked Mike angrily.

"Only if you count the part where he stuck his tongue down my throat," said Chastity.

"Admit it, you loved it Chas," said Paul.

Mike ran straight at Paul for a tackle. Paul simply stepped aside as Mike flew headfirst into the pool, almost landing on Chastity.

Paul jumped up and down like Rocky Balboa with his hands in the air. "Both of you are in the pool without me throwing a punch. This is priceless!" said Paul.

Just then two policemen walked into the backyard with Betty close behind. Betty pointed to Mike and Chastity.

"Those two are the ones who started this whole fiasco. Mr. Cousins called me to look at this home, and this other man and woman showed up with him. They started fighting over the home, and I saw this girl kick Mr. Cousins into the pool. Then the other man tried to tackle Mr. Cousins, and he fell in the pool."

"Both of you, out of the pool now!" yelled one of the cops. They were each handcuffed as they emerged from the pool. The cops led Mike and Chastity back to their car.

"I'll visit both of you in jail. Don't worry," said Paul.

"You're not going to get away with this," said Mike as water dripped off his face.

"I'll get you out after I sign a contract to buy this house," said Paul.

"That's okay. I didn't want it anyway," said Mike as the policemen led them away.

Betty had the presence of mind to close the sale. She had heard Paul say how much he liked the outside and that he wanted to buy it.

"Would you like to sign the contract outside or do you still want to see the inside?" asked Betty.

"Let's take a quick look inside," said Paul. "I hope I don't drip everywhere."

Betty opened the front door for Paul. She grabbed a towel from a closet so that Paul could dry up some. Paul's sneakers were soaked and made a funny squishing sound that reverberated off the high ceilings. The house had a 26-foot ceiling and a huge brass chandelier hanging in the foyer. The foyer gave an unobstructed view of the river through a large window in the living room. Paul loved the hardwood floors. The kitchen had been modernized with a sub-zero refrigerator and custom cabinets. A den with two drop-down steps could easily be converted into the dance floor Paul wanted. The den had a large bay window, crown molding and a fantastic view of the river.

"I love it," said Paul. "Will the owners take $899,000?"

"We can draw up an offer for that, but the bank has final approval since this is a short sale," said Betty.

"Let's do that," said Paul.

"I'll need a deposit to go with the contract. Can you write a check to Watson Realty for $5,000?" asked Betty.

"No problem," said Paul as he whipped out his soaked checkbook. Do you take wet checks?"

"I don't see how you can write on them. Is there one in the back that isn't so wet?" asked Betty.

Paul looked at his checkbook, and the last few checks were only half wet. He wrote his deposit check and signed the contract.

"I'll present this offer to the owners today and get back to you as soon as possible. I must say, I have never had a day like this in my life," said Betty.

"Neither have I," said Paul. "I can't wait to hear from you. Can I spend a few more minutes inside?"

"Sure," said Betty.

Paul walked through his future house and let its subtle elegance fill his mind. *This is exactly what I've wanted.* He saw the den turned into his lighted dance floor with a big disco ball spinning from the ceiling. He wanted Bose 901 speakers suspended because he loved the way they filled a room with sound. He envisioned huge parties with everyone on the dance floor, and he saw a celebration of life unfolding before him. Paul realized the person who helped him succeed was probably sitting in a jail cell now. He would let him sweat a little bit before he got him out.

Chapter 13

The private investigator Rob Thigpen had nothing to report back to Kitty, so he had been ready to drop the investigation into Bo's philandering. Kitty pleaded with him to continue, and he was ready to continue any job as long as the client was willing to pay. He had Bo's cell phone number and the most sophisticated equipment to listen in on calls. He also put a GPS tracer on Bo's car to track his whereabouts, and he decided to be patient and wait for Bo to make a move again. It was exciting to Rob when he taped an incriminating conversation or caught someone in the act of cheating. He became excited after reading an email he intercepted from Bo and called Kitty.

"Kitty, hey it's Rob you-know-who. Bo has just emailed a couple old flames in Toronto to say he was going to be in town and wanted to see 'em. We've got him now."

"I knew he had been playing it too close to the vest recently," said Kitty. "Good work, Rob. I'll follow him out tonight. He said he was going out to dinner with a Bio Strength prospect. I want to see who he's with."

"Kitty, you really shouldn't try to follow him. He'll spot you, and I'll have a harder time following him," pleaded Rob.

"No, I want to see him with my own eyes. Then I'll divorce him and take half of everything. My goal is to make the rest of his life miserable, and I'm gonna do it on *my* terms."

"If he sees you, just pretend you were meeting someone else for dinner. Okay?"

"You got it," said Kitty. "Besides, I'm going to be wearing a big blonde wig. He'll never recognize me."

Kitty left for Joe's Crab Shack because she knew that was his favorite restaurant and that was where he would likely be. It was a pretty busy place, so Kitty felt she could blend in pretty well. She sat at the bar where she could get a good vantage point on people coming and going. If she saw him come in, her plan was to duck into the bathroom and wait to see where he was seated.

Kitty ordered a frozen margarita with salt and scanned the restaurant. The place was hopping as usual, and every hour or so the entire wait staff came out and danced in the middle of the floor. The restaurant sat right on the ocean and had a large deck with tables overlooking the water. Kitty was sitting beside two nicely dressed middle-aged women having a drink.

"Quite a place here, huh?" asked Kitty.

"Yeah, we like it. As long as you don't mind yelling to be heard," said the woman directly beside Kitty. "First time here?"

"No. This is my husband's favorite restaurant, so we've been here many times."

"We love this place, too. It's so much fun. There's nothin' else like it around here. Is your husband here?"

"Not yet," said Kitty. "Are you eating tonight or just having some drinks?"

"Just drinks now. We're going out dancing later."

"Nice dancing shoes you're wearing. Is this a girl's night out or are you meeting your husbands later?"

"We used to be married. By the way, my name is Melanie Waters and this is my friend Kim Davis."

"Nice to meet you. I'm Kitty Valentine."

"That name sounds awful familiar," said Melanie. "The only Valentine I know is Bo Valentine."

"That's my husband."

Both Kim and Melanie looked at each other with utter disbelief.

"We both know your husband," said Melanie.

"Oh, how do you know him?"

"We were both in Bio Strength with him a few years ago. We're not really active now," said Kim.

"Oh, here comes my husband now," said Kitty as she turned her back to the entrance.

"Aren't you going to eat with him?" asked Melanie, confused.

"Uh, not tonight. I'm not here to eat."

"Then why are you here?" asked Kim.

"I….listen, I know I just met you, but I'm here to check on my husband. You see, I think he's been cheating on me. I've got this wig on for disguise. I'm sorry to lay this on you, but I'm playing detective tonight and I'm a little nervous he'll catch me. Do you mind telling me who he's with?"

Melanie turned around in time to watch Bo being seated in a corner booth with another man.

"He's sitting in the corner with a man," said Melanie.

"Okay. At least he's not with a woman. I wonder who it is."

"We've actually been meaning to talk to Bo. Would you like us to be a mole for you and check this guy out?"

"Really? You'd do that?"

"Sure. Come on, Kim. Let's go talk to Bo."

"But…what if he recognizes me over here," said Kitty nervously.

"Just keep your back to us," said Melanie as they stood up. Both women grabbed their drinks and headed to Bo's table. Kitty put both hands on her forehead, sipped her drink and tried to keep from turning around.

Bo spotted Melanie and Kim approaching him and started choking on the sip he had just taken from his drink.

"Melanie *and* Kim! Boy, it's great to see both of you," said Bo. "How have you been?"

"We've been great," said Melanie. "Kim and I were just out having a few drinks when we saw you here. How is your Bio Strength business going?"

"Oh, fantastic! Hey, this is my friend Don Robinson."

"Nice to meet you," said Don. "How do you know Bo?"

"I was a distributor in Bio Strength under him," said Melanie.

"Yeah, we've both been under Bo," said Kim trying hard not to laugh.

"I'm telling Don a little more about Bio Strength tonight. He finally agreed to meet me even after I pestered him for years about it."

"That's great. Bio Strength has helped a lot of people," said Kim.

"Yeah, I tried the lotion, and it really helped my arthritis," said Don.

"By the way, sorry about what happened at the convention center. Things got a little out of hand, I heard."

Melanie was taken aback by his sudden if bogus apology, and she didn't know what to say.

"That's okay, security people overreact sometimes," said Melanie.

"I know, but it shouldn't have happened that way."

"Thanks, well it was good to see you, Bo. Nice to meet you, Don," said Melanie as they turned to go back to the bar.

"Goodbye."

"I thought you were going to let him have it back there," whispered Kim. "After what he did to us, you were way too nice to him."

"I know. But after he apologized, I couldn't let him have it. I guess I found a little place in my heart to forgive him. I do kinda feel sorry for him, though I don't know why."

"What did he say?" asked Kitty as they joined her at the bar.

"He's with an old friend named Don Robinson talking about Bio Strength," said Melanie.

"Did he see me over here?"

"I don't think so," said Kim. "Melanie actually accepted his apology for something that happened in Toronto. I couldn't believe it."

"He apologized?" asked Kitty. "That's a first. It must have been a strategy of his since it looked like you two were going to gang up on him."

"Kim, I've gotta go to the restroom," said Melanie as she motioned to her.

"We'll be right back," Melanie said to Kitty as they turned to go to the restroom.

"Should we tell her the truth about our relationship with Bo?" Melanie asked.

"Not right now," said Kim. "We don't know her well enough, yet. Maybe as we get to know her better we can say something. I would feel weird telling her that now. Besides, she already doesn't trust him. For god's sake, she wore a wig to spy on him."

"I guess you're right, though. I feel bad for her. What a sleaze Bo is."

"If we get to know her better, we'll have to tell her," said Kim.

"We'll cross that bridge when we come to it."

Melanie and Kim walked back to the bar to find Kitty gulping down a margarita.

"Ladies, I've gotta leave now!" said Kitty.

"Why, what's the matter?" asked Kim.

"The bartender gave me a margarita and said it was compliments of the man in the corner booth. I turned around and Bo smiled and waved at me. I quickly turned back around hoping he didn't recognize me."

"He was hitting on you, Kitty. No way he recognized you," said Melanie.

"I'm not taking any chances, so I'm outta here. Oh, here's my card if you want to get together sometime. Do you play golf?"

"Yes, we'd love to."

"Well, call me. You two were so nice to be a mole for me and talk to Bo. I'm gonna leave before he comes over. See ya later."

Kitty grabbed her purse and walked quickly out of the restaurant. Bo tried to grab her attention as she walked out, but Kitty ran out quickly. Kim and Melanie watched Bo in amusement.

"Look, he's trying to pick up his wife and doesn't even know it," said Melanie.

"Hilarious. There's an old saying that applies to Bo," said Kim.

"What's that?"
"What goes around, comes around."

Chapter 14

Ernie sat at his desk and stared out the window. He couldn't stop thinking about Joanne and wondered if she felt anything towards him. Even if she didn't, he was okay with that. For the first time in years, Ernie felt like he was in love. He wanted to call her, but he needed some excuse. He had been drinking the Bio Strength nutritional drink for the last four days, and he thought he did feel a little better. Ernie thought perhaps it could be from the euphoria of feeling in love. Floating on cloud nine was a good place to be, and he kept thinking of the two of them riding in her convertible with the music blasting. He downloaded the Fleetwood Mac song "You Make Loving Fun" on his iPod. The song kept running an endless loop through his brain all day long. The more he tried to stop thinking about Joanne, the more he thought of her. Marlo had stopped talking to him at home, so she didn't notice how distracted Ernie had become. Ernie's boss stood watching him daydreaming at his desk.

"Ernie," said Joe. Ernie did not turn around.

"Ernie," he yelled a little louder. Joe noticed Ernie had earplugs in.

"*Ernie!*" yelled Joe loudly. Ernie spun around to face Joe, and he quickly pulled out his earplugs. His face was red with embarrassment from being caught so blatantly goofing off.

"Get out of whatever la-la land you are in and tell me what you've found out about Bio Strength so far," said Joe angrily. Ernie gathered himself together and fiddled with some papers on his desk. He had not gotten any work done all week, but he tried to appear busy by keeping files nearby.

"Here is some background checking I did on the company," said Ernie. "No problems with the IRS or creditors. They are growing rapidly and have plenty of cash. No problems yet."

"Were you able to get some product so we can start testing?"

"I ordered some from a distributor, and it should arrive in a few days," said Ernie nervously.

"Let me know when you get them so we can take them down to the lab. We are ready to move forward with the investigation. Some doc in Miami made a stink about the product to us, so we have to follow up on it. Seems like the Bio Strength stuff is working so well it took some of this doc's patients away," said Joe.

"It's a shame that it takes some pissed off doctor to try to blow the lid on some of these natural products," said Ernie.

"I know, I know. But we can't just ignore them. If we do nothing, the complaints will get louder, and then my boss will ask me why we didn't do anything. By the way, how did the meeting go the other night?" asked Joe.

"Just fine. They tell the same hype about the product and the business opportunity as every other multi-level out there," said Ernie.

"Didn't they have any product there you could have bought? Why did you order it?" asked Joe.

"They only had used samples. I wanted unopened bottles to avoid any cross contamination. You know the lab only wants new samples," said Ernie confidently.

"Yeah, that's right. I forgot. Just let me know when your new samples come in. I want to get moving on this," said Joe.

"No problem," said Ernie.

Ernie knew he didn't have much time to milk this Bio Strength case, so he figured he had no time to waste in contacting Joanne again. He felt butterflies like a nervous teenage boy trying to call a girl for the first time. He found Joanne's card and stared at it for a few minutes. What would he say? He decided to tell her how much he liked the nutritional drinks. Ernie closed his office door and called Joanne. The phone rang and rang, and just before he ended the call he heard Joanne's voice on the other end.

"Hello," said Joanne.

Ernie hesitated a moment before answering. He was surprised she answered.

"Uh, hi," said Ernie. "This is Ernie Zimmerman from the Bio Strength meeting the other night."

"Ernie, hey, it's good to hear from you."

"I wasn't sure you'd remember me or not," said Ernie meekly.

"Of course I remember you," said Joanne. "How could I forget Firehouse Subs and the car ride? I've been meaning to call you to see how you've liked the Bio Strength products you bought. Which ones have you been using?"

"I've been drinking the anti-oxidant drink, and I think I've been feeling a little better the last couple of days," said Ernie.

"That's great! Keep drinking it and you'll feel your energy levels rise, too," said Joanne excitedly. "Hey, you should consider becoming a distributor so you don't have to pay retail prices for the products. And if you sell some at retail, you can make a 25 percent profit. Doesn't that make sense? Who knows, maybe you will decide you want to be a Royal Diamond one day like me!"

Joanne always liked to invite men right away to join. She feigned just the right amount of interest in the guy to reel him in, and when they met a second time, she would go in for the kill. Ernie was just another sucker in her long list of distributors, but her outward appearance was really a façade. Her soft feminine side bubbled just below the surface, waiting to emerge from the shadows.

Ernie thought about what Joanne had just proposed. What would the harm be in becoming a distributor? His boss didn't need to know. It would enhance his investigation since he could see and hear the inner workings of Bio Strength better on the inside. Besides, he would be able to spend more time with Joanne.

"Sure, why not," said Ernie. Ernie felt so free saying yes to something without having to check with his wife. It was the first spontaneous decision he had made in 20 years. "What do I have to do to join?" asked Ernie excitedly.

"There is a business starter kit for $49 that you order. I'll take care of signing you up to get you a distributor number. Why don't we meet for lunch today?"

"Sure," said Ernie trying to sound cool and collected.

"There's a neat little Loop Restaurant not far from here. How about 1:00?"

"Hold on, let me check my calendar just to make sure," said Ernie. He pretended to look for a moment though he knew he had nothing going on.

"Yeah, I can do that. I know where The Loop is. See you there."

"Great, see you then!" said Joanne.

Ernie hung up and started dancing around his office. He plugged in his iPod and lost himself in Fleetwood Mac again. An unfamiliar energy surged through Ernie, and he lost all memory of being married with little kids. The feeling was strange but exciting, and he didn't want it to end.

He glanced at his watch and saw he had two hours to kill before lunch, so he tried to look busy. He was so totally distracted that he did not hear his cell phone ringing. He finally looked at his phone and saw Marlo was calling. No sense spoiling a great day, Ernie thought as he let it roll to voicemail.

He sat down at his computer to kill time. He remembered he had some friends that talked about Facebook constantly, so he decided to check it out. He typed in Joanne Griggs's name to see if he got a match. Thirty-two Joanne Griggs entries appeared, and Ernie quickly searched for a picture of the only Joanne Griggs that mattered to him. On the last page was a picture of Joanne and her background info. His heart raced as he read her bio. She was born in 1975, so that made her 35 years old. She was born in Providence, Rhode Island. There were several pictures of her with men he didn't recognize. Were these Bio Strength distributors? Ernie's mind raced as he tried to figure out who they might be.

Ernie had never considered starting a Facebook page of his own, but he thought he should start one to have another way to contact Joanne. It was easy and free, but he had to use a pseudonym so people at work would not know he had a page. He was an investigator with the FDA, and he was supposed to be working in a clandestine manner. Ernie thought there was no way he would get caught if he used a fake name. He only wanted access to Joanne Griggs and not the rest of the world. Ernie wanted a pseudonym that Marlo would never think of, so he typed in Larry Zeiger. That name happened to be the real name of the CNN talk show host Larry King. Marlo would never know that since she hated Larry King because of his eight marriages. Larry King's propensity to divorce and remarry was all the info Marlo ever wanted to know about him. Ernie was certain Marlo would never find him through Larry Zeiger's name.

He put very little information on his page, and he didn't bother to put a picture on it yet. He wanted a really good picture for Joanne to see. Ernie was amazed at how many high school friends he found on Facebook. Some of his classmates were really into it, and he could tell which of them was online. Ernie had never bothered to go back to any of his reunions, and he had completely lost touch with everyone from high school. He realized his life had a big, gaping hole in it from lost relationships past and present. What had happened to all his friends? Why did he marry who he did? What was his life all about now? The weight of all these questions was too heavy for him to deal with, so he plugged in some good music and got back to his previous cloud-nine dreamlike state.

Finally it was 12:45 and time for Ernie to leave for lunch. He walked out of the building pretending to talk on his cell phone so no one would bother him. He read that it was a trick that Tiger Woods used to do in public places to avoid people harassing him. It usually worked pretty well.

Ernie pulled into the parking lot at The Loop, and he spent a few extra minutes combing his hair until it was Fonzie-perfect. He saw Joanne pull into the parking lot, and his heart jump started. She was wearing tight tan pants and a blue button-down shirt. She was dressed professionally, but her pants definitely showed off her curves. Ernie adored her from afar and imagined her spread on a bed naked. He quickly came to his senses and realized he shouldn't keep her waiting. Or should he? He thought he could build up suspense by making her wait for him. He couldn't decide what to do. Should he get out of the car now and meet her right away, or should he make her wait? "This is ridiculous," Ernie told himself. He checked his hair again and got out of his car. Joanne was waiting for him in the front of the restaurant.

"Hey, good looking," said Joanne.

Ernie had never had a lady say that to him. He looked around to see if she was talking to someone else.

"Yes, I'm talking to you, Ernie Zimmerman."

Ernie felt himself blush. "You're the only good looking one here," said Ernie. Ernie felt a strange confidence around Joanne. Marlo had emasculated him years ago, and it was refreshing for Ernie to have someone see something in him.

"How's my next Royal Diamond?" asked Joanne with a smile.

"Don't get too far ahead of yourself," said Ernie. "I haven't even signed up yet, and you've got me headed to the top."

"That's the only way to think," said Joanne. "Why go halfway with anything you do. We only get one chance, so why not go for it. Does that make sense?"

Ernie felt like Joanne was speaking directly to his soul. He wondered if going for it meant she was interested in him.

"Yes, that makes perfect sense," said Ernie.

"The pizza here is fantastic. You wanna split a barbecue chicken pizza? That's my favorite," said Joanne.

"Sure," said Ernie as they took a table in the corner.

"Lunch is on me," said Joanne.

"You don't have to do that."

"My pleasure. It's the least I can do for my newest Royal Diamond," said Joanne. "I have to ask you Ernie, what made you change your mind about becoming a distributor? You were not too hip on network marketing when we first met."

Ernie reflected for a few seconds before answering her.

"You made me realize that there is more to life than simply waiting for some future event to bring happiness. We only have now, and you can't ever wait for it to come. I've been waiting for it to come to me for a long time. Waiting to retire, waiting for the kids to get out of diapers, waiting to fall in love again…." Ernie's lips quivered ever so slightly as he spoke his heartfelt feelings. He was so used to bottling up his emotions. His mantra during his marriage was to never do anything to upset the apple cart. Whenever he spoke his mind, his wife would jump down his throat. He found his best way to deal with things was to just keep quiet and do what Marlo wanted.

Joanne could sense an emotional shift in Ernie. She knew she had touched something deep in him.

"You've waited for something to come along and change your life for a long time, haven't you?" asked Joanne as she reached out and touched Ernie's hand. "It's okay to let these feelings of frustration out. It's good for your mental and physical state to release frustrations. They'll kill you if you keep them bottled up too long. Does that make sense?"

"In fact, everything you say makes more and more sense to me," said Ernie. "I'm not used to anyone speaking to me in such a positive way, and I like the way you make me feel."

"Ernie, I will do everything I can to help you make it in this business. I see that having something you can call your own is important to you. I see you are not fulfilled at all at home. I hope Bio Strength can help fill that void for you."

"Joanne, Bio Strength has some great things to offer, but what I'm really talking about is…."said Ernie when Joanne's cell phone rang.

Joanne glanced at her iPhone to see who was calling.

"I'm so sorry. I've been waiting for this call. Do you mind?"

"No, not at all," said Ernie. He would have to wait to tell her how he felt about her.

Joanne stood up and walked outside to take her call. Ernie could see her laughing and smiling through the window while she was on her call. He hoped it was not a long lost boyfriend calling to get back into her life. Ernie fumbled through some Bio Strength promotional materials she had left on the table. The slick looking brochures painted a rosy picture of successful distributors standing in front of their fancy cars and big houses. The people all looked so happy. Ernie wondered if they could be real. *Did anyone really live the life of their dreams?* He didn't want to believe the endless network marketing hype. Ernie thought most people just trudged along like him and were content with only a smidgeon of happiness every now and then. Why raise your expectations only to see them crushed? He thought about changing his mind about signing up with Bio Strength. Marlo would kill him. Joanne walked back to the table and sat down, and any negative thoughts about network marketing instantly disappeared. Ernie knew the reason he was signing with Bio Strength was sitting right in front of him.

"Sorry about that," said Joanne. "I've got a great lead with a doctor in town. He knows Dr. Garfinkel but doesn't want to sign under him. Having a doctor in your downline is a wonderful thing. They have instant credibility."

Joanne was always jealous about the easier success she felt doctors had in signing up distributors and selling product. They had a natural market, and people looked up to them. Actually, many doctors felt they were at a disadvantage in the multi-level business because their credibility was on the line. If they put their reputation on the line behind a poor product or company, the consequences to their reputation would be catastrophic.

"That's great," said Ernie. "Maybe he can get other doctors to sign under him, too."

"That's the whole idea," said Joanne. "That's how I'm going to make my million. It's simple, really. It's just a whole lot of people doing a little bit of work. I compare it to the miracle of compound interest. Does that make sense?"

"Absolutely," said Ernie. Ernie was ready to soak in everything Joanne said. He had lost all sense of reason and objectivity talking to Joanne. The restaurant was crowded, but Ernie sensed only the two of them there.

"How do I get started as a distributor?" asked Ernie.

"Wow, you *are* an eager beaver. Just fill in your address and social security number here. I'll also need your credit card info."

"Why do you need my social?" asked Ernie.

"We need that to report any income over $600 a year to the IRS. It's required. I hope you don't mind. Besides, what's wrong with some extra money coming in every month? Your wife shouldn't mind that at all."

"Oh, yeah. That reminds me. I can't use my home address to ship stuff. She'll get suspicious. I have a neighbor whose address I can use."

"Are you sure?" asked Joanne.

"Yeah, I've had stuff sent there before. He'll do it for me." Ernie had ordered some porn movies before and had them sent to his neighbor's address.

"What about your work address?" asked Joanne.

"I don't want people at work knowing my business," said Ernie.

"Whatever you want. You're the boss. I just need your autograph at the bottom of this page."

Ernie quickly scribbled his name.

"Congratulations!" said Joanne. "You tell me how fast you want to go with the business. We can do it fast or slow. It all depends on you. I know your family life is demanding, so keep that in mind."

"I won't have any problems there," Ernie said. "I can start on a fast track. I'll wait a while before I tell Marlo."

Ernie just wanted to spend as much time as possible with Joanne. He knew he would have a mountain of trouble telling Marlo he had just signed up with a multi-level marketing company with a bombshell blonde as a sponsor. She wouldn't buy for a second that it was all part of an undercover scheme.

"I'll help you get started with your website," said Joanne. "That's going to be critical to your success because customers will be able to order product without you doing a thing. All you do is direct them to your website, input your distributor number, and Bio Strength does the rest. You sit back and collect the commission."

"How about training? How do I learn about the products and the business?" asked Ernie.

"That's my job," said Joanne.

"I'll need your help," said Ernie. "I hope you don't mind if I call with some questions?"

"No, not at all. Here is your distributor kit. I carry several extra with me so you don't have to wait for it to arrive. There's a CD about Bio Strength and the products, brochures about autoship and distributor sign-up forms, and a flyer on the upcoming world convention. You should order a couple of distributor kits yourself so your new recruits can get started right away. It's important to keep the momentum going quickly with new people because quite often the initial enthusiasm wears off. I'm not going to kid you and say that this business is easy, because it's not. But the rewards are huge at the end. Most people get discouraged at first because there is a lot of effort without much reward. But just keep with it. Your rewards will come later. I'll help you any way I can," said Joanne.

Ernie was getting ready to ask a question when his cell phone rang. It was his work number, so Ernie felt he needed to answer.

"Excuse me, Joanne. This is my work number. I'm sorry."

"That's fine. Go ahead," said Joanne.

Ernie stood and walked outside so Joanne could not hear him.

"Hello," said Ernie nervously.

"Ernie, this is Joe. Who is the blonde bimbo you're with?"

Ernie was stunned. He knew he couldn't lie to his boss now.

"How did you know I was here?" asked Ernie.

"One of the secretaries in the office just left The Loop and saw you there with a gorgeous woman, and you know how some of these women can gossip. Listen, I don't care if you are fooling around as long as it doesn't affect your work. Your personal business is just your business. But if it starts to affect your work, then it becomes my business, too," said Joe.

"Joe, this is related to the Bio Strength investigation," Ernie shot back. "I am becoming a mole to get the inside scoop on this company. This lady is a big shot distributor I'm going to get a great deal of information from. I can't help it if she's got boobs," said Ernie.

"I'm sure her boobs had nothing to do with why you picked her," said Joe. "There are thousands of distributors to sign under, and you pick a dadgum blonde beauty pageant winner. I suppose that was just coincidence."

"I'm a happily married man," said Ernie, utterly unconvincingly.

"Yeah, so am I," said Joe sarcastically. "Listen, I don't care if you wanna play detective in Bio Strength. Just don't screw it up by letting your little head do the thinking. Got it?"

"Yeah, I got it," said Ernie as he turned to look back at Joanne. She smiled and waved. He smiled back and waved. "Listen, I gotta run. I'll see you back at the office."

"Remember, you can't get away with anything these days, Ernie. Marlo will find out eventually. But it won't be from me," said Joe. "There's a another group of ladies going to The Loop to eat now, so I suggest you finish up so they don't see you there."

"Okay, thanks," said Ernie as he hung up. He was anxious to get back to Joanne.

"Sorry about that. I need to get back to the office. Some sort of emergency. Can I call you later?"

"Of course. And think about going to the world convention in Toronto. That's a great way to get the big picture of what's going on with Bio Strength," said Joanne.

"Sure. Sounds great. I've never been to Toronto," said Ernie.

"We'll have a blast. Call me later, okay?"

"Okay," said Ernie as he turned to go.

Ernie was fired up as he got into his car. He felt like something great was going to come from all of this. He wasn't quite sure what would happen, but his energy level was soaring. Getting this Bio Strength case was the best thing that had ever happened to him.

Chapter 15

Paul was busy piecing together his income history for the lender for his dream home purchase. He knew he had to explain how his income had grown from zero a little over a year ago to over $25,000 a month now. He was not so good at record keeping, and his dealings with tax preparers usually involved receipts stuffed in shoe boxes.

Paul had convinced the police to let Mike and Chastity out of jail shortly after their incident. Mike apologized to Paul for trying to buy the house out from under him, and Paul was sorry for letting Mike get arrested. Mike even signed up the arresting officer as a Bio Strength distributor on the way to the station. Paul called Mike daily to talk about their growing businesses.

"Only you could sign up the cop that arrested you," laughed Paul.

"I also signed up the sheriff while I was in jail. He had tried some of the nutritional drink while he was in the restaurant and really liked it. He's already turned me on to his whole family. He has nine brothers and sisters. You think they are going to say no to their brother the sheriff? Us fighting was the best thing that happened to our business. Let's do it again sometime," said Mike.

"I don't know about that," said Paul. "That might get a little old for the police. Maybe I'm the one that should get arrested next time instead of you!"

"Jail's no big thing. I've been there before. Three square meals and lots of time to read. The worst part is the snoring at night. Good lord, it's impossible to sleep with the whole place snoring like a buzzsaw. By the way, I've been thinking about the best angle for you to take with your income situation with the bank. I know for a fact banks are real suspicious of self-employed incomes, particularly ones that have come out of nowhere like yours has. And being a network marketer doesn't help either. Most people assume they won't last. They forget about the Amway guys. They are set for life. Hell, they even named the

Orlando Magic basketball home the Amway Arena. Mary Kay is still going strong, so there's a lot of misperception out there."

"What did you have in mind?" asked Paul.

"I'm good friends with the head of the mortgage department at BB&T. I can make a call for you and make sure you get your loan approved," said Mike confidently.

"You're kidding," said Paul.

"Hell no, I ain't kidding. He's an old fraternity buddy of mine. I know so much dirt on him from our younger days, and he's scared I'll tell somebody. He can push it through. Heck, I might as well sign him up as a distributor while I'm at it," said Mike.

"That's awesome," said Paul. "But are their rates good?" asked Paul.

"How is your credit?"

"Better now. It was pretty sucky before I came to Bio Strength. Now I have zero debt."

"You should be okay. But don't cancel your credit application with your current bank yet until you hear from me. We should make sure you're approved first," said Mike.

"Okay, I really appreciate your help. I'm sorry I got so pissed at you at the showing, but I really thought you were trying to buy the house out from under me," said Paul.

"I was," said Mike. "Don't apologize to me. I like to shake things up every now and then. Otherwise my life gets too boring. I just take the attitude of whatever happens is okay. Whatever happens was supposed to happen anyway, and it all comes out all right."

Paul thought about what Mike had just said. No wonder Mike attracted people like a magnet. Everything was always okay with him. He never complained about or worried about anything. He lived one minute to the next in a state of bliss waiting to see what the fun truck was about to deliver. A party followed Mike wherever he went, and he never planned anything because he always liked what happened spontaneously better. It was the only way Mike knew how to live.

"You don't worry about anything. Have you always been like that?" asked Paul.

"My dad ran a large carpet and tile business, and I'll always remember a saying he had on the wall in his office. His job was very stressful, and he had to find a way to deal with the everyday problems he encountered. The saying on his wall was *What difference does it make*? It was his way of coping with all the stupid stuff that happens every day that doesn't go quite like you had planned. Whenever he would start to get mad, he told me he would look up at the saying, and it would help him realize that those stupid things bothering him were so trivial in the whole scheme of things. Twenty years from now, who would care? So I decided a long time ago to never let little things bother me. And you know what? Ninety-nine percent of things that happen *are* little things. Most people just blow them way out of proportion," said Mike.

Paul thanked Mike again for his offering to help with his mortgage. He realized that it is not always what you know but who you know that helps you in life. Mike was someone who knew lots and lots of people. His circle of influence was huge, and Paul had stumbled on him at a time when he was about to quit the business. Paul often wondered what would have happened if Carlos hadn't told him about the book *Excuse Me, Your Life is Waiting*. It was right after he had finished the book that he started practicing its lessons, and it worked right away for him. Did it work for everyone else? Paul wasn't sure. He hadn't talked to Carlos in a while, so he decided to give him a ring.

"Carlos, hey it's Paul. I haven't talked to you in a while."

"Yeah, I know. Once you big shots get all successful you forget about all the little people who helped ya along the way."

Paul wondered whether Carlos was kidding him.

"I know you're joking. Hey, I want to show you the house I just put a contract on. It has a beautiful view of the St. Johns River and has a pool and everything I've dreamed about," said Paul proudly. He was anxious to show the teacher how the student had excelled.

"How much are you payin' for this dream house of yours?" asked Carlos.

"I'm getting a steal for $899,000."

A few seconds of silence followed Paul's last words.

"Are you still there?" asked Paul.

Carlos was choosing his next words carefully. Finally he said, "Ya know how I feel about raisin' your standard of livin' too fast. I'm proud of what you've accomplished, I really am. But to do something like this so quickly is just plain crazy. I know I told you to go out and live your dreams, but good things happen to those who wait, too. This is way too much too soon. I really think you had success come too quickly. Do ya think that everybody has your kind of success in this business?"

"No, but it's because they haven't put their feelings at the forefront like the book you gave me said to do. She said that there are no coincidences in life and that we attract everything good and bad to us by the energy we put out." Paul was hoping that Carlos would be happy for his achieving his dreams. Having goals was what he preached to him when they first met on his street while Carlos had been selling donuts.

"The law of attraction does mean that like attracts like. But it doesn't mean that gettin' stuff is what life's all about," said Carlos.

"I don't think I'm obsessed with material things. But what I really wanted to ask you is how many other people in your downline have had success like me?"

"I have two other guys earning about a third of what you are pullin' in, and the rest are makin' around one or two hundred a month," said Carlos.

Paul was stunned.

"What? Is that all? How can that be? Have you shared the *Excuse Me* book with everyone?"

"Every single person that wants to treat this as a business gets that book," said Carlos.

"Then how come it doesn't work for everyone? Why did it work for me?" asked Paul.

"To be honest Paul, you were just damn lucky. Runnin' into Mike Melito is the only reason you are where you are. Without him, your checks would be nothin'. There are only a few Mike Melito types in this world, and you hit the jackpot. I've seen people struggle in this business for years while doin' all the right things. They use the product, they meet people, they keep their attitudes positive. But success comes at different times to different people. Unfortunately, most people can't wait around for years for success to come. They want it to come quickly just like what happened to you. But your case was different. Most people quit long before they run into a Mike Melito."

"So my attitude and energy flow had nothing to do with my success?" asked Paul.

"I'm not sayin' that at all. All I'm sayin' is for some reason I can't explain, yours came early. Would the others have succeeded eventually if they'd hung on for a while longer? Maybe, but most quit way before then. Paul, I've been in this business for many, many years. I've seen too many distributors raise their standard of livin' just like you're about to do when somethin' unexpected comes along and pulls the rug out from under 'em."

"You're just afraid to take a chance, that's all," said Paul.

"I might be cheap, but I live comfortably and have no regrets."

Paul couldn't believe that so few people were making money at Bio Strength.

"In your experience, is this how it is with all network marketing companies?"

"Yep," said Carlos. "The eighty-twenty rule applies to all types of businesses, includin' ours. That's where 80 percent of the money comes from 20 percent of the producers. Hell, I'd even bet that at network marketin' it's closer to 90 percent of income coming from the top 10 percent."

"So the guys at the top make all the money while the rest at the bottom are simply wannabe dreamers making a couple hundred a month" said Paul.

"Exactly," said Carlos. "You're one of the lucky ones. It's people like you that have made it that keeps everyone at the bottom filled with hope. This whole business is built on hope, man! Hope keeps everyone buying more product, hope keeps them buying more motivational books, and hope keeps them feelin' alive. It's all some people got. Your job is to keep givin' 'em that hope. Keep em' comin' back for more. The more you give 'em hope, the more money you make."

Paul pondered what Carlos had just said. No one had ever explained it quite that way to him before. Hope. An entire business model built on hope and dreams. It seemed so impossible for people to make it, yet he had. This was a huge paradox that Paul was having trouble grasping.

"I guess it's kinda like what happens to soldiers on the battlefield. The survivors can't understand why they made it and their buddies didn't. There doesn't seem to be any reasonable explanation of why. They feel guilt for surviving when death was all around them. I have a hard time sometimes telling people they can become wealthy in this. I guess it comes down to the fact that I was just damn lucky."

"That's right. Don't try to overanalyze it. It is what it is. You found the luckiest guy in the world to work with. You know that people make their own luck, don't ya?"

"Yeah, I've heard that before."

"Well, it's true. Lucky people are always open to possibilities. They see opportunity where others see nothin'. Every potential encounter is seen as a chance to have a life changin' experience. Lucky people have a huge network of friends. Have you noticed how many friends Mike Melito has? Hell, he's never met a stranger. You had a serendipitous meeting up with Mike. You were meant to meet him, and he was meant to meet you. Your energies synched up, and *boom*."

"Yeah, I don't think it was coincidence at all."

"Also, have you noticed how relaxed Mike is all the time? He's not conscientious at all. He's never married and probably never will. He's not a great task master, but that's why he is who he is. He's flexible enough to see somethin' good that comes along anytime, anywhere."

"Yeah, he had immediate relief from his shoulder pain when I put some lotion on him in the restaurant. He seized on this as a business immediately. He asked almost no questions. He saw an opportunity and took it."

"Mike's not afraid to fail," said Carlos. "Ownin' a restaurant is one of the riskiest business ventures to start, but he's been a smashin' success. I'm glad you're sayin' yes to life just like Mike Melito. But there's a smart way of doin' business, and this house thing is too much too soon."

"I appreciate that," said Paul. "But I'm going ahead with it anyway. Do you think people are just going to stop buying Bio Strength all of a sudden? We haven't even touched the surface with this company yet. My income has doubled in the last six months. I want you to come see my new dream house. I've waited all my life for something like this."

"Okay, okay, I'll come see this house. But first let's have a little fun. I wanna' do a little experiment on the science of luck. I'm gonna' prove to you that serendipity is a science. I don't think you're totally convinced yet."

"What did you have in mind?"

"Get one distributor of yours that you think is lucky, and get another who thinks of himself as unlucky. We both know the lucky one is going to be Mike. Now, who do you have in your downline who's a complainer and wonders why they never make any money? Got anybody like that?"

"Of course. Her name is Jenny Wyman. I get whiny emails and messages from her all the time. Nothing is ever right. It's either the compensation plan or lack of a producing downline that is killing her business. I've tried to talk to her, but she won't listen."

"Call her and tell her you've gotta' great potential lead for her and that you wanna' help jump start her business. She'll listen to you then."

"I can't lie to her about giving her a lead."

"Actually, she really will have a chance for a good lead. All she's gotta do is open her eyes. Prospects are around you all the time. You just have to be open to them. Here's what I wanna do. Let's tell Mike and Jenny that we want them to meet an influential prospect at Starbucks that could help their business. We'll send them in one at a time and tell 'em to just buy some coffee and wait for further instructions. I'll have a guy planted at a table near the cash register. He'll slip a twenty dollar bill on the floor for them to spot after they pay for their coffee. Then we'll see what happens next."

"Sounds crazy, but I'll call both of them to ask. Who are you going to plant in the Starbucks?"

"Arthur Lantor. He's an old buddy of mine who owes me a favor, so he'll help me out. Arthur is very wealthy, but he's bored. He's been lookin' for somethin' good to jump into. I've never been able to convince him to sign up with Bio Strength. He's leery of network marketin' companies in general."

"Alright, Mike will be all over the idea. Jenny will be harder to convince, but I'll give it a try."

Paul pulled out his phone to search his contact list and dialed Mike's number.

"Mike, hey it's Paul again. Hey, I've got a good prospect for you. Can you meet me at the Starbucks tomorrow at 10 a.m.?"

"Sure. I usually wake up at 10, but I can get up a little early for a good prospect."

"Great. Meet Carlos and me at the Starbucks at Racetrack and San Jose at ten."

"Cool, see you then."

"That was easy," said Paul to Carlos.

"Now call Jenny and see what happens."

Paul looked up Jenny's number and called her cell. Jenny was 39 years old and was struggling to pay bills on her salary as an administrative assistant. She had never married and dressed conservatively and wore funny looking black glasses with a big rim. Her lenses were huge, which made her eyes appear twice as large.

"Hello."

"Jenny. Hi, it's Paul Cousins."

Jenny was startled to hear Paul's voice. She called him at least once a week, and he rarely returned her calls. He usually just texted her a brief response.

"Hello Paul. It's unusual for you to call me, I must say."

"Listen, I've got a great opportunity for you. There is a great prospect that I want you to meet tomorrow. I'm trying to jump-start your business for you because I know things are slower than you would like…."

"I'll say they're slow. Nobody wants to spend money in this recession. People are losing their jobs everywhere. I'm not making any money at this Bio Strength stuff. Who is it that you want me to meet?"

"I don't have his name yet, but my sponsor Carlos wants to pass it to me, and I want to give him to you. We are meeting tomorrow at 9:30 at the Starbucks at Racetrack and San Jose. Can you meet us there?"

"That's not a convenient time for me since I have to work."

"Don't you work five minutes from that Starbucks?"

"Yeah, but my boss doesn't like me to leave my desk except for lunch."

"Jenny, this will be worth it. I promise it will be quick."

"Are you sure? I don't want to get in any trouble at work."

"I'm sure. Just come to the Starbucks at 9:30 and meet Carlos and me."

"Okay. But it better be worth it."

Paul hung up with Jenny. "Wow, that was hard."

"Notice how both of them reacted to your phone call," said Carlos. "Mike was immediately available while Jenny complained and asked questions. It will be interestin' to see what happens tomorrow."

"Maybe Jenny will quit Bio Strength and stop pestering me after this."

Carlos and Paul arrived at Starbucks at 9:15 to meet Arthur Lantor. Arthur was six foot six and had been a star basketball player in high school. He wore khaki pants and a blue button-down shirt with a sport coat. His hair was gray and cut short, and he looked like a big-shot type who could run a Fortune 500 business. Arthur walked in and ordered his coffee, spotting Carlos and Paul across the room. Carlos got up to greet him.

"Arthur, great to see you man. What's it been now, six months?"

"At least. So what kinda cockamamie scheme have you concocted for me today."

"First, let me introduce you to my business partner Paul Cousins. Paul this is Arthur Lantor."

"Nice to meet you, Arthur. I've heard a lot about you."

"From this guy? Oh, no. You've got the wrong impression of me already. You're not in one of those pyramid schemes with Carlos are you? He got me in one of those years ago and the whole company imploded after I bought thousands of dollars of product. I've still got some of the stuff in my garage."

"Carlos introduced me to a company called Bio Strength, and it's made me financially independent in just over a year."

"We're not here to sell you on Bio Strength, Arthur. We're conductin' a little test on serendipity for the benefit of Paul."

"*Seren* what?"

"Serendipity. It's the art of seizing the power of chance."

"Oh, you mean how some people seem to be luckier than others."

"Exactly. Here's what I want ya to do. Take a table near the cash register, and we're gonna send a lady in at 9:30 and tell her to get some coffee. When she comes to the cash register, take this twenty dollar bill and put it on the floor near you to see if she sees it. If she takes it, fine. If not, just pick it up after she walks by. Then, at 10 we'll send a man in through the line and you repeat the twenty dollar bill trick on the floor. We'll be sittin' over in the corner watchin'."

"You're nuts Carlos. But that's what I like about you. You keep my life interesting."

"Oh, here comes the first victim now. I don't want her to see us talking. Here's a crisp new twenty. Don't say I never gave you anything."

"Can I sell you back all the crap in my garage?"

"Shut up and sit down. We'll be over there."

Carlos and Paul moved to a window seat while Jenny pulled up in an old beat-up Honda Accord. She walked in at 9:35 looking hurried and worried. She looked anxiously around for Paul. They waved to her, and she walked over to their table.

"Good morning, Jenny," said Paul as he stood up to shake her hand. "Do you remember my sponsor Carlos?"

"Hi." Jenny offered a limp-wristed handshake to each of them. "I've only got a few minutes. My boss gave me a hard time about leaving. Who am I supposed to meet?" asked Jenny nervously.

"He's not here yet, so why don't you buy some coffee while we wait. The coffee is on me," said Paul as he handed her a ten-dollar bill.

"Thank you," said Jenny as she turned to walk to the counter.

"I hope Arthur doesn't screw this up," whispered Paul.

"He won't. The worst that'll happen is I'll lose twenty bucks."

Arthur watched Jenny place her order, and he quietly slipped the twenty on the floor in front of his table. Jenny paid for her coffee and glanced quickly at her watch. She checked her phone for messages while she waited for her coffee. Finally, her coffee was ready, and she grabbed it and took a step towards the twenty-dollar bill. Arthur was quietly reading the paper no more than three feet from Jenny. Paul and Carlos were sure she would see it. How could she not? Jenny took another step towards the twenty and stood on top of it with her left foot as she stirred cream in her coffee. She headed back to meet Paul and Carlos having never seen the twenty.

"So where is this guy?" asked Jenny.

"I just got a text from him that he couldn't make it. I'm sorry. How about if I arrange a conference call with him for you?" asked Paul.

"Don't bother. I can't believe I wasted my time here. I've got to get back to work now-this is just typical. I'll talk to you later," said Jenny as she walked away dejectedly.

Arthur picked up the twenty and walked over to Carlos and Paul.

"Did you see how she stepped on top of the twenty? A blind person could have seen it," said Arthur.

"Yeah, her vision wasn't the problem," said Carlos. She just wasn't perceptive enough to look at everythin' around her as a possibility. Mike should be here shortly. This'll be an interestin' comparison."

Mike pulled in the parking lot at 9:50. His black Cadillac Escalade was plastered with Bio Strength advertisements. The back window was covered with the white words "Get Health and Wealth with Bio Strength, Mike Melito 867-4240."

Mike bounded into Starbucks dressed in khaki pants, a blue button-down shirt and a sport coat. He opened the door for a woman walking in at the same time and smiled at her.

"He's dressed just like Arthur," said Carlos. "This is so weird. Did you tell him what to wear?"

"Hell no. I'm just glad he didn't show up with another of his bimbo waitresses."

Mike walked briskly back to Paul and Carlos while Arthur took his place at his table. He peered from behind his paper to see a man dressed just like him talking to Paul.

"What's happening," said Mike.

"You're a few minutes early for our prospect. Why don't you go get some coffee while we wait for him," said Paul while offering him a ten.

"I can pay for my own, thanks," said Paul as he turned to go place his order.

Paul and Carlos could see Mike making small talk with the Starbucks employees. Several of them were laughing, and Paul was obviously flirting with the pretty young employee taking his order. Arthur discreetly placed the twenty in the same spot on the floor he had before. He made sure Mike's back was to him when he did it, and he went back to quietly reading his paper.

Mike paid for his coffee and glanced around the restaurant while waiting. He immediately spotted the twenty on the floor and walked over to pick it up.

"Is this yours?" Mike asked smiling at Arthur.

Arthur was surprised Mike spotted it so quickly. It had been on the floor for less than ten seconds.

"Why, yes it is! Thank you very much. It's nice to see there are still some honest people left."

"Well, I *have* to give money I find to my identical twin. Nice threads."

"Yes, we are twins aren't we. Where do you buy your clothes?"

"Brooks Brothers," said Mike.

"That's where I shop, too."

"The manager Andy Ford comes into my restaurant all the time. He's a great guy."

"I've known Andy for years. I played golf with him last week."

"I love golf. I'm always looking for a partner. Hi, I'm Mike Melito," said Mike extending his hand.

"Mike Melito. That name sounds familiar."

"Ever been to Melito's Restaurant?"

"Of course."

"That's my restaurant."

"Well, I'll be damned! I thought you looked familiar. I *love* that place. How's business?"

"Fantastic. But I'm always open to new possibilities, and my friends Paul and Carlos got me into a new business with them, and it's working out great. In a year or so my income from this venture will exceed what I'm doing in the restaurant, and I've been running that for almost 25 years."

"Really? What is it? I've been looking for something to do now that I'm retired."

"It's a company called Bio Strength, and I had never heard of them until Paul rubbed some of their lotion on my arthritic shoulder. I hadn't been able to lift my right arm above my head for years, and this stuff worked a miracle," said Mike as he whirled his right arm around and over his head. "Now I'm selling this stuff out of my restaurant, and I can't keep enough of the stuff in stock. It's incredible! People love it!"

Mike had Arthur's complete attention now.

"You know, I've had arthritis in my hands and knees for years, and I'm willing to try anything. Got any of that stuff on you?"

"Sure," said Mike as he reached in his coat pocket for a tube. Paul had taught him to always have product handy, and Mike was a good student.

"Just rub some of this on your hands," said Mike as he squirted a glob of lotion into Arthur's hands.

Paul and Carlos watched in amazement as Mike gave lotion to someone he had just met. It looked like Mike and Arthur were long lost friends. Mike then took a seat at Arthur's table.

"Should we go over and tell Mike that we had just set him up?" asked Paul.

"Hell, no. Let's see how far this goes with Arthur. If we go over now, Arthur will become suspicious that we got him here to sign him up in a network marketing scheme. He hates network marketing since the only time he tried it he got stuck with a bunch of unsold product. Fifty bucks says he signs Arthur up."

"Oh, I know better than to bet against Mike Melito. He's so damn convincing, even to complete strangers."

Arthur sat with Mike for a good 20 minutes talking animatedly. They both were army veterans, and both liked golf and the Jacksonville Jaguars.

"Wanna play golf this weekend?" asked Mike. "I need a fourth."

"Where are you playing?"

"Ponte Vedra Inn and Club. I've got a regular time on Sundays at noon."

"Great. I'll let you know how this stuff works on my hands. Now that I mention it, my hands do feel a little better already. Can I have a little more of that lotion until I see you Sunday?"

"Here, take the rest of this tube. Just rub it where it hurts. I am a brand new person on this stuff. Plus, I'm making a killing selling it. Tell me how it works out for you when I see you Sunday."

"I sure will. Hey, thanks for the invite. I'll see you then."

Mike and Arthur shook hands. Arthur waved to Paul and Carlos as he walked out the door. Mike saw Arthur wave in their direction.

"You guys know Arthur Lantor?" asked Mike.

"For a long time," said Carlos. "I've actually tried to recruit him into Bio Strength before. Seems like you might have him interested. I saw you givin' him lotion."

"We're playing golf this Sunday, and I told him to let me know how it works out for him. You can't come on too strong with people, or they'll sniff it out that you're over eager. Ya gotta let them come to their own conclusions."

"Hear that Paul? Let people come to their own conclusions. Did you teach him that?"

"I wish I had. I learn something new from Mike every time I'm around him. Just don't ask him to go house hunting with you."

"What does that mean?" asked Carlos.

"I never told you what happened when I took Mike with me to look at my dream house?"

"No."

"Well, I'll tell it to you on the way to look at the house. Do you wanna come again to buy it out from under me, Mike?"

"No thanks. Oh, by the way. I talked to my buddy at BB&T today, and he said with two more months of earnings like you've been having he could approve your loan as long as you had 20 percent down."

"Really?" said Paul excitedly.

"Yeah. Just keep up your earnings and you'll be okay. I go back with this guy a long ways, and he knows I don't call him up for favors unless I really need one."

"Man, you're *awesome*!" said Paul as he held up his hand for a high-five.

"Could you call Chastity and tell her that? She's mad at me right now."

"Lovers' quarrel, huh? What did you do to piss her off?" asked Paul.

"I was just showing a little too much attention to a new bartender."

"And what kind of attention did you give her exactly?" asked Carlos.

"Well, I was doing some training with her after hours, and Chastity walked in on us. She screamed at us while we were both half undressed."

"What did Chastity do next?"

"She just ran outside. I've tried leaving several messages, but she hasn't returned my calls."

"I'd let her go," said Paul. "She's never gonna forget that. Is that the kind of training you give all your new bartenders?"

"Nah. Only the ones with the most potential."

"You're incredible," said Carlos. "Let's go see this dream house of yours."

"Okay," said Paul. "You sure you can't come, Mike?"

"Yeah, I've gotta get to the restaurant. Lots of training to give."

"I've never had training like that before," said Paul. "Hey, call me after you play golf with Arthur. Let me know if you sign him up."

"Sure thing. I'll talk to you soon." Mike walked towards the door and gave a broad wave to the girl at the register he had flirted with. She gave him a big smile and wave back.

"That guy is amazin'," said Carlos. "Look at the difference in how two people dealt with the same exact situation. One saw inconvenience, and the other saw an opportunity to make a friend. Keep lookin' for more people like Mike. They're the ones that'll send you to the top."

"I know. Would you like to ride with me to look at my future home?"

"Let's go. I've got an hour to kill."

Paul told Carlos about the incident at the original showing for the house he was buying. Carlos laughed out loud after hearing about the fight and plunge into the swimming pool.

"I promise I won't buy it out from under you!"

"I know you mean well by telling me to wait. But I've been waiting for something like this my whole life. And nobody has tomorrow guaranteed, so I'm taking advantage of what I've got today. Just because you never bought a house like this doesn't mean I can't. I kinda get the feeling you're jealous."

Carlos stopped in his tracks in the parking lot.

"You think I'm jealous?"

"Yeah. You haven't been supportive of me at all through this process. All you've tried to do is talk me out of it. I think it's because you want what I'm getting."

"How the hell do you know what I'm thinkin'? Did it ever occur to you that I might be proud of what you've accomplished? I did bring you into this business, after all."

"I wanted you to be excited for me. You're the reason I've made it this far, and I appreciate it. Of all people, your opinion matters the most."

"Well let's stop arguin' and go look at this dream house of yours."

"Okay, I don't want to kick your ass like I did with Mike."

"Don't tempt me, Paul. I'll drive. Just get in the damn car before I start something."

Paul hopped in Carlos's car. The front seat was covered with papers, empty soda cans, and candy wrappers.

"Don't you ever clean this thing?"

"Once a month. But in between it is what it is. I ain't got time to clean a car. I'm too busy tryin' to make money. Where is this house anyway."

"Go down San Jose and turn onto Mandarin Road."

Carlos pulled down Mandarin Road and immediately noticed the large brick homes with huge oak trees and manicured yards.

"You definitely are taking a step up, man. You don't believe in takin' baby steps, do ya?"

"Nope. I've imagined this home my whole life, and I'm not waiting for it any more. There it is right over there!" said Paul pointing like a child spotting Santa.

Carlos turned the corner and spotted a beautiful two-story brick home on the river. Two large, white columns stood on the front porch, and old-growth oak trees had Spanish moss hanging lazily off their branches. It looked like something from *Gone With the Wind.*

Carlos stared at it for a few seconds. Paul waited anxiously for Carlos to say something, and after a seemingly forever silence, Carlos spoke.

"It's absolutely beautiful. It's prettier than you described. Ya know you have to get a boat when you live on the water."

"I know. Don't you remember you asking me what my dreams were when we had our first meeting? I told you I wanted a boat and a house on the water. You got my juices going for the first time in years. It's all because you decided to let kids sell doughnuts to me on a Saturday morning. Funny how life works out sometimes."

"Yes it is. See how thoughts are things? Powerful things. The human mind can create some fantastic realities, or it can create misery. I've seen misery, and I want no part of it. I'm happy for you, Paul. I really am. But you're much more spontaneous than I ever was. But let's not celebrate with champagne until you actually close, ya know."

"I know, I know. But Mike said the loan was a done deal as long as my income stays the same for two more months. That's a piece of cake."

"Should be. I checked the downline orders this mornin', and I'm up 20 percent over last month. That means your check should be up even more than that next month."

"Awesome! Everything is falling into place so easily. Is this how it's supposed to be?"

"For a few. Everyone can't make that kind of money like you have. Otherwise, you'd have a top heavy pyramid. Everythin' depends on a whole bunch of people doin' a little with a few leaders picked up along the way."

"What could possibly happen to screw things up? Bio Strength has just started to grow."

"I've seen some crazy things happen, Paul. You never know."

"I'm going all for broke, man. I see my future, and like the song says, it's so bright I gotta wear shades."

"Just don't go broke wearin' 'em. I like the Boy Scouts motto."

"What's that?"

"*Always be prepared.*"

Chapter 16

Ernie turned in his Bio Strength samples after procrastinating for several weeks. He had never enjoyed life so much during that time. He talked to Joanne every day during the week for Bio Strength strategy sessions, and he was a regular at the business previews. Even his boss Joe noticed how perky Ernie had been around the office. He knew puppy love when he saw it. Ernie wanted this feeling to last forever, but he couldn't put his boss off any longer. He turned his samples over to the laboratory head Ralph Smedley.

Ralph's nickname around the office was "The Rat" because his eyes were close together, and he had small glasses on his thin nose and a narrow face that made him look like a rat. Ralph was the guy who you could never cheat off of in high school because he always followed the rules. It didn't help that he talked down to people since he felt he was smarter than everyone else. He would have made more friends if he wasn't so caught up in following every minute detail to the letter. It took him forever to get lab results back, but he always got things right. His reliability saved his job more than once when people complained about his petulance and annoying attention to detail and procedures. But Ralph the Rat was right every time.

Ralph took the Bio Strength samples and started his analysis of the listed ingredients. He poured a couple ounces of each product into a test tube and labeled each. He liked to use x-ray fluorescence and nuclear magnetic resonance spectrophotometry testing among several others.

Ralph left the lab for lunch after completing the Bio Strength product testing. All he had to do was read the computer results that afternoon, and he would know what the ingredients were in each product. Ralph locked his lab door and headed to the cafeteria for lunch.

Ernie was anxious to hear Ralph's results on Bio Strength, so he walked to the lab to talk to him. The door was locked, but

Ernie could see through the window that no one was in there. Ernie had stolen Ralph's office key years before and made a copy in case Ralph ever came under suspicion for fraudulent testing. Ernie had asked Ralph for a little lab training when things were slow a year before. He looked down both ends of the hall before pulling his key out and entered the lab. He turned on the computer screen that Ralph had been working on and looked for a Bio Strength heading. A tab with the heading "Testing Complete" appeared at the bottom of the screen. Ernie clicked on the tab and held his breath.

    A screen full of numbers and chemicals appeared. Most seemed innocuous and were on target with what Bio Strength had advertised. But one chemical caught Ernie's eye: Methylprednisolone 20 percent concentration. *What the hell is that?* He quickly Googled "methylprednisolone." He discovered it is a steroid used to treat allergies, arthritis, skin conditions, and breathing disorders. *Why is a steroid being used in a nutritional drink?*

    The computer also listed high levels of anabolic steroids in the Bio Strength lotion. Testosterone and epitestosterone were indicated at compositions of 25 percent. Ernie remembered reading about baseball players using the "cream" to avoid detection in doping tests. He Googled "epitestosterone" and discovered it was used to beat doping tests based on ratios of testosterone to epitestosterone. Epitestosterone provided all the advantages of testosterone without any of the chances of detection. *What in the world are anabolic steroids doing in Bio Strength products*? He looked at the screen to make sure it was the Bio Strength samples he was reading, and he verified that they were. The sunscreen products turned up with steroids as well. Ralph the Rat didn't make mistakes. It appeared that whoever put the anabolic steroids in the Bio Strength lotion was attempting to avoid detection. Ernie felt they must have assumed any test would come from checking urine specimens and not from the product itself.

    Ernie was in shock. His face was turning beet red and he looked nervously around to see if Ralph was returning. A revelation like this would shut down Bio Strength, but worst of all would effectively end his relationship with Joanne. He was not going to let anything get in the way of his happiness, and he especially didn't want Ralph the Rat screwing up his life.

He clicked on the heading for Bio Strength products and switched the name to another company named "Preventa" which Ralph was testing as well. He carefully made sure he spelled Preventa correctly under each product tab. They had similar products to Bio Strength, so Ralph would not get suspicious when he saw Bio Strengths' results compared to Preventa's.

He left the lab and locked the door behind him. He had never done anything so illegal in all his life, and it thrilled him. *This is what it must feel like to rob a bank!* Adrenaline surged like a river through his veins. Ernie quickly made his way back to his office. Ralph returned to his lab after lunch to see if the results on Bio Strength had been compiled yet. He was excited to see that the results were ready. He clicked on the tab for Bio Strength, and the results popped up on his screen. There were a number of irregularities in the product ingredients from what Bio Strength had advertised. Several ingredients were common ones in most lotions like glycerin and cetyl alcohol, but a number were present that were not listed at all. Ralph had found problems, but there was no smoking gun of proven hazardous ingredients. He was a little perplexed since his boss had indicated that there had been a number of complaints from Bio Strength users of rising cholesterol readings and men losing hair, but that could be attributed to people just getting older.

Ralph decided that he would test the Bio Strength products again the next day just to make sure. He wanted to duplicate his findings to make sure they were accurate. He had a number of other samples to work on that afternoon, and he never trusted only one sample. It was possible for one sample to be cross-contaminated in production.

Ernie had never been so nervous in all his life. He had just put his entire career on the line, and he was operating on impulses that had completely taken over. The only thing he cared about was being in love again. He picked up the phone to call Joanne.

"Hey, Joanne. It's Ernie."

"Hi, Ernie. Made any new friends with Bio Strength today? You've probably got a ton of people at work who would love it."

"I've got somebody looking at it as we speak," said Ernie unaware of the irony of what he just said.

"Cool. Hey, you should sign up for the world convention in Toronto. Paul, Carlos, Dr. Garfinkel and I are going. It would be a great way for you to see how big Bio Strength is around the world and the growth that is still coming."

"I'd love to." Ernie didn't hesitate whenever Joanne suggested something. It was a simple relationship-Joanne barked, Ernie jumped, and it didn't matter that Joanne had no interest in Ernie. All he needed was the feelings that he longed for, and the fantasy of it all was alright with him. He felt that with time she could fall for him, so he had to be the perfect little downline distributor for now.

"Great! I'll forward the sign-up sheet to you. Are you sure your wife is okay with you going?"

"Don't worry about her. She'll let me go."

Ernie knew Marlo would have a cow over him going to Toronto for a network marketing world convention. He would have to come up with something good to get away with this.

"It's only a month away, so you should sign up now. I think it makes perfect sense for you to go to Toronto and get the big picture. Don't you?"

"Absolutely." Ernie was making snap decisions again without consulting Marlo. It felt wonderfully liberating.

"I'll see you at the Thursday night preview at Dr. Garfinkel's. Okay? Gotta run now. Call me if you need me."

"Bye."

Ernie checked his home email and quickly filled out the form and deleted it. He didn't need an argument with Marlo yet, and he didn't feel like begging to go. He liked acting with bravado, and breaking into Ralph's lab was his *coup de grace*. His biggest challenge would be handling Marlo.

Ernie surprised his family by coming home in time for dinner at six o'clock. He usually came home after the kids were put to bed. He decided to be especially nice to Marlo tonight.

"Honey, I'm home."

Marlo was busy getting dinner on the table. She didn't look up at Ernie when he walked in.

"Honey," said Ernie louder. "I'm home for dinner." Ernie was going trying to overcompensate for his lack of attention recently.

"Well, woop-de-doo. Ya want me to turn a cartwheel or something?" said Marlo sarcastically.

"I thought you'd like it if I came home early."

"Maybe five years ago. Now I don't even know you anymore."

"What do you mean?"

"Oh, don't give me that crap. You know you've been avoiding us by working so late. And by the way, I saw an email about some convention in Toronto sent by a woman named Joanne. What is in Toronto, and who is Joanne?"

Ernie felt his forehead turn red hot. He thought he had deleted the email too quickly for Marlo to notice. He realized she must have been online when Joanne sent it.

"It was just a junk email. I don't know who sent it, so I deleted it," said Ernie as calmly as he could.

"Not much gets by me. Are you having an affair?"

Ernie was shocked she asked that question. She had said it so matter of factly that it was as if she already knew the answer.

"Of course not," said Ernie emphatically.

"Would you tell me if you were?"

"That's not even an issue, honey. What's gotten into you, anyway?"

"I don't think I want to be married anymore. No, let me say that differently. I *know* I don't want to be married anymore. I've met with a lawyer, and you're going to be served papers next week. You can stay in the guest room until everything is finalized. It's better when the kids are younger so they won't really understand what is going on. I've been thinking about this for a long time. The spark is long gone, Ernie. You know it, and I know it. I would rather be alone with the kids than be with you and be ignored."

Ernie didn't know whether to laugh or cry. His mind was swirling with so many mixed emotions, and he imagined running off together with Joanne. Then he thought of child support and alimony. He had seen too many of his friends struggle to get by after a divorce.

"You want to quit just like that? No discussions, no warnings, no counseling? You just want a divorce, period."

"I couldn't have said it better."

"Well, you've got it. You think it's been easy living with you?" said Ernie as his voice rose to match his emotions. "I don't think you ever wanted kids because they get in the way of your social life. All you want to do is leave when I get home and go see your friends and play bunko. How do you think that makes me feel?"

"You're never home in time for me to go anyway. And what's wrong with wanting to get out of the house? I'm stuck in here all day, and seeing my friends is the only thing that keeps me going," yelled Marlo.

"I don't need to hear this. I'm leaving," yelled Ernie.

"Good. Sleep in your car for all I care," screamed Marlo.

Ernie slammed the door to the garage and got in his car to leave. Marlo stuck her head out the kitchen door. The kids started crying and the dog barked loudly.

"Yeah, go ahead and walk out of an argument like all you men do."

Ernie calmly started his car and opened the garage door. "I may be walking away from an argument. But you're walking out on a marriage. That's a big difference."

Ernie could see the stunned look on Marlo's face as he gave his last zing. She was speechless as Ernie spun his tires on the driveway and sped down the street. He was proud of the last line he gave her about walking out on the marriage. He thought of that spontaneously, and this newfound impulsiveness thrilled him. He had years of bottled up emotions bursting forth.

Ten minutes ago he came home to a wife and kids, and now Ernie was driving around aimlessly wondering where he was going to spend the night. He thought of his kids and if they would miss him. His thoughts turned to Joanne. He wanted so much to see her. "Should I call her now?" he thought. He didn't want to sound too desperate to see her. He decided to wait another day before calling. He wanted to practice what he was going to say to her anyway.

Ernie stopped at a Bob Evans for dinner. During his meal he noticed how lonely it was to eat by himself. Is this how it is going to be the rest of my life? *Eating out by myself every night? Seeing the kids every other weekend?* Then he remembered he wouldn't have to see Marlo every day, and everything was going to be all right.

Ernie checked into a Ramada and stared out the window for 30 minutes. He didn't know what to feel, so he turned the television on to distract the numbness. He was not going to tell anyone at work right away because he needed to keep things running smoothly there. The last thing he needed now was to be fired. His boss was already mad at how long the Bio Strength case was taking. Ernie prayed that Ralph the Rat would not notice the changes he had made on his computer. He watched television until midnight and finally drifted into sleep.

The next day at work Ernie kept walking past the lab in hopes of talking to Ralph about the Bio Strength sample results. He walked past the lab four times before finally catching Ralph coming out of the restroom.

"Hi, Ralph. Anything come back on the Bio Strength samples?" Ernie asked politely.

"As a matter of fact, I am waiting on my second set of tests right now. They could be ready any minute. Would you like to come in and see for yourself?"

"Of course. I'm the one who brought those samples in. My boss is breathing down my neck for these results."

"Come on in," said Ralph as he unlocked the lab door. He sat down at his laptop and the words "results complete" appeared at the bottom of the screen.

"Here we go," said Ralph as he clicked on the results. Ernie held his breath as the screen went blank for a second as the results tabulated. He was sure he had covered all his tracks by changing the heading name from Bio Strength to Preventa.

"Very interesting," said Ralph. "This test shows a large concentration of methylprednisolone. That's a steroid used to treat asthma and a host of other conditions. Quite unusual to find this and also very illegal."

Ernie's face turned ashen. He tried to appear calm, but his insides were churning.

"Are you sure? That's really strange. Maybe there is some mistake."

"There is no mistake. This is the second test I have run on the Bio Strength samples. There also are large concentrations of epitestosterone and anabolic steroids. I don't know why steroids are in these products. They were not listed in the ingredients at all, and besides that a doctor's prescription would be required to take these. These are medical products requiring approval by the FDA. They're in big trouble," said Ralph with a smirk on his face.

Ernie bent down to the screen to take a closer look. He was sure he had changed the entries and saved them properly. He couldn't believe what he was seeing.

"Ralph, maybe you should run a third test. Perhaps there was some cross contamination involved here."

"Nope. I don't need to run another test. This company has a lot of explaining to do. This revelation will certainly shut them down. But the real interesting thing is that someone attempted to tamper with the first test results. Do you know who would have done that?"

"Oh, no. What makes you think someone tampered with the test?"

"Funny you should ask. Here, watch this video." Ralph clicked on a video which showed Ernie breaking into his lab and sitting at the computer.

"What were you doing breaking into my lab yesterday?" said Ralph suspiciously.

Ernie knew he was busted. There was no mistaking that it was him on the video.

"You never told any of us you had a closed-circuit camera in here."

"Exactly. Why would I tell anyone of the existence of a camera? And why were you sneaking into my office? Your boss would love to see this."

"Have you sent it to him yet?" asked Ernie nervously.

"Not yet, but I will now," said Ralph as he reached to forward the video to Ernie's boss.

Ernie quickly reached his arm over to grab Ralph's hand.

"Not so fast, Ralphie." Ralph hated that name since kids in school used to tease him with it all the time.

"You really don't want to do that," said Ernie sternly.

"I have to. Not only did you break into my office, but you changed the results of a test. That is such a blatant ethics violation. Hell, you could go to prison for this. And it's all caught on tape! You are so gone from here. Nice knowing you, buddy," said Ralph as he tried to wrench his wrists away from Ernie's firm grasp.

Ernie and Ralph flailed away at each other's arms in front of the computer. Ralph tried to hit send on his computer while Ernie pulled his wrists back. Finally, Ernie pushed the laptop on the floor making a loud crash as it hit the hard tile.

"You idiot," yelled Ralph. "You may have screwed up my hard drive."

Ralph got out of his chair to retrieve his laptop. Just as he picked up his laptop, Ernie made a charge and bowled Ralph over like a bowling pin. Ralph's glasses flew off, and he ended up under a table with Ernie on top of him. They wrestled briefly until Ernie had Ralph pinned on the floor.

"Give me your laptop now!" yelled Ernie.

"Hell no, you'll have to take it over my dead body!"

Ernie started pressing down harder against Ralph. He had at least 40 pounds on him, and his shoulder came close to Ralph's head. Ralph seized his opportunity and bit hard on Ernie's right shoulder.

"*Aaaggghhhh*," screamed Ernie as he rolled off of Ralph. He was sure the Rat had drawn blood.

"So, Ralphie the Rat likes to bite, huh? Is that the best you can do?" said Ernie mockingly.

Ralph hated being called Ralphie almost as much as The Rat. Ernie had called him both names, and Ralph was livid.

"Nobody calls me Ralphie the Rat!" screamed Ralph.

"Well I just did. *Ralphie the Rat. Ralphie the Rat.* Want some cheese, little rat?"

Ralph was full of rage at this point, but he had never been in a fight in his life. He didn't know what to do, so he looked for something to throw at Ernie. He grabbed a can of pencils and slung them at Ernie. He always kept his pencils sharpened, so he knew they were sharp projectiles. Ernie reflexively held his hands up in front of his face. One of the pencils landed squarely in the palm of his hand and stuck.

"*Owwwwwhhh!*" screamed Ernie as he grabbed the pencil and winced as he pulled it out.

"You probably just gave me lead poisoning!" yelled Ernie.

When Ralph heard the word poison, he remembered some blow darts someone had given him to test a year ago. He had completely forgotten about them until now. He remembered his brief research indicated the poison could cause a heart attack. He slowly moved to the cabinet where they were stored. Ernie inched closer to corner Ralph.

"What are you gonna do now, Ralphie. Throw your lunch box at me?" teased Ernie.

Ralph pointed to the window behind Ernie's back.

"Your boss Joe is looking for you," said Ralph pointing his finger.

"Oh, sure. That's the oldest trick in the book. You think I'm going to fall for that?"

Ralph kept his finger pointing towards the window. Ernie decided to take a quick glance behind him. He saw no one, and Ralph lunged towards the cabinet and grabbed a container of blow darts. Ernie rushed towards Ralph and knocked the container on the floor scattering the blow darts everywhere. They both jumped down on the floor to grab a blow dart. Each came up with one simultaneously, and Ernie and Ralph held the blow dart up to their mouths daring the other to blow first. They circled around the room, each pretending to blow first. Whoever missed would be a sitting duck for the other to hit.

"You always carry blow darts in your lab? What kind of researcher are you?" said Ernie as he positioned himself to attack first. He jumped behind a chair for cover and popped his head up to see his enemy.

"No. Someone gave me those to test a year ago and I just remembered them."

Ralph had never tried to blow the darts before, but he wasn't going to let this maniac ruin his lab results. He was going to blow his lungs out to nail Ernie in the head. Ernie kept popping his head up and down to see Ralph, so he waited until Ernie had hidden his head behind the chair again. He placed his mouth over the blow dart and took in a mighty breath. The dart blew right into Ralph's mouth as he inhaled, and Ralph immediately gasped for air. Ernie popped his head up in time to see Ralph choking.

"You inhaled the blow dart, didn't you," said Ernie. He crept closer to Ralph who now was desperately trying to hack up the dart stuck in the back of his throat.

"Didn't anybody ever tell you to never inhale on the blow dart, you idiot?" Ernie took aim and blew the dart at Ralph's head. The dart nailed Ralph in his neck, and he grimaced and grabbed at the right side of his neck.

"*Agghhhh,*" moaned Ralph as he fell back against the cabinet. His eyes rolled back in his head as he slowly fell to the floor and slumped over.

"That ought to put you to sleep for a while," said Ernie as he walked over to Ralph. He looked around to see if anyone had witnessed their fight, and he was relieved to see the coast was clear. He put his hand in front of Ralph's nose to see if he was breathing. There was no air coming out of his nose. Ernie quickly checked for a pulse and felt nothing. He didn't know CPR, and he couldn't call 911. How was he supposed to explain a blow dart in Ralph's neck? Ernie panicked. He never counted on killing Ralph, and he never suspected there was anything lethal in the darts. He just thought it was some kind of sedative.

"That's what I'll tell the police," thought Ernie as his mind raced for what to do next. "We were just playing around and neither of us knew they were lethal." How was he then going to explain the video showing him breaking into the lab. He couldn't let that video get exposed either. He grabbed the laptop and deleted the email with the video of him breaking into the lab. Ernie looked around for a hidden camera and saw one in the corner. He jumped up on a table and pulled it out of the ceiling. He quickly jumped down and started straightening the room up so there was no evidence of a fight. What was he going to do with Ralph? There was no way to sneak him out of the building in the broad daylight. Maybe he could do it at night. No, where would he put the body? Ernie knew no one visited Ralph in his lab since no one liked him. Who would miss him if they thought he was just working?

Ernie grabbed Ralph from behind to place him in his work chair. Ernie was amazed at how heavy a dead person was even though Ralph weighed barely 130 pounds wet. He struggled to place Ralph in his chair, but he slumped over too much. He had to get him sitting up straight, so he grabbed some duct tape and wrapped it around his chest then to the back of the chair. Ernie draped Ralph's lab coat over the back of the chair to cover the duct tape.

Ralph's head was still a problem because it dangled to one side. Ernie was trying to get it to look like Ralph was hard at work. No one would notice for days, and that would give him some more time to figure out what to do. He noticed a microscope on another desk, so he grabbed it and placed it in front of Ralph. He placed Ralph's eye socket over the microscope like he was looking at a sample. It took at little balancing act, but he finally got Ralph's head to stay still. He placed both Ralph's arms on the table and found Ralph's glasses on the floor and placed them beside the microscope. He then turned the table so Ralph's back was completely to the window. Not wanting any evidence of his cause of death, he pulled the dart out of Ralph's neck and mouth. After a few days, someone might check on him and think he died of a heart attack.

Ernie made one last check around the lab and went outside to see how it looked. "Perfect," he thought. It looked just like Ralph was working. Ernie walked briskly back to his office when he thought he better slow down. He didn't want to be seen as hurrying to leave the scene of a crime. He wanted to talk to Joanne, but he was in worse shape than yesterday after Marlo told him she wanted a divorce. He needed to calm down first.

Ernie drew a few deep breaths at his desk. In less than 24 hours, his wife had asked for a divorce, and he killed someone at work. At least he still had his imaginary lover. He needed to pick up some clothes from home if he was going to be staying in a hotel indefinitely. He called Marlo's cell phone and wondered if she would answer seeing that he was the caller.

"Hello," said Marlo.

"Oh, hi. I wasn't sure if you were going to answer or not."

"I started not to. Listen, you can stay here until everything is final. We can't afford for you to stay in a hotel. I met with an attorney today, and he is drawing up all the papers."

"Wow, this is really happening, isn't it?"

"Yeah, well you ignored me forever. I just couldn't take it anymore."

"I'm sorry. I've been real distracted at work recently. I know I could have done more at home."

"Well, just come home and see the kids. They missed you last night."

"I missed them, too. I'll be home soon."

Ernie realized that this was the most honest conversation he had had with Marlo in years. Each had been bottling up feelings, so it felt good to finally speak freely. Ernie had heard several of his friends say that they got along much better with their spouse after divorce papers were filed. No one had to pretend anymore.

When Ernie got home, both his kids shouted, "Daddy, Daddy!" as he hugged them. Even if his wife didn't want him anymore, he knew he always wanted his kids in his life. After dinner he set up the guest bedroom to stay in, and he fell asleep quickly. It took a great deal of energy to kill a co-worker. Meanwhile, several people commented that night on Ralph's work ethic as they saw him in the lab. He was working so hard that his head never budged from his microscope.

Chapter 17

Paul was finishing up packing in his apartment when the phone rang. He was due to close on his dream home at noon, and he was on a roll in every aspect of his life. He had started getting in shape again, and his paychecks had grown to over $34,000 per month in the last two months. Life was good, and the only thing missing from his perfect life was the perfect woman. Paul reached for his phone as it rang.

"Hello."

"Hey, it's Carlos. What time you need me there to help ya move?"

"Now would be good. I don't have too much stuff fortunately. I've already ordered some furniture so the new place doesn't look so empty."

"I'll bring my pickup over. See you shortly."

Paul looked around his house and remembered how down and out he was when he first met Carlos. He would never forget the eyes of the little black boy peering through his mail slot to sell him some doughnuts. That morning was a turning point in his life although he did not realize it at the time.

Carlos walked in with bottle of champagne and two glasses.

"Time to celebrate, man!"

"Why don't we wait until I close? I'm a little superstitious."

"Fine by me. Thank god you don't have no piano to move. In fact, we might be able to do all of this in one trip."

"Yeah, I've made several trips to Goodwill. I couldn't put all my junk in that beautiful new house. I've got to basically start over. I do plan on getting a baby grand. I've always wanted one."

"As long as I don't have to move it. Hey, what time is your closin'?"

"Noon."

"Well, let's get your bed downstairs."

"Can't. I threw it away."

"You threw your bed away? What the hell are you gonna sleep on tonight?"

"I have a bed being delivered this afternoon. It's a four-post king size with fancy bars connecting the posts."

"You really don't have a stitch of furniture, do you?"

"Nope."

"Well, why did you make me bring my truck?"

"I didn't ask you to bring your truck. You brought your truck."

"Don't get sassy with me, son. I ain't gettin' paid to do this. They say you can always tell who your friends are when it's time to move. I can be an ex-friend if you want me to," Carlos snapped.

"I'm just playin' with ya. I do have a couple of beers. Is it too early?"

"Hell, no. I'll take one. I'll save the champagne until you close."

Carlos and Paul sat on the living room floor amongst stacks of boxes and sipped on their beer.

"Have you turned power on in your name at this new place?" asked Carlos.

"Of course. You don't think I know what I'm doin', do ya?"

"Sure I do," said Carlos as he sipped on his beer. "Have you gotten your cashier's check ready to pay at the closin'?"

"What do I need a cashier's check for? I was just going to write a check."

"Man, they don't take personal checks at closings. You ain't never bought a house before have you? I shoulda known you didn't know what you were doing. We need to get you to the bank right now." Carlos and Paul chugged the rest of their beer and hopped in Carlos's old beat-up black pickup truck.

"Nobody told me about that. And my ex handled all the money stuff on this house. Hey, what year is this thing?" asked Paul.

"'77 Chevy. Best damn vehicle I ever had. It's moved too many people to count. Who do you bank with anyway?"

"Bank of America. It's right around the corner here."

Carlos pulled into the parking lot, and they walked into the branch together. They each were wearing old gym shorts and tattered t-shirts for the move.

"I bet they think we're gonna rob this place the way we're dressed. You sure you got enough money to close?"

"Of course I do. They wouldn't have loaned me the money if I didn't have a down payment," said Paul under his breath as they waited in line. Paul stepped up to the teller with Carlos right behind.

"I'd like to get a cashier's check please."

"Yes sir. For how much?"

"$182,047 made to this firm," said Paul as he handed her the name of the law firm.

"Can I have your checking account number, please?"

"Certainly," said Paul as he handed her his debit card.

"You got that much in your checkin' account?" asked Carlos.

"That will leave me with about ten thousand or so left. I'll get my next Bio Strength check next week. It's going to be a big one."

"Have you held money back for estimated taxes?"

"Sort of."

"I guess that's a no. Man, you are gonna be in a fix next April if you don't send in your estimated payments. You've got a lot to learn. That's why I'm your sponsor."

The teller came back with the cashier's check.

"Is there anything else I can do for you today?" she asked with a smile.

"You can help me move. I'm closing on a house today."

"That's wonderful. Congratulations, Mr. Cousins. Sorry I can't help you, but I'm stuck here."

"Thank you."

Paul glanced down at the cashier's check. He had never seen such a big number written on a check in his life. He showed it to Carlos as he smiled broadly.

"Thanks for everything, Carlos. I owe it all to you."

Standing behind Paul was a young white man with a blue Nike baseball cap and sunglasses. He stepped up to the teller after Paul and Carlos moved aside and pulled out a gun he had concealed in his pants.

"Give me all your money and quick," he screamed at the teller. She appeared to be in her early twenties, and she turned white with panic and froze not knowing what to do. All the training in the world doesn't matter when someone sticks a real gun at you to hold you up.

"*Now*! Give it to me now or I'll shoot," he yelled waving his gun around.

Carlos and Paul were no more than 10 feet from the robber. The teller at the next window slowly moved over with her hands up to help her.

"I can do this for you. Tammy, slowly move back and let me get the money for this man," said the older teller.

"Keep your hands where I can see them!" the robber yelled at the older teller.

Carlos and Paul stood stone cold, still watching the drama unfold.

"What do we do?" said Paul under his breath to Carlos.

"Just keep cool until he gets the money bag. Then I'll distract him and you grab his arm."

"Are you nuts? Why me? You grab him," Paul whispered.

"*No talking*," screamed the robber as he turned to Carlos and Paul. He kept the gun pointed at the teller who was putting money in the bag for him.

Paul and Carlos stood still and quiet as the teller handed the bag to the robber. As he reached over to grab the money bag, Carlos dropped his keys on the floor. He had 10 keys on his key ring, and they made a loud clinking sound as they hit the hard tile floor. Carlos reached down to retrieve them as the robber pointed the gun in his direction.

"*Keep still!*" the robber yelled nervously.

Paul figured this was the diversion Carlos planned. In an instant he reached out to grab the robber's arm. Just as Paul grabbed his wrist, the gun fired. The tellers and customers shrieked with horror. The bullet went between Carlos's legs and exited through the front glass door. Paul grabbed the man's arm with both hands as they struggled for control of the gun. They both tumbled over the ropes in the lobby, and the gun became dislodged and rolled neatly to Carlos's feet. The robber panicked and clutched onto the money bag and ran to the front door. Carlos calmly picked up the gun, and Paul followed the robber out the front door. Carlos aimed the gun but was afraid he would hit Paul while he was in hot pursuit.

Paul kicked his legs into high gear and chased the robber down. He tackled him from behind, and they struggled in a heap on the ground for a few seconds. As they wrestled, the dye in the money bag exploded, covering each of them from head to toe with blue dye. Paul tried to wipe the dye away from his eyes, but his hands were covered, too. The robber seemed stunned at the sudden turn of events, and he got up to run away just as two police cars with sirens blasting careened into the parking lot. Four officers exited their cars with guns drawn. They weren't sure which of the two blue men in the parking lot was the actual thief.

Carlos chuckled as he saw Paul emerge from the wrestling match covered in blue dye. He still held the gun from the robber, but he decided to leave it on the counter. A black man walking out of a bank with a gun in hand is never a good thing, he thought.

"Both of you, hands behind your head, *now!*" yelled an officer. Paul and the robber both stopped and put their hands behind their head.

"Officer, there's your man. He tried to rob the bank, and I tackled him here in the parking lot," said the robber pointing at Paul.

"Don't listen to him," said Paul. "He's the bank bandit. The dye pack exploded on both of us when we were wrestling."

"We'll have to cuff both of you and get some witnesses here to ID both of you," said the officer.

All four officers slowly walked towards Paul and the robber with their guns drawn. Each was handcuffed and taken to separate police cars for questioning. The bank manager and all the tellers were called over to ID Paul first.

"Can you tell me, is this the man who robbed the bank?" The teller had to study Paul's blue face for a few seconds first.

"He's not the robber. He was a customer who had just gotten a cashier's check. He grabbed the robber's arm, knocked the gun away and tackled him in the parking lot. The policeman turned to the bank manager.

"Can you confirm that story, sir?"

"Yes, sir. This man did stop the robbery. Your thief is standing right over there," said the bank manager pointing at the blue-faced man standing in front of the police car.

"Okay, I'm going to take your cuffs off now, sir. But I would like you to produce some identification and ask you a few questions, please. I'm sure you will be asked to testify in court at some point."

Paul told the story from start to finish as the officer took notes. The bank employees both positively identified the robber, and he was taken to jail. The officers retrieved the gun from the bank. Carlos introduced himself to the officers and told them they would find his prints on the gun as well as the robbers. They asked if he would mind coming to the station for some fingerprints and to give his witness statement. Carlos looked at his watch-it was 11:45 a.m.

"Can I speak to Paul first? He's gotta be somewhere at noon, and he was ridin' with me."

"We can drop him off where he needs to go," said the officer. "We really would like your statements while everything is fresh in your mind. Since your prints are on the gun, you really need to come with us. You are not being charged with anything. This is just for your protection."

"Okay," said Carlos reluctantly. "Let me tell Paul what is happening."

Carlos walked over to the police car where Paul was being questioned.

"Hey, aren't you in the Blue Man Group?" said Carlos with a straight face.

"Very funny," said Paul.

"The police want me to come to the station for a fingerprint now since my prints are on the gun. No matter that 15 people testified to what they saw today. You blue people get off while us blacks have to explain ourselves all the time. It just ain't right," said Carlos sternly.

"Life's not fair, is it? We blue faces have been discriminated against all our lives, so I don't wanna hear any whining from you."

"By the way, the police can drop you off at your closin' when you're done. I have to go the station now. You might want to call them and tell them you'll be a little late."

"Good idea," said Paul as he pulled out his phone and called the law office.

"Yes, this is Paul Cousins. I have a closing at noon today, and I'm going to be a little late. Is that alright?" Paul did not feel like getting into the details of why he was late. They wouldn't believe him anyway.

"I shouldn't be too much longer. Thank you for your understanding," said Paul.

Carlos got in the front of the police cruiser and left for the station for fingerprinting. Paul finished up his questioning with the police as the bank tellers lined up to give him a hug.

"Thank you so much for stepping up. You were so brave," said the young teller, Tammy.

"I'm just glad no one was hurt," said Paul.

Paul spoke to each bank employee and customer who was in the bank. He didn't feel like a hero. He just did what Carlos told him to do.

"My friend Carlos was the real hero," Paul told everyone. "He's the one who created the diversion that allowed me to jump him." Paul made sure everyone got his Bio Strength business card.

"Officer, if we're done, could you give me a ride to the law offices of Burton & Burton? I'm closing on my dream home today."

"Absolutely. I think we're done here."

Paul hopped in the police car and looked at his watch nervously. They were already 20 minutes late.

"Fortunately, the law offices are only five minutes away on San Jose Blvd. Do you know where Burton and Burton is?"

"Yes sir. No problem at all."

Paul took a look at his face in the mirror. His face and hair were completely blue. He did look like he belonged in the Blue Man Group. He had skinned his knee while wrestling with the robber. His t-shirt was ripped halfway down the back, and his shorts were muddy. He looked like a homeless person dropped in from Mars. He thought about cleaning up some first, but he figured all they cared about was the money anyway. Besides, thought Paul, this would give them something to talk about for years.

Attorney John Burton loathed tardiness, and he watched out of the second floor window for signs of Paul's arrival. He was a former Navy man, and his attention to detail suited his occupation as a closing attorney. Paul's real estate agent Betty Tisdale was waiting with Mr. Burton. He caught sight of a police car pulling into his parking lot, but he didn't pay much attention to it until Paul got out. He saw a blue man in a ragged t-shirt emerge from the car.

"Betty, come see this," said Mr. Burton. Betty came over to the window.

They watched Paul wave to the officer and walk in the front door of his building. "Certainly, this can't be Mr. Cousins," said Mr. Burton.

"It does look like a blue version of the Paul Cousins I met," said Betty.

Paul opened the door and walked up to the receptionist. She was staring intently into her computer as Paul walked up to her.

"Excuse me, I'm Paul Cousins. I'm so sorry I'm late."

The receptionist glanced up to see a bloody, muddy, ragged man with a blue face standing in front of her desk.

"*Ahhhh*...my lord, you scared me," she said as she pushed away from her desk.

"Oh, I guess you've never done a closing for a blue man before. Well, consider this your first."

The receptionist stayed 10 feet away from Paul as she eyed him head to toe.

"Can I see some ID please? I'm going to need it for your closing."

Paul handed her his license. She carefully stuck her hand out and walked briskly to the back of the office.

The receptionist burst into Mr. Burton's office without knocking.

"Sir, there's a blue man out front who claims to be Mr. Cousins."

"I saw him enter the building after getting out of a police car. Did you get his ID?"

"Yes sir, but I didn't look at it yet."

"Let me see it." Mr. Burton examined Paul's Florida license and it looked legitimate. "We're already 25 minutes behind. I don't care what color he is as long as his money is green. I've got three more closings this afternoon. Send him on back."

The receptionist went back to Paul in the lobby. Paul was afraid to sit on the couch since he didn't want to mess up their nice furniture. He stood casually by her desk as if this was a common appearance for him.

"Mr. Burton will see you now," said the receptionist while keeping her distance.

"Thank you."

Paul entered Mr. Burton's large office with an oval mahogany table and hunting pictures on the wall.

"Hello, Mr. Cousins. Nice to meet you." He didn't want to embarrass Paul, so he decided to ignore his appearance. Betty stood up with her mouth wide open since she thought she was in the presence of an alien.

"Mr. Cousins?" said Betty incredulously. "How come every time I see you the police are involved somehow?"

"There's an explanation for the way I look. I was a witness to a bank robbery at Bank of America today. I won't go into all the details. I suppose you'll read about it in the paper tomorrow."

"I'm sure I will," said Mr. Burton. He was not much into chit-chat, so he moved along with the paperwork. Paul had never signed so many papers in his life. He left a blue imprint on each page he signed.

"I'm sorry for the mess I'm causing on the paperwork," said Paul.

"It's quite alright. After this last page we'll need your cashier's check, please.

Paul signed the last page and reached into his pocket for the check. He pulled out a crumpled up cashier's check and handed it to Mr. Burton.

"At least it's not blue," said Paul dryly.

"It's acceptable. Congratulations, Mr. Cousins."

"Congratulations," said Betty. "Here are the keys to your new home. Maybe you should have someone hose you off."

"I'll just jump into the pool. Then I'll have the neighborhood's first toilet bowl colored pool."

Paul reached out to shake Mr. Burton's hand then withdrew it after seeing how blue he had turned everything.

"Don't be so blue, Mr.Cousins. Everything will turn out alright," said Betty.

"Nice one, Betty. Would you mind giving me a ride to my house?"

"Sure. I've got an old blanket in the trunk you can sit on. I don't want you messing up my car."

Paul walked out with Betty to her car. He drew quite a few stares from people in the parking lot. Betty pulled the blanket out for Paul to sit on.

"Thank you so much for giving me a ride. It's been one hell of a day."

"You really witnessed a bank robbery?"

"More like I jumped on the bad guy before he got away."

"Really? Wow. Were you scared?"

"It all happened so fast there wasn't time to be scared. The dye pack exploded after I tackled the robber, and both of us got covered with this blue dye. I don't know how this stuff comes off."

"I really don't mind finding a hose to clean you off."

"Thanks, but I don't want it to get around that I got hosed by my real estate agent. I think I'll just jump in the pool."

"Whatever you want. By the way, you got one hell of a deal on this house. I can't believe how you stole it. You will enjoy this house for years to come."

"I hope so. Here's my place. You can drop me off here. Thanks for everything, Betty."

"You're welcome. Try to stay away from the police, please."

"Sure. Goodbye."

Paul opened his door and retrieved a few clothes and essentials so he could spend his first night in his house. Carlos was still at the police station, so Paul had no truck to start packing. He put several boxes in his car and headed to his dream home.

Paul drove to his new house and sat in his car just admiring it from the road. He slowly pulled down the driveway and parked in front. It had a large circular driveway like he always wanted. The sound of a passing motor boat on the river filled the air. Paul envisioned his own boat docked on the water. A steady chirp of crickets filled the air as he closed his eyes and saw his red sports car. He could feel the leather seats in the car and the wind blowing in his hair as he drove his convertible. He saw a beautiful blonde standing in the front doorway, and a broad smile crept on his face. In his mind, he already had those things, so they were already his. It was not *if* he would attain them but *when*. He walked up his front porch stairs admiring every detail of the craftsmanship of the home. He loved the large red crepe myrtles in the front of the house. He pulled out his key and opened the door to his dream house.

Paul walked in the foyer and looked straight out the back to the view of the river. It was a beautiful, late afternoon without a cloud in the sky. He walked out the back door to the pool and dove in with his clothes on. A blue streak trailed Paul as he glided across the pool. He rubbed his scalp and face to clean up, and he couldn't believe all of this was really his. He felt like he was dreaming. Paul cleaned up as best he could with an old golf towel he kept in the trunk of his car. He kept those wonderful positive vibes going through the evening until Carlos finally called.

"Man, they kept me forever at the police station. I think they secretly took my DNA while I was there."

"I don't blame them. Your prints were on the gun after all."

"Thank god there were witnesses. Otherwise, I'd be in jail."

"Can you help me pack the rest of the boxes tomorrow? I'm a little beat to finish it tonight."

"Sure. Just promise me one thing."

"Yeah."

"Don't take me to the bank with you ever again!"

Chapter 18

Ernie arrived at work early hoping no one had gone in the lab to check on Ralph. He held his breath as he turned the corner to the lab. Ernie worried that Ralph's head may have slipped off the microscope and clonked on the table. Or worse, what if he had completely fallen out of the chair?

He slowly approached the lab window and peered inside. Ralph was still there plopped on his microscope, so he let out a huge sigh of relief. Fortunately the lab was in the back of the building where most people never ventured. He unlocked the door and walked over to Ralph. He had to change Ralph's position today or people might get suspicious. He pulled the microscope out quickly and placed it on another table. He forgot to hold Ralph's head, so there was a dull thud when Ralph's head hit the table. Ernie had to find a way to prop Ralph's head up in a different position, so he got Ralph's laptop and placed it in front of him. Then he remembered the duct tape he had used to wrap around Ralph's body, and he applied the tape to Ralph's palm so the sticky side was facing out. He put tape on Ralph's elbow and stuck his palm to his cheek. Next he secured Ralph's elbow to the table so it looked like Ralph was looking at his laptop while resting his palm on his face.

Ernie stepped back to the window to get a view of what it looked like from outside. It really looked like Ralph had his palm on his cheek while studying the screen. He came back and made a few adjustments to Ralph's arm and then turned Ralph's laptop on to a screen with some lab results showing. Ernie knew most laptops have a screen saver option, so he turned it off so the screen would be on continuously. Ralph sitting in front of a blank screen all day would be a "dead" giveaway.

Ernie knew his boss would be asking for the Bio Strength results, so he forwarded the tampered results to his office. Ernie did not know how long he could keep this caper up, but at least it was biding him some time. He wasn't sure how long it would be before Ralph started to smell rank. He decided to read a few Patricia Cornwell novels for some insight into how long it takes for dead bodies to smell.

Ernie slipped out of Ralph's office and locked the lab door. He walked briskly back to his office before he slowed down. It was 7:15 a.m., and Ernie was sure he had beaten most people into the office. Just before he turned the corner to his office, he was startled to run into a co-worker.

"Hey, Ernie how's it going?" said Bob. He was a new guy and a little bit too eager beaver for Ernie's liking.

"Fine. Just fine," said Ernie curtly. He was in no mood for idle chit-chat now.

"Hey, have you talked to Ralph lately?"

Ernie stiffened up. He tried to appear calm in his response.

"No, why do you ask?" said Ernie coolly.

"Everybody's talking about how much he's been working lately. His car is the first one here in the morning, and it's still here at night when everybody leaves. He must really be working on something big!"

"I really haven't noticed. I've been very busy."

"Why don't we go see what he's working on?" said Bob as he turned to head towards Ralph's lab.

"Oh, no, no, no," said Ernie as he grabbed Bob by the shoulder. "He's much too busy to be interrupted. He's doing some work for Joe and me now on the Bio Strength case. He just emailed me some info on some of his findings. Do you want to see that in my office?" Ernie was desperate for any diversion now.

"Sure!" said Bob eagerly.

"Follow me."

Bob was impressed that a veteran like Ernie had asked him to see results on an active case. Ernie turned the corner away from the lab towards his office.

"Please, come on in," said Ernie invitingly. Ernie's office was easily twice the size of Bob's.

"Wow, you've got a window and everything!" said Bob.

"Yeah, and I've got a laptop, too," said Ernie sarcastically. "Let's check out these Bio Strength results."

Ernie clicked on the email that he had forwarded from Ralph's computer. He clicked on the results heading for Bio Strength.

"Most of the product testing came back within normal limits for Bio Strength. They shouldn't have any problems."

"I wonder why so many people are complaining about side effects from them now. Some of them are pretty incredible," said Bob.

"Oh, there are many reasons people could have side effects. There are many factors involved. I'll go ahead and forward this to my boss. He's been waiting for these results."

Ernie forwarded the email to his boss Joe. "Now if you'll excuse me, I've got a conference call to make. Good to see you, Bill."

"It's Bob."

"Oh, sorry. I knew that. I'll talk to you later, Bob."

Ernie drew a huge sigh as Bob walked out of his office. He slumped down in his chair and wondered how much longer he could conceal a dead person at his workplace.

Joe was sitting at his desk when Ernie's forwarded email from Ralph appeared. He had been eagerly awaiting these results for weeks, so he quickly clicked open the results. They were nothing like he was expecting. They were so boringly normal, and Joe immediately called Ernie to discuss them.

"Ernie. Joe here. I take it you've seen these Bio Strength results."

"Yes, sir. Everything appears fine."

"Have you talked to Ralph about them?"

"Yes, sir. He was surprised too, so he did a second round of tests. They both came back in the normal range."

"Could there have been some cross-contamination?"

"No sir. You know how meticulous Ralph is."

"I'd like to discuss this with Ralph directly. Is he in today?"

Ernie started sweating bullets. He couldn't lie because everyone could see Ralph's car still in the parking lot.

"He's at lunch now. Would you like me to have him call you?"

"Yes, please. Maybe we'll do another round of tests. I'm still getting lots of heat from people about Bio Strength. Hell, more than 50 men are attributing baldness, high cholesterol, low sperm count and shrinking testicles to this stuff. One guy even said he had started developing breasts after using Bio Strength daily for six months. There's got to be an explanation."

"I'll let him know your concerns. He's been working really hard lately."

"Yeah, I've heard. What a guy. I wish everyone had his work ethic around here."

"He is an inspiration, sir."

"Yeah, but he's also an annoying little shit sometimes, ya know."

"I know. But he hasn't been wrong yet."

"Have him call me this afternoon."

"Yes, sir. Goodbye."

Ernie hung up wondering how in the hell he was going to pull this off. He thought about impersonating Ralph over the phone, but their voices were nothing alike. Ralph had a nasal type voice, and Ernie tried to eke out a few "Ralph sayings" in his office. Ernie knew his attempts at voice impersonating would surely backfire. He had to figure out a way to get Ralph out of the building. Luckily, Joe had been called into a meeting that lasted the rest of the day, so he had lost track of wanting to speak to Ralph. He decided to wait until dark to try to figure something out.

He waited until all of the cars in the lot were gone and the sun had set. He walked over to the lab and used his spare key to enter. Ralph was still propped up in front of his laptop. Ernie ripped off the duct tape and attempted to lift Ralph over his shoulders. He now knew what people meant by "dead weight." He almost got Ralph on his shoulder when he tripped over the chair leg and fell straight to the floor with Ralph directly on top of him.

"*Aaagggh*," moaned Ernie as he tried to get out from under Ralph. He was disgusted to be so close to a dead body, especially Ralph the Rat's. Ernie finally pushed Ralph off him, and he tried to pick him up three more times with no success. He had to think of something else. If he tried to drag him down the stairs his head would get bruised from clonking on each step. That wouldn't do. He then remembered the security cameras in the lobby that would capture him for sure. Ernie spied a coat locker and rushed over to peek inside. It was a little larger than the one he had as a high school locker. There was an extra lab coat hanging on the hook, and Ernie pulled it out.

Ernie managed to set Ralph in his chair and roll him over to the locker. He grabbed his white lab coat lapels and with a mighty heave stuffed Ralph into the locker. The hardest part was getting the loop on the back of Ralph's lab coat to latch onto the coat hook. Ernie struggled for a few minutes and finally hung Ralph by his coat on the hook and quickly closed the locker door.

He figured if he could take Ralph's car, then people would think he had gone home. Nobody ever bothered Ralph in his lab, so Ernie felt confident he could pull it off. It was a Friday, and it would have been suspicious for Ralph to have his car there all weekend anyway.

Ernie searched for Ralph's car keys in his desk and found nothing. He forgot to check Ralph's pockets, so he swung open the locker door. He found the car keys in Ralph's front left pocket and exited the building to a dark parking lot. He approached Ralph's white Buick and looked in the window. There were scientific journals on the front passenger seat and empty fast food bags in the rear floorboard. Ralph kept a neat lab, but his car was a disaster. Ernie hopped in and sat on top of something thick. He reached down and pulled out a photo album. Opening it up, he discovered hundreds of photos of child pornography. Feeling sick to his stomach, he quickly closed the album. "What a sick bastard," thought Ernie.

Praying the car would start, Ernie turned the ignition. The engine started easily, and he heaved a sigh of relief. He backed out of his space and slowly left the parking lot. Ernie had to make a plan for getting his car home the next day. He couldn't call Joanne to come pick him up since it would give away where he worked. He knew where Ralph lived since he once had to give him a ride home once. Ralph's house was only ten minutes way, so he would park the car in his driveway.

Ernie pulled onto Ralph's street and turned off the car lights as he approached the driveway. He parked the car towards the back of the driveway so no nosy neighbors would see him get out. He called information for a cab, and within 20 minutes the cab driver arrived. Ernie got in and told the driver the address for his workplace. When they arrived, he got in his car and headed straight home. He and Marlo were at least civil to each other these days.

He stepped into the kitchen from the garage when his two-year old screamed "Daddy!" He loved to hear that.

"Anything exciting happen at work today?" asked Marlo as she put away dishes.

He thought about everything he had gone through that day. How was he supposed to answer that? He and Marlo were being more open with each other these days than ever before. Something about an impending divorce brings out honest emotions in spouses, Ernie thought.

"No just the usual, boring old stuff."

"Don't worry, honey. Something exciting will happen one day for you. It might be after we are split, but I can just feel it."

Ernie thought about Joanne and how much he needed to talk to her but couldn't right now.

"Yeah, I feel like something exciting will happen, too."

Chapter 19

Paul was excited to get furniture for his house in time for his upcoming party. He invited 200 people, and he got RSVP's from over 100. Carlos shook his head when he heard how many people were coming.

"Do you know how much this party is going to cost you?" asked Carlos incredulously.

"Yes, and I don't care. I've waited all my life to have a house like this, and I'm going to break it in right. Besides, most people will be out in the yard or in the pool."

"Alright, whatever you say. But don't say I didn't warn you about spending too much money. You should at least stick to a budget for this party."

"Budget schmudget. I'm going all out, man. Mike Melito will be spinning records, so he's saving me some money in deejay fees. Does that satisfy you?"

"As long as he plays my kinda music."

"I'm sure he'll play some from your era."

"What the hell do you mean, from my era?"

"You know, oldies stuff."

"Man, I oughta slap you upside your head. You think you know music. Good music is just good music, no matter when it was made."

"Don't take it so personal, Carlos. I'll play whatever you want. Chill out."

"Motown, man. Lots of Temptations and Smokey Robinson."

"You got it."

Paul spent $20,000 on a stereo system for his home. The dance floor had flashing lights and a disco ball, and speakers were wired in every room. This was going to be a party that everyone would talk about for years. Mike Melito would keep everyone on the dance floor all night.

Bo Valentine told Kitty there was a Bio Strength meeting at Paul's home, but he didn't mention anything about a party. He wanted to be there without Kitty so he could scope the scene for available women.

People started arriving by 7:00, and Paul made sure everyone had a margarita in their hand when they entered. He had rented two margarita machines for the party with both frozen lime and strawberry margaritas.

Mike Melito brought most of his waitresses from his restaurant. Mike had a prerequisite for hiring female waitresses and bartenders that they all looked good in a bikini. Mike should have been sued for sexual harassment years ago, but his charisma protected him like a giant shield. Mike was bulletproof. He was manning the deejay booth wearing a Hawaiian shirt, yellow shorts, and sandals. A young blonde waitress was hanging all over him and spilled her drink all over Mike's leg.

"Hey, babe, watch out. You can't get sloppy yet. It's too early. I need you to get me drinks tonight while I deejay."

Joanne had called Ernie to tell him about the party, and she assured him that she had cleared it with Paul for him to come. He had not received an invitation since Paul did not really know him, but Ernie was excited to be able to hang out with Joanne for the evening.

Joanne arrived at the party dressed in a beautiful maroon sun dress. Every guy's head turned when she strolled in the front door. Paul noticed her from across the room, and he couldn't take his eyes off her. He excused himself from his conversation about network marketing and approached Joanne.

"Glad you could make it," said Paul. "You look absolutely stunning tonight."

Joanne actually felt herself blush. "Why, thank you. Your home is gorgeous. Oh, and the view of the St. Johns River is fabulous. You're going to make some woman very happy one day with this house."

"One day, yes. I'm sure I'll meet her," said Paul as he made direct eye contact with Joanne. "Let me get you a drink.

What would you like? We have wine, beer, mixed drinks, and a margarita machine on full blast."

"Oh, that margarita sounds wonderful."

"You got it."

Paul led Joanne to the margarita machine. She waved hello to Mike at the deejay booth. Mike noticed Joanne strolling beside Paul, and he noticed how Paul was looking at her. Mike motioned for Paul to come over.

"Excuse me, Joanne. Mike needs to talk to me about something. He must be having trouble with the stereo. Will you excuse me?"

"Of course. I'll wait for you."

Paul walked over to the deejay booth to see Mike.

"What's up?" asked Paul.

"You know what's up," said Mike.

"What do you mean?"

"I see how you're eyeing Joanne. She does look like a million bucks tonight, but man, she'll tear your heart out. I've seen it a hundred times from that lady."

"What? You're just jealous. You're just trying to keep me away from her, that's all. Besides, all I've done is get her a drink. Don't jump to any conclusions."

"I know where all this is headin', buddy. Don't kid yourself. She's a beautiful, driven woman coming to a party hosted by a man more successful than herself. She's got you as a target. As soon as you fall for her and drop a ton of money on her, she'll dump you faster than Larry King dumps wives."

"You have no idea what you're talking about. Don't make me throw you in the pool again."

"You didn't throw me in the pool. It was a fluke accident. I could take you out in a heartbeat, but then you wouldn't get to be with Joanne. Go ahead and knock yourself out. She'll eat you alive."

"I don't know why I invited you. If you weren't responsible for over half my monthly check, I'd kick your ass outta here," said Paul loudly.

Carlos heard Paul and Mike arguing from across the room and decided to become the peacemaker before things got out of hand. He walked across the room and stepped between the two of them.

"Gentlemen, what's the problem here? This is a party, and we don't need you two knuckleheads spoilin' it for everyone. You two need each other, so make your peace before the cops are called. I don't wanna' see no police anytime soon. Can you two manage to get along tonight?" said Carlos sternly.

"Yeah, man," said Mike holding up his drink. "I'm not the one who's gonna get his heart broken. I'm perfectly content spinning records."

"Just come with me," said Carlos to Paul as he pulled him away. "No sense in you two getting' into it again."

"He can be such an asshole sometimes. He pushes all the wrong buttons on me."

"It's people like him that can become your greatest teachers."

"Mike Melito my greatest teacher? Give me a break!"

"Absolutely. If you can learn to keep your peace around someone who naturally agitates you, then you can keep peaceful around anybody. And peace-a mind is what it's all about."

"Sounds like you're preaching to me."

"Heck, no. I stopped going to church years ago. I just realized long ago that being peaceful and lovin' to everyone I meet is the best way to a happy life."

Paul looked at Carlos and realized the wisdom of his words.

"Okay. You're right. I'll just keep my distance from him."

"Now go back to that beautiful woman. Man, she is somethin' else."

Paul walked back to Joanne as she was finishing up her margarita.

"Is everything okay with Mike? It sounded like you were arguing."

"Yeah, everything's cool," said Paul.

"Did you hear that Mike signed Arthur Lantor up? He played golf with him and convinced him Bio Strength was the real deal."

"That's great. I'm not surprised."

"So, why don't you show me around your beautiful home?"

"Sure. The dance floor is the highlight for me. I loved the step down into the family room, so I thought it would make a great dance floor. I put in these hardwood floors, flashing lights in the ceiling, and Bose 901 speakers to fill the room with sound. You should hear the sound system I put in. It makes your chest shake."

"Really? I've never had speakers shake mine before," said Joanne glancing down at her chest.

Paul realized what he had just said. "I didn't mean just the chest. I meant your whole body," said Paul now embarrassed.

"That's okay. I know what you meant."

"And here's the kitchen. I haven't used it much yet, but I will eventually. It has a built-in coffee maker over there."

"Wow, and I love the granite. It's absolutely beautiful." Joanne saw over Paul's shoulder that Ernie had just walked in.

"Excuse me, Paul, but a friend of mine just walked in. I'll be right back."

Ernie appeared nervous as he scanned the room for a familiar face. His face lit up when he saw Joanne approaching him, and she gave him a hug which startled him. He wrapped his arms around her as if he would never see her again. Ernie was in heaven in her arms even if it was only for a fleeting moment.

"I'm so glad you came," said Joanne. "Do you remember meeting Paul at the Bio Strength meeting?"

"Of course."

"Come over here and meet him again."

Joanne grabbed Ernie's hand and pulled him across the room like a parent drags a child. Ernie didn't really want to talk to Paul. He just wanted to talk to Joanne all night since no one else mattered to him, but he decided to just go through the motions of pleasant conversation.

"Paul, this is my friend Ernie Zimmerman. I hope you don't mind that I invited him."

"Of course not. Nice to meet you again, Ernie."

"You have a beautiful home."

"Thanks. Can I get you a drink?"

"You can just point me to where the beers are and I'll help myself."

"Just go to the back deck and you'll find a tub of ice cold ones."

"Thanks."

Ernie walked through the growing crowd across the dance floor. Mike was wearing sunglasses and moving and grooving to the beat reminding Ernie of a disco. He stepped onto the deck and was struck by the incredible view of the river. He was jealous of Paul's success, but Paul's success meant his chance to be with Joanne.

Bo scoped the room for available women. Most local distributors knew his reputation and stayed away from him, but there was always one or two newbies who were impressed with his success. Bo would offer to help them until he got what he wanted. It was an old trick that he had down pat, but his reputation preceded him in Jacksonville. He spotted two ladies in the corner talking and approached them. He liked the tan, blonde one with a white dress slit far up her long legs.

"Hi, I'm Bo Valentine. Either of you ladies like to dance?"

"Bo Valentine. Where have I heard that name before?"

"I'm the only Royal Diamond Bio Strength distributor in Jacksonville," said Bo proudly.

The blonde's eyes widened.

"Can you tell me how you did it? I've been doing Bio Strength for six months, and I haven't made a dime yet."

"Sure. I'll tell you everything you need to know to succeed if you dance with me."

"Sounds like a deal to me. Let's go!"

Bo put on his best dance moves to impress his newest protégé. The dance floor was packed as people were drinking more and more. From outside you could hear the incredible bass thumping from the music. Mike Melito loved playing at bone-shattering decibels.

Next door, Billy Wazeka was fishing on his pier. He lived in a modest brick house built long before the mansions around it appeared. Trees and tall shrubs concealed most of his yard, and that was fine with his neighbors. Several neighbors had tried to buy Billy's property from him, but he wasn't selling. His view of the river was too good. He was going to die on that lot with a fishing pole in his hands. The neighborhood wanted to get rid of his tiny house so another mansion could be built, but he was determined to beat them.

Billy was mad that Paul had been blasting his stereo for two straight weeks. Fishing is what Billy lived for, and the loud music disturbed his fishing. While everyone else had a speed boat, Billy had a small fishing boat. He was definitely a fish out of water in his neighborhood, but everyone pretty much left him alone. Tonight Billy was going to make an unusual introduction to his partying neighbor.

No one knew that a week before Billy had purchased a baby pig from a local farm. He kept it in a small pen out of sight from his neighbors. He fed it leftover scraps, and he named him Arnold after the pig in the television series *Green Acres*. Arnold was a small, cute potbellied pig, and Billy felt it was high time that his new, noisy neighbor got to meet his pig.

Billy waited until it was dark and carried little Arnold over to Paul's house. He kept one hand over Arnold's snout to muzzle his squealing. He could see people splashing in the pool and dancing inside. He was going to make this a party they would never forget.

He crept up among the trees and into Paul's front yard clutching Arnold. He waited in the dark while a couple entered the front door. When the coast was clear, Billy ran to the front porch and set Arnold down. He had placed a leash around Arnold's neck to keep him from escaping. Billy pulled out a tub of butter and quickly lathered Arnold up. Arnold started squealing loudly.

"*Shusshh* Arnold, you'll get to squeal as much as you want in a minute. These rich folks prob'ly never seen a live baby pig before, much less a greased one."

Billy finished covering up the last inch of Arnold's body and slowly opened the front door. He placed Arnold on the floor and untied his leash.

"Run, Arnold, run!" yelled Billy as he slapped the pig on the back. Arnold took off like a cannonball, and Billy peered through the window to see the action.

Bo Valentine was in the foyer putting his finishing moves on his newest blonde prize. Arnold made a beeline straight at Bo who had his back to the front door. The blonde saw something from the corner of her eye and let out an ear deafening scream when she saw a small pink pig come barreling straight for them.

"*Aaaaahhhh*!" she screamed right in Bo's face. Bo had no idea what she was screaming about, and as he turned around Arnold ran under his legs. He threw his glass in the air, and Arnold caused her to fall as he brushed up against her legs. Her red wine glass became airborne and crashed on the tile floor.

Paul looked up to see what the commotion was about. Bo ran after Arnold and made a dive to catch him. Billy laughed outside because he didn't know a soul who could hold onto a greased pig. Bo grabbed onto Arnold's back, and his arms slipped off like flip-flops on ice. Arnold let out a huge squeal as Bo's grip let loose, and he headed straight for the dance floor.

"Somebody grab that pig!" yelled Bo.

There was mayhem on the dance floor with women screaming, drinks crashing, and people running like the house was on fire. Mike Melito saw the dance floor part like the Red Sea, and he saw Arnold running around trying to find his way out of the house. Mike saw this as a wonderful time to be the hero, but he didn't realize how hard it would be for a drunk to catch a greased pig.

"I'll get him!" yelled Mike as turned down the music and stepped out from the deejay booth. Mike faced Arnold on the dance floor less than 10 feet away, and a crowd had gathered around the dance floor urging Mike on. Arnold took a few steps away from Mike.

"Come here, you little sausage," said Mike. "I'm going to have you for breakfast," he said in a sinister yet soothing tone. Mike made a lunge for Arnold and managed to grab his back. His hands slid right off Arnold's buttered body, and the crowd went nuts. Everyone was screaming, but Billy Wazeka was laughing his ass off watching the pandemonium he had induced.

Paul opened up the door to the deck in hopes they could corner the pig.

"Mike, see if you can chase him out here."

Mike stood up and took on the chase again. Arnold was in no mood to be grabbed again, and he ran circles around the island in the kitchen with Mike in hot pursuit. Women were up on the counters screaming like there was a snake in the house. Arnold spotted the open door and made a dash for it. Paul and Mike followed Arnold out and closed the deck door behind them.

"We've got 'em now," said Paul.

"I'll get him," said Mike calmly.

"No, I'll get him," said Paul as Arnold hid under a chair.

"Paul, I've been professionally trained in the art of pig capture."

"Is that so? Since when is pig capture an art?"

"I grew up on a farm, man. Just watch this."

Mike crept to the chair where Arnold was hiding. Arnold darted out and headed for the corner of the deck. Mike pursued Arnold and cornered him.

"Gotcha now. You're mine, baby." Mike inched closer and grabbed Arnold in a bear hug. Arnold squealed and wriggled for his life.

"Got him!" yelled Mike.

Down by the pool Ernie had been enjoying his time with Joanne when he saw Mike holding Arnold up on the deck.

"Mike Melito is holding a pig on the deck," said Ernie pointing up.

"Well he's dated some questionable women before, but I wouldn't go so far as to call them a pig. I'm surprised at you, Ernie," said Joanne.

"No, a real pig. Look up on the deck."

Joanne had her back turned and looked up to see Mike struggling to hold a tiny pink pig.

"What the hell kinda party is this?" asked Joanne in disbelief at what she saw.

Just then Arnold made a frantic squirm and slid out of Mike's grasp only to sail over the railing. The crowd let out a silent gasp in unison as they watched a baby pig fly through the air. Arnold made a perfect splash in the pool and sank straight to the bottom.

"Can pigs swim?" asked Paul as they both peered over the deck railing to the pool below.

"I don't know, but I'm not gonna wait to find out," said Mike as he climbed up on the railing.

"You're seriously not gonna jump into the pool are you?" asked Paul.

"Are you saying a pig's life is not worth saving?"

"It's not worth breaking your neck over. Now get down now-I don't want you to file a claim on my homeowners."

"I won't sue you. Gotta go," he said as he jumped with his arms flailing into the pool. Everyone had already exited the pool when Mike came crashing in, and he drenched everyone around the pool with his surprise entry. He swam down to the bottom of the lit pool and spotted Arnold on the bottom. He grabbed him and surfaced quickly. The entire house party was either gathered on the deck or by the pool. They gave Mike a huge ovation as he walked up the steps of the pool holding a semi-conscious pig.

"Always the center of attention," muttered Paul as everyone high-fived each other over Mike's successful rescue.

"Anybody know pig CPR?" yelled Mike as he stood dripping wet holding Arnold.

"I do," came a voice from the back of the crowd.

Mike saw a little old black lady approach him.

"Miss Ellie?" said Mike.

"That's me. I grew up on a farm, and I had to give mouth-to-snout CPR on a piglet once. Saved his life. Give me the little fella."

Ellie put Arnold down on the grass and started CPR. Paul watched from the deck above in amazement. He had invited Ellie, but he had been so busy he hadn't had a chance to speak with her yet. After a few minutes, Arnold sprung back to life and let out a loud squeal. Everyone cheered their new hero, Ellie.

"Nice work, Ellie," said Mike.

"Oh, it was nothin'. Just don't go eatin' this little fella. We've gone to a lot of trouble to save his hide. How'd he get in the house anyway?"

"Nobody knows," said Mike.

"Miss Ellie, when I invited you, I didn't know you could perform CPR on a party- crashing pig," said Paul who had come outside to see her.

"That's okay, honey. All in a day's work. The Lord wanted me to be here, I guess. By the way, what a wonderful house you have."

"Thank you. I'm so glad you could make it. I'm sorry I haven't been by to see you sooner."

"That's okay. My house is fixed so nice thanks to you and Builders Care."

"My pleasure," said Paul. "But the best part of it all was meeting you. You are an inspiration."

"You stop all that nonsense, ya hear? I did nothing special."

"What are we gonna do with this pig?"

"Do you have a fenced in area or fencin' material that we could use to make a makeshift pigpen for him?"

"I think there's some leftover fence in the shed. I'll go look."

Paul came out a few minutes later with a roll of wire fence.

"Will this do, Ellie?"

"Sure, but just for tonight. That pig would dig under that fence easily if he were a little bigger."

"I'll help you put it up," said Mike.

"Thanks," said Paul. "I'll go get a towel to keep him from shivering."

Paul and Mike put up the fence in a half hour while dozens of people took turns holding the baby pig. He looked so cute wrapped up in a beach towel with his little pink snout sticking out. Billy had crept back to his side yard and peered through the shrubs at what was going on. He didn't know that Arnold had become airborne and had had CPR performed on him. It looked like his new neighbor was building a fence to keep Arnold in.

"I'll just hafta steal 'im back when they're asleep," Billy mumbled to himself.

"That's enough swimming for me tonight," yelled Mike. "Does anybody wanna dance?"

"Yeahhhh," the crowd screamed.

"Let's go," said Mike as he slogged back to his deejay booth wiping his hair dry with a towel. The dance floor stayed packed until 2:30 a.m., and Ernie danced with Joanne while Paul was playing the good host to everyone. He felt he had connected with Joanne on the dance floor and began to picture the two of them doing Bio Strength together. He didn't mind a woman making more than him as long as he was in love with her and not her money. Joanne knew how Ernie felt about her by the way he looked at her.

Bo stood on the edge of the dance floor looking for a woman, any woman at this point. He was very drunk and not very picky about who he ended up with. All the women he had talked to earlier had gone home. It was depressing for him to think he would go home alone, but it wasn't in the cards for him tonight. He sought out Paul to tell him good night.

"Thanks for a fantastic party. I'll never forget this one. Pig and all."

"Sorry about the pig. I have no idea where he came from. I'll have to come up with a name for him."

"Your home is beautiful. Keep up the good work. Bio Strength is going to take us all the way."

"It already has," said Paul. "This is the house I've always dreamed of. Now, all I need is my dream boat and my red convertible, and my picture will be complete."

"You've done it right, Paul. You held that dream out in front of you and didn't let it go. It wasn't an accident for you. You made it happen. I'm proud of you," said Bo as he put his hand on Paul's shoulder.

"Don't get all mushy on me now. Are you okay to drive home?"

"Yeah, I'm fine."

Joanne walked into the foyer as Bo was leaving.

"I can follow you part of the way home to make sure you're okay," said Joanne.
"I'm on my way home, anyway."

"You can follow me all the way home if you want," said Bo slyly.

"Don't push it, Bo."

Ernie walked up when he saw Joanne at the door.

"Are you leaving?"

"Yeah, I'm going to follow this drunk fool here part of the way home to make sure he's okay."

"I guess it's time for me to go, too. Paul, thanks so much for the party. Your home is beautiful. Your kitchen is incredible."

"Nobody's using it right now. I need a wife."

"No you don't," said Bo and Ernie in unison.

"My, what a couple of poster children for marriage you two are."

"Don't get me going on marriage," said Bo.

"Don't worry. I know where you're coming from," said Ernie.

Joanne took both of them by the arm as they made their way out the door.

"Now guys, don't be so down on marriage. Some can work out, ya know. Thanks for the great party, Paul," said Joanne as she turned around to see Paul standing in the doorway.

Paul waved and watched the three of them walk down the sidewalk arm in arm. Ernie walked Joanne to her car while Bo fumbled for his keys.

"You sure you're okay?" yelled Joanne.

"I'm fine. You can go on home. You don't need to follow me. I'm only three miles away," said Bo.

"Okay. Be careful."

Ernie felt like he was on a first date in high school. Now was the awkward time where small talk is made before you decided on going in for a kiss.

"I had a great time," said Ernie.

"Yeah, can you believe that pig?"

"I'll never forget Mike jumping off the deck into the pool," laughed Ernie. "He could've killed himself."

"He should have killed himself. That man is crazy."

"I'll give you a call tomorrow," said Ernie not knowing what else to say.

"Good. I'll talk to you then." Joanne leaned toward Ernie and gave him a quick kiss on the cheek. He awkwardly stuck his arms out for a hug, but Joanne had already opened her car door to leave. Ernie pretended he had an itch on his shoulder since he was standing there with his arms wide open. Joanne started her car and pulled away giving a big smile and wave to Ernie.

Ernie had a huge smile on his face. It was just a kiss on the cheek, but it was the first kiss he had received from anyone other than his wife since he had gotten married 15 years earlier. He put his hand up to his cheek where she kissed him. He hopped in his car, and on the way home let the events of the night run over and over again in his mind. He was so excited that he knew it would be a long time before he went to sleep.

Meanwhile, Paul said goodbye to the last of his guests. Carlos had gone home right after he saw the flying pig. He didn't need to see any more. It was way past his bedtime anyway. Paul's house was trashed, but he didn't feel like cleaning any of it up. He checked on his new pet pig to make sure he hadn't escaped. The temporary pen was holding up fine. Paul threw some scraps from the party into the pen, and Arnold lapped them up quickly.

The party was everything he wanted it to be even with the pig incident. He went upstairs to watch a little television before drifting off to sleep. He dreamed of a fast car, a fast boat, and a beautiful woman, and he knew they were all his. He could just feel it.

Chapter 20

Ernie woke up with his kids pulling on his hair at 8 a.m. His head was killing him, and he had only a few hours of sleep. Marlo was dressed and ready to go out shopping.

"The kids are yours now, honey."

Ernie didn't know where he was for a second. All he wanted to do was roll over and sleep some more.

"Where are you going?"

"Didn't you remember I'm going shopping?"

"Honey, I'm in no shape to watch the kids. My head is killing me."

"Oh, I feel so sorry for you. You get to go out and party all night, and now you want to sleep in. Our deal was that you got to go to the party, and I get to go shopping. So just deal with it. I'm leaving."

"But honey...." Marlo slammed the door on the way out. Ernie had to figure out what to do with the kids. The television was always a good babysitter, so he turned it on in the den and plopped the kids on the sofa. He downed a big glass of water and popped a couple Advil and fell back asleep on the sofa beside his kids.

Ernie was awakened by what sounded like a barrel rolling down a hill. His two- year old boy had climbed up the stairs and slipped and was rolling down them. It ended with a resounding thump of his head on the floor and then an ear piercing scream followed by crying. Ernie jumped up from the sofa in a panic and ran over to his son. He was horrified to hear his child rolling down stairs and not be able to do anything about it. He picked up his son and held him close. A large bump was already forming on his head, so Ernie took him straight to the freezer for some ice.

"It's okay, Ray, little buddy, it's okay," said Ernie as he put ice on his bump and wiped his tears. It was 12:15, and he had slept another four hours after Marlo left. She would be livid if she found out he had fallen asleep while watching them. His headache was mostly gone, but he was very thirsty. He drank some more water and held Ray while he went to get the paper. Ray was still crying his eyes out, and Ernie hoped the neighbors wouldn't hear. Ernie ran out to get the paper and came in to look for his glasses. He always put them in the same drawer, but they were not there. Ernie suddenly realized he had taken them off at Paul's party. He couldn't read without them, and they were expensive prescription glasses. He had to go get them.

Ernie gathered up his one-year-old daughter and Ray into his car. Poor little Ray whimpered and held his head as Ernie headed straight to Paul's house.

It was a dark, cloudy day as Ernie pulled into Paul's driveway. He left the kids in the car, hopped onto Paul's front porch and rang the doorbell. He nervously looked back in his car to check on the kids. Ray was still crying and holding an ice bag to his head. Ernie prayed Paul was home. All he wanted to do was grab his glasses and leave.

Ernie rang the doorbell a second time, and after what seemed like 10 minutes, the front door opened slowly. Ernie knees buckled at what he saw.

Joanne was as shocked to see Ernie standing there as he was to see her. She was wearing one of Paul's dress shirts, and her hair was messy as if she had just awoken.

"Ernie, I'm surprised to see you here," said Joanne nervously.

"Not any more than I am to see you."

"I can explain. When I was halfway home, I realized I had left my purse here, so I turned around and...."

"You don't have to explain. I understand. I just came back to get my glasses."

"Where did you leave them. I'll look for you."

"I'm pretty sure I set them on the table by the pool. I'll go around and get them myself."

"Oh, okay. It's good to see you, Ernie."

"Yeah, you, too."

Ernie turned to walk to the back of the house. The temporary pen for Arnold was empty since Billy Wazeka had reclaimed his baby swine during the night. Ernie spotted his glasses on a poolside table where he had been talking to her. He took them off because he thought he might jump in for a midnight swim with Joanne. It was clear to Ernie that Paul was the only one doing midnight swimming with her. Maybe they even went skinny dipping.

Ernie trudged back to his car to find both of his kids crying. He felt like he had just had his heart ripped out of his chest and was too numb to even try to calm his kids. He closed his door and pulled out of the driveway with both kids screaming. He felt betrayed even though he had never dated Joanne. Ernie knew she was in a different league than he, but it sure was nice to dream a little. Now it was back to reality with two crying kids and a looming divorce.

Paul came downstairs to find Joanne slouched on the sofa looking morose.

"You look like your pet puppy just died."

"Well, sort of."

"What happened?"

"Ernie came by looking for his glasses, and I, like a big dummy, answered the door."

"What's the big deal? We're all adults here."

"The problem is he's kinda had a crush on me," said Joanne sternly. "And I think I just broke his heart when he saw me standing in the doorway."

"Wow. Did you have a thing for him?"

"No, but he's just a really nice guy."

"I didn't think you were the sentimental type."

"I'm not, but I really didn't want to hurt his feelings."

"You did nothing wrong. Besides, he's married isn't he?"

"He's living at home with his wife, but she's filing for divorce."

"Listen, he's going to be just fine. I need to get you out of this funk. What do ya' say to some shopping?"

"Shopping for what?"

"A boat."

"You mean you want to go buy a boat today just like that?"

"Sure, why not?"

"You sure are a spontaneous kinda guy. I like that."

"Well, let's go. Maybe we can get some boating in this weekend if we hurry."

"Alright, I'm in. I love being on the water. Can I wear your shirt? The one I wore to the party is a mess," said Joanne as she stood up and played with her hair.

Paul wrapped his arms around her. "You would look good in absolutely anything," he said as he gave her a long kiss.

"Just let me fix my hair. I can't go out with it looking like this."

Within an hour Paul and Joanne were walking into a local boat store. The salesman on floor duty was glad to see a prospect come in since the recession had hit the boat industry hard.

Paul was immediately struck by the boat on display in the showroom. It was an inboard/outboard with a full cabin and enough room for at least 15 people. What really caught his eye was the color. It was just what he had imagined it to be in his dreams all those years. He had found his red, white and blue boat. It was a floating American flag.

"How can I help you today?" asked the salesman.

"How big is this boat?"

"Thirty-five feet. It is last year's model, and we have a good price on it."

"How much?"

"One hundred fifty thousand."

"I'll give you one twenty-five."

"Oh, I don't know if we can do that. Let me speak with my manager."

"Are you sure this is the boat you want?" whispered Joanne.

"Yup. It's just like the one I've dreamed about."

"But you haven't even shopped around at all. You're going to buy the first one you see?"

"If the price is right, sure. Listen, I've wanted a boat like this all my life. I can afford it, and I have a great place to dock it. I can't have that view without a boat."

The salesman came back from his manager's office.

"I can do one thirty-nine. That's our lowest price."

"I'll take it."

The salesman was not used to such an easy sale and he was not sure what to do next. He stood there dumbfounded because he had made a huge sale so effortlessly.

"Is there some paperwork to fill out now?' asked Paul.

"Oh, sure. I'm sorry. Follow me."

The next morning Paul and Joanne sat under a beautiful, cloudless sky awaiting the 9:30 arrival of his new boat.

"This is a great day to be on the water," said Paul.

"It sure is." Joanne paused for a moment before continuing. "It's been even nicer to be with you this weekend."

Paul was stunned. He wasn't sure what Joanne was thinking, but he knew he was falling in love with her. He paused for a second so he didn't screw up the moment. Joanne took this hesitation as a bad sign.

"You haven't enjoyed this weekend?" asked Joanne nervously.

"Oh, of course I have. I….I was just searching for the right words to say. This weekend has been incredible. We have so much in common. The same dreams, the same goals. I don't want to put the cart before the horse, but I was wondering if you would like to move in with me. This house is way too big for one person, and we could help each other with our Bio Strength businesses. I know this is happening so quickly, but I believe in going for what I want just like you do. Life is short, so I've learned to ask for what I want. I can fill my life with a nice house, boat and money, but it's all empty without someone to share it with. I'd like to share it with you."

Joanne's eyes filled with tears. She had never heard such heartfelt words coming from a man before. She was always the one with the steely surface, but this time was different. She knew Paul could be the one.

"I feel the same way," said Joanne.

Paul looked her in the eyes and ran his fingers through her hair. He leaned over for the gentlest, most loving kiss he had ever had. They held each other while sitting on the edge of the dock with their feet splashing in the water. No words were spoken, and none needed to be. This was the kind of communication Paul craved for with a woman. The only sounds were the birds in the trees and the distant sound of a motor boat. For the first time in years, Paul had the feeling of perfect contentment.

Finally, Joanne spoke. "Are you sure you want me to move in? I can be a real bitch sometimes, ya know."

"Yes, I've never been surer of anything in my life," said Paul.

The sound of the distant boat was getting closer. Paul strained his eyes to see. He could tell the boat approaching was red, white and blue.

"There's my other dream come true coming right towards us," said Paul. They both stood up to get a better look. Paul was as excited as a kid on Christmas morning. This boat was the most beautiful thing he had ever seen. The salesman wore a big smile as he pulled up to dock.

"Good morning, Paul!" said the salesman.

"Good morning,…I'm sorry, I forgot your name."

"Jim Akers. Man, oh man are you gonna love this boat. It rides so smooth. And what a day to be on the water. But first I'd like to spend an hour or so going over a few things about your new boat."

"Is there a manual?" asked Paul.

"Of course, but it's always better to have questions answered in person."

"That's okay, I'll read the manual later. I know how to drive a boat. Let's go for a ride."

"Are you sure?" asked Jim.

"That's my man," said Joanne. "He shoots first and asks questions later."

"Well, alright. But you can call me anytime with questions. My card is in the glove box. Can you drop me off back at the store?"

"Sure thing. I wanna drive this baby now."

Paul helped Joanne step on the boat.

"Wow, this is an awesome boat, Paul," said Joanne. "I'm going down to see the cabin." Joanne found the mini kitchen with microwave, maple cabinets and a flat screen television. She plopped down on the sofa and bathed in the luxury of the cabin when Jim stuck his head around the corner.

"That sofa pulls out to a sleeper with an air mattress. It's quite comfortable to sleep on."

"I'm sure. This is incredible." Joanne stepped up out of the cabin as Jim held his hand out to assist her up. He admired Joanne's long, tan, slender legs as she came up.

"Here we go! Hold on," said Paul as he put the boat into gear. Joanne stood beside Paul and put her arms around his waist. He turned and smiled at her as the engine roared and the boat lurched forward quickly. The boat moved strongly and effortlessly across the water, and a broad smile came across Paul's face. The breeze blew Joanne's long blonde hair, and Paul reveled in the scenery and the silent companionship of the woman he loved. This was what he had been dreaming about all those years. He had achieved his dream of feeling free with the wind brushing across his face on the water. He recalled his first meeting with Carlos where he was invited to dream again. He remembered telling him how he always wanted a red, white and blue boat. Paul gave a silent thanks to God for bringing his dreams into fruition. He wanted to stay on this boat with Joanne for the rest of his life.

Jim kept trying to tell Paul about all the features of the boat, but all Paul wanted to do was dump the boat salesman off. Paul knew he was only doing his job, but he grew tired of the incessant boat talk. That could come later or never for all Paul cared.

Thankfully the dock at the boat marina came into view, and Paul dropped Jim off. He promised to call him with questions. Jim waved goodbye from the dock as Paul and Joanne cruised back into the open water.

"Where do you wanna go?" asked Paul.

"Anywhere with you," said Joanne as she embraced him. Paul let Joanne stand in front of him to steer the boat as he held her from behind.

"I've always loved watching sun sparkle on water. I don't know why. When I die, will you spread my ashes over sparkling water?"

Joanne was startled at Paul's request and talk of death.

"Why are you talking about that now? Is there something I should know about?"

"No, I'm not dying. I just thought you should know that."

"Wow, can we talk about something else?"

"Okay, why don't we talk about our Bio Strength business. I've been thinking we should combine our downlines. Do you think they would let us do that? We could work so much better as a team."

"I've never heard of that being done. It doesn't mean they can't, but just I've never heard of it. We could still work together and help each other. Let's just give this a little more time before we try that. Hell, I've already agreed to move in with you after a long weekend together. I think we can wait a little before combining our business. Does that make sense?"

"Sure, I'm just thinking out loud. Sorry, I get a little excited sometimes."

Paul and Joanne spent the next two hours cruising the St. Johns River. As they approached Paul's dock, his cell phone rang. Paul turned the steering wheel over to Joanne as he talked on the phone. Joanne had driven a boat once as a teenager, and that was the extent of her experience.

"Just slow it down more as we get closer," whispered Paul as he pulled his head away from the cell phone to talk to her. He thought he remembered Joanne said she could drive a boat. He was a little distracted by a call from a distributor. A new downline wanted to do a three-way call with a prospect so Paul could answer some questions. He never turned away these calls since he had a vested interest in his downline succeeding. He was engrossed in his conversation in the back of the boat while Joanne steered closer to the dock. In an effort to slow further, Joanne pushed the throttle forward instead of backwards. The boat raced directly at the edge of the pier. Paul would have fallen off had he not been sitting down.

"Pull *back* on the throttle!" yelled Paul. Joanne pulled back too late as the boat crashed into the corner of the dock with a sickening thud.

Joanne's head smashed into the windshield, and Paul was thrown from his seat in the back and down into the cabin. Joanne rushed back to check on Paul and found him lying on the floor face down in the cabin.

"Paul, are you okay?" screamed Joanne as she peered into the cabin holding the top of her bruised head.

Paul slowly got up on all fours. "Never mind me. How's the boat?"

"I don't know. I haven't looked yet. I'm sorry, honey. I got confused about which way the throttle went." Joanne reached out a hand to help Paul up.

"It's alright. I thought you said you could drive a boat. At least we got two hours in before crashing."

The boat was partially grounded as it had made a glancing blow on the corner of the dock. Paul hopped out to investigate the damage.

"It's scraped up pretty good but no holes, fortunately. I think I'm doing the driving from here on out, sweetie."

That night Ernie took a cab to Ralph's house to retrieve his car. Ernie drove it back to work and parked it in the same space that Ralph had always parked in. He went back to the lab to check on Ralph. He had to place him back in his chair for another week of hard work. He wasn't sure how much longer he could pull off this ruse. The building was completely empty, and Ernie felt safe from anyone surprising him there.

Ernie opened the lab door and approached the lockers. He suddenly had a weird vision of opening the locker to find roaches crawling out of Ralph's eye socket. He stopped for a second to shake off that image. He had work to do, and he told himself to focus. Ernie held his breath as he slowly opened the locker door. He couldn't believe the locker was empty and stood there paralyzed with fear. Someone had found out about Ralph, and he was in big trouble now. But where was he? What would anyone want with a dead body? The police were never called, so Ernie figured it was someone who was glad Ralph was dead. Ernie's mind raced as he tried to figure out what to do next. He randomly opened the adjacent locker only to scream at what he saw.

Ralph the Rat was hanging from a hook in the next locker. There were no roaches crawling from his eye sockets, but he still looked pale and creepy. Ernie couldn't remember if he had put Ralph in the locker on the left or the right. Did someone move Ralph, or did he just forget which locker he had put him in? Ernie panicked that someone was on to him. He decided he still had to move Ralph back to his chair and assume no one knew he was dead.

Pulling Ralph off the hook was much easier than placing him in the locker. Ernie still hated handling a dead person, particularly someone he detested. He plopped Ralph back in the chair and pushed it back to his spot in front of the microscope. He thought it best to not use duct tape again in case he was discovered. Ernie felt his time was running out hiding Ralph. It would not be a good thing for Ralph to be found duct-taped to his chair.

Ernie positioned Ralph just right, and he looked at his handiwork from the window outside the lab. It looked like Ralph was hard at work yet again. He walked outside into the night and called a cab for a ride home. Marla and the kids were asleep by the time he got home, and he had trouble sleeping as he tried to remember which locker he had put Ralph in. He finally convinced himself that Ralph was never moved. He just had a momentary lapse in memory.

Ernie's boss Joe arrived early Monday morning and spotted Ralph's car in the parking lot as usual. That prompted him to make a personal visit to the lab to talk to Ralph about the Bio Strength results. More and more complaints were coming in about strange side effects from Bio Strength products and he wanted an explanation.

Joe had not been in the back part of the building for months, and the hallway lights were turned off leading back to the lab. Joe peered into the lab window, and sure enough, there was Ralph working hard again with his face stuck to his microscope. Joe rapped on the window to draw Ralph's attention. Ralph didn't move. Joe knocked harder this time, and Ralph still didn't budge. This time Joe knocked hard with his fists and started calling out his name.

"Ralph! Open up. Are you okay?" Joe yelled loudly. There was still no movement from Ralph, and Joe became worried something was terribly wrong.

"Ralph! *Ralph*!" yelled Joe even louder. Joe pulled out his cell to call security. He really did not want to call them since they were lazy, good-for-nothing slobs in his opinion, but he had no choice.

"Yeah, this is Joe up on the second floor outside the lab. Ralph is in the lab and he's not responding. Call 911. The door is locked, so we need to get in. Do you guys have a key?"

"Ralph was real particular about who had access to his lab, so he never gave us a key. We'll have to break the glass in the door and open it from the inside," said the security guard. "We'll be right up."

Joe continued to pound on the door and yell Ralph's name. Two security guards with axes came running down the hall. One swing of the ax was all it took to break the glass in the door. Joe stuck his arm in and unlocked the door from the inside.

"*Ralph!*" yelled Joe as he ran up to his chair. His shoes slid and crackled as he stepped on top of broken glass. Joe put his hand on Ralph's shoulder only to see his head clunk down awkwardly on the table. Joe pulled up Ralph by his shoulders and his head flailed helplessly to one side.

"This guy's dead," said the first security guard. "Check his pulse."

Joe put his hand on Ralph's wrist and detected nothing.

"His wrists are ice cold. I think he's been dead for days," said Joe.

"Aw, man," said the second security guard. "Ralph owed me $200 from last year. I'm never gonna get it back now."

Joe shot the guard a menacing stare.

"We've got a dead guy here, and all you think about is getting your damn money back. You heartless piece of shit."

"I'm sorry, Joe. I just lost myself for a minute there. You're right."

"Let's show some respect here."

Just then the first guard bumped into Ralph's chair and caused his limp body to collapse into a heap on the floor. Before Joe could verbally assault the guards again, they heard a loud commotion from down the hall.

"It's the rescue squad," yelled Joe. We can't let them find Ralph here in the floor like this. Let's put him back in the chair there on the right," said Joe.

Joe grabbed Ralph's legs while each guard grabbed an arm.

"On the count of three let's hoist him up. Okay, one, two, *three....*"

All three made a strong jerk of Ralph's limbs to throw him in the chair. The only problem was that each guard pulled Ralph's arms in a different direction. It suddenly became a quick tug of war. Their hands slipped off Ralph's cold wrists, and Ralph's body rose several feet into the air before his head clonked firmly on the tile floor.

"You idiots," said Joe. "What the hell were you thinking?"

"I thought you said the chair on your right," said the first guard.

"I thought you said the chair on *my* right," said the second guard.

"The rescue squad guys are getting closer. They're gonna think we're a bunch of idiots," said Joe.

"I'll start doing CPR," said the first guard. He jumped in the air and landed a flying elbow smash on Ralph's chest. The rescue squad technicians had just gotten to the door only to witness their first-ever professional wrestling CPR move.

"What the hell are you guys doing?" said the first EMT on the scene.

"We're trying CPR," Joe stammered nervously. "We found him unresponsive here on the floor."

"Get out of the way," said the EMT as his assistant entered the lab. He started checking for vital signs on Ralph.

"No pulse and no breath," said the EMT. "He's been dead for a while. When was the last time anyone spoke to him?"

"He's been working pretty much around the clock for the last week," said Joe. "He was last seen working here in the lab on Friday."

"He died sometime over the weekend," said the EMT. "We'll take him to the morgue at the hospital until funeral arrangements are made. Who is his next of kin?"

"We really don't know much about Ralph's personal life or family. He was a loner and just lived for his work. We'll have HR look in his file for some contact information," said Joe

Just then two police officers arrived at the lab door.

"Whadaya got here?" asked the first cop. We weren't far away when we heard the 911 call over our radio."

"The deceased was found unresponsive here in the lab by a fellow worker who called 911. We checked his vitals and determined he died sometime over the weekend. He was last seen here in the lab working on Friday."

"Which one of you saw him last?" asked the second cop.

"I'm pretty sure Ernie Zimmerman said he saw him working," said Joe.

"Can we speak with him?"

"Sure, he should be getting to work soon."

"Did you speak to the deceased?" asked the first cop.

"No, but everybody told me how busy he was. He was always staring into that damn microscope of his. He didn't move for hours. His work ethic was legendary around here. He was always the first to arrive and the last to leave at work. I guess he just worked himself to death."

"I like my work," said the first cop, "but I don't like it that much. Do you mind answering a few more questions?"

"No, not at all," said Joe.

"Call St. Luke's Hospital when you find out about the deceased's relatives," said the EMT as he reached down to pick up Ralph. His assistant set a stretcher down, and they both picked up Ralph and laid him on it. They pulled a sheet over his head and walked out of the lab carrying Ralph's body.

Ernie was pulling into the parking lot at 7:45 a.m. when he spotted the police cars and ambulance in front of the building. He then spotted two EMTs carrying a body wrapped in a sheet out of the front door. His heart sank into his stomach.

"Please tell me that isn't Ralph," Ernie said to himself. He parked his car and walked quickly over to the ambulance just as they were closing the back door.

"What happened here?" asked Ernie as nonchalantly as he could.

"A man died over the weekend. He had no pulse and wasn't breathing when we arrived," said the EMT.

"Who was it?"

"Can't divulge that, sir. But the police want to talk to a guy named Zimmerman. If you see him, tell him the police have a few questions for him in the lab upstairs."

Ernie's face turned ashen, and his knees almost buckled. He gathered himself and walked as calmly as he could into the front door.

"I'll be sure to tell him," said Ernie as he turned and walked away. Ernie's mind raced in a million different directions about what he would say to the police. Was it Ralph who was found? Did someone turn him in? Who else already knew that Ralph was dead? Ernie pictured himself in jail for the rest of his life. Killing Ralph was a pure accident, but he did it out of love for a woman. Now the woman was with someone else, the business she did was a fraud, and he was going to jail for murder. Ernie could see how some people rationalized suicide. For some it was the only way out. Maybe if he turned himself in, he would get some leniency. It was an accident, after all.

Ernie entered the foyer and waved meekly at the receptionist.

"Oh, Ernie. Did you hear about Ralph?"

"No, not yet."

"They found him dead in the lab this morning. They think he died sometime over the weekend. It's pretty creepy to think he died in this building. I don't think I'll ever go upstairs again."

"That's horrible!" said Ernie feigning surprise. "Does my boss know?"

"Oh, yeah. He's the one that found him."

"I'll go find out some more from him. Thanks."

Ernie walked up to the second floor and down the back hallway to the lab. He practiced his answers to the questions that he thought he would get from the police. He couldn't appear nervous at all, or it would raise suspicion. "Maybe they already have it figured out," thought Ernie. "Maybe I should just turn myself in."

Ernie could see the policeman standing in the doorway down the hall. It seemed like a half-mile walk to reach the lab. Ernie raised his hand to shake the policeman's hand.

"I'm Ernie Zimmerman. Did something happen to Ralph?" he asked with what he hoped was the right amount of concern on his face.

"Yes, sir. Your boss found him dead here in the lab this morning."

"Oh, that's terrible!" said Ernie. He was getting better at acting surprised.

"We'd like to ask you a few questions Mr. Zimmerman. Do you have a moment?"

"Certainly."

"When was the last time you saw Mr. Smedley alive?"

"I believe that would have been Friday," said Ernie confidently. "I walked past the lab and saw him working at his desk."

"Did you speak with him that day?"

"No, I don't think so. He always seemed so busy. I didn't want to interrupt him."

"That's what your boss said. We are not suspecting foul play or anything. We just have to ask questions like this when there is uncertainty over the cause of death. I'm sure the autopsy will answer a lot of questions."

"I hope so," said Ernie. "By the way Joe, did you ever get a chance to talk to Ralph about the Bio Strength results?"

"That's what I was going to ask him about today when I found him unconscious here in the lab. I had to call security to come break in when he wouldn't answer."

"We're going to ask around the office some more to see if anyone saw or talked to Mr. Smedley this weekend. Do you have any objections?"

"Of course not," said Joe.

"Thank you, sir. We'll let you know if we find anything out," said the first policeman as they headed out the door.

"I can't believe he's dead," said Joe.

"Me, neither," said Ernie.

"He had such a bright future here. He was a pest sometimes, but I don't know how we are going to replace him."

"Does Ralph have any family?"

"I don't know of any, but I'll get HR involved. Tough way to get started on a Monday, huh?"

"I know. This lab will never be the same again," said Ernie.

"I've got to get with HR now and find a family member to contact. I'll talk to you later," said Joe as he left the lab.

Ernie stood in the lab alone amongst the shattered glass. His mind raced back to the blow dart fight, and he was glad he had removed the camera Ralph had installed. Ernie felt he had dodged a bullet for now. He was nervous over what would come back in the autopsy, but there was nothing he could do about that now. He would just have to wait.

Chapter 21

The following week Paul and Joanne spent every day on the boat. His boat was still damaged but not enough to keep him out of the water. The weather was beautiful, and Paul loved the feeling of the wind rustling through his hair while listening to Bob Marley tunes. A cool beer, a beautiful boat, a house, and a hot babe made Paul feel like he was in heaven. He had dreamed of days like this for years, and now it was actually happening.

"There's only one thing missing from my dreams right now," said Paul as they cruised the St. Johns River at sunset. The sun was bright orange as it touched the treetops on the riverbank.

"And what's that, Paul Cousins?" said Joanne as she put her arm gently on his shoulder and smiled.

"A red Ferrari."

"You've got to be kidding."

"No, I'm not. I've always wanted one."

"Can you afford it? You've bitten off a good bit lately."

"Sure. My checks are going up each month. I'll just lease one if I have to."

"I love your spontaneity. You see something, and you just go for it."

"Just do me a favor and don't tell Carlos I'm getting it. He will have a cow."

"I know he will. This is going to be so cool. I've never ridden in a Ferrari. Have you?"

"Only in my dreams. Let's go get one now."

"Right now?"

"Why not? You only live once." Paul turned the boat around and sped back to his dock.

Paul turned on his laptop back at his house and found a red Ferrari for sale on the Internet at a luxury dealership.

"Look honey, here is a 1999 Ferrari F355 Spider on sale for $62,000. It only has 17,000 miles on it. And the best thing about it is the color…candy apple red."

"Wow, it's beautiful!"

"I can see you riding in it with me down the interstate. Let's go!"

"Honey, it sounds as if you've already bought it."

"In my mind I have."

An hour later Paul and Joanne strolled into the dealership. Paul wore a dark suit and red tie while Joanne wore a short red skirt to show off her long, tan legs. They looked like Donald Trump with one of his young trophy wives. Bubba Jones was in his first week of selling cars. He was 57 years old with a large beer gut, and he pulled up his pants by the belt and approached his new prospects like a tiger stalking prey.

"Can I help you?" said Bubba in a thick southern accent.

"Yes, I saw the red Ferrari for sale on the Internet and would like to test drive it."

"Absolutely." Bubba didn't bother to ask any questions since Paul was so sure of what he wanted.

"I'll just need a copy of your license."

"Here you go," said Paul.

"Hi, I'm Bubba Jones. My friends just call me Bubba."

"Nice to meet you, Bubba."

"If you wait around front I'll pull the car around."

A few minutes later Paul and Joanne heard the loud roar of a racecar engine coming around the corner of the dealership. The red low-riding Ferrari was a soft top convertible and looked like it was ready for the race track. Paul fell in love instantly. This was the car he had dreamed of. He didn't want to appear too eager in front of the salesman.

"With a car like this, I am required to be in the car for the test drive. Unfortunately, there are only two seats. Miss, do you mind waitin' a few minutes in our lounge while we take it for a spin?"

"No, not at all," said Joanne. "Be careful, honey."

Bubba got out of the driver's seat and held the door open for Paul. Paul put on his Oakley sunglasses and casually sat behind the wheel as if he had been doing this all his life. He pushed the button to put down the top. He never felt as cool as he did at this moment. He was sold, and he hadn't even driven it yet.

"Take a right out of the parking lot and we'll get to the interstate. I'm sure you'll want to push it a bit."

Paul clicked on his seat belt and blew Joanne a kiss as he peeled out of the parking lot, leaving skid marks behind.

"Whoa, whoa," said Bubba. "Don't get a speedin' ticket before we hit the interstate."

Paul could not help himself as he weaved in and out of traffic. The pure power of a Ferrari engine made it impossible for him to drive it like a grandma. Paul turned on the ramp for the interstate and gunned the accelerator. It felt like he was driving a rocket. Bubba was too scared to speak as Paul moved across three lanes of traffic in a flash.

"Mr. Cousins," said Bubba as he clutched the door handle. "Do you have any questions about the car?"

"How fast does it go?"

"It'll approach 190 mph. But I wouldn't try that, sir...."

Paul mashed the accelerator down further as the speedometer blew past 110 mph. The car seemed to run smoother at 110 mph than it did at 90. Paul passed cars in a blur. Any semblance of neatly-combed hair disappeared as soon as he hit the road with the top down. His head was pushed against his headrest, and he gripped the leather steering wheel even tighter. He could see Bubba holding on for his life. Paul didn't want to give him a heart attack, so he slowed down to 85 mph. It felt like he was crawling along after having reached 120 mph.

"Kinda nice, ain't it?" said Bubba as he loosened his grip on the door.

"Yup."

"Ya know, that's what Dale Earnhardt used to say when he was racin'. His crew would be talkin' to him durin' a race, and his only response was 'Yup' over and over again. Were you an Earnhardt fan?"

"Yup."

"Ha! I shoulda known you were gonna say that! That's pretty good. You can turn around right up there," said Bubba pointing a half-mile down the road.

Paul turned around and drove a little more cautiously back to the dealership. He knew he would be buying the car, so he wanted to make sure he got it back in one piece. Joanne was waiting patiently out front.

"That's some fine lookin' woman ya got there," said Bubba.

"Yes, she is," said Paul proudly. He pulled in front of the dealership and screeched to a halt in front of Joanne.

"This man drives like a lunatic!" said Bubba. "Are you sure you wanna ride with him?"

"I'm sure. How was the ride, honey?"

"Very nice. Hey, Bubba. Let's go in and talk some numbers."

Bubba tried to contain his enthusiasm. This would be his first sale as a car salesman, and it was going to be a whopper of a sale.

"Sure, Mr. Cousins. Just follow me."

Paul and Joanne walked arm and arm back to Bubba's desk.

"I'll give you ten grand less than your asking price," said Paul.

Bubba seemed startled. "I don't think we can do that, but let me go talk to my manager," said Bubba as he got up from his desk. He pulled up his pants and tucked in his shirt. His protruding belly made it hard for his shirt to stay tucked. Bubba came back a few minutes later.

"My boss said he could split the difference and take $5,000 off the asking price. How does that sound?"

Paul thought for a moment and looked at Joanne for approval.

"Don't look at me," said Joanne. "This is your car."

"How much would you give me for trading in my Camry?"

"Let me go take a look at it."

Paul saw Bubba and another man looking over his car. A few minutes later Bubba returned.

"You've got 142,000 miles on it. We can give ya $2,500 for it."

Paul thought for a moment. "Okay, I'll take it."

"Fantastic. You're gonna love this car. We just need to fill out some paperwork now. Can I see your insurance card?"

An hour later Bubba handed the keys to Paul.

"Now promise me you won't drive like a maniac outta here. I want to see you get home safe, ya hear?" said Bubba.

"Joanne, do you wanna drive it home? Bubba here doesn't trust me."

"After the boating incident, you trust me to drive your new Ferrari?"

"Just be careful. You'll do just fine."

"Okay. I'll drive," said Joanne as she grabbed the keys from Paul.

Bubba waved goodbye from the front door of the dealership as Joanne and Paul pulled out of the parking lot. He scratched his belly and admired what a fine looking couple they were in their new sports car.

Joanne felt the hum of the engine and listened to it purr like a kitten at low speeds.

"What's it like to drive this thing fast?" asked Joanne.

"It's better than sex," said Paul. "And it just keeps on going."

"Why don't I let 'er run a little on the interstate."

"Be my guest. It's the fastest car I've ever driven. Zero to sixty in 4.6 seconds."

Joanne made a sharp turn for the exit ramp and felt the engine roar as she quickly accelerated to 70 mph. Her blonde hair was blowing relentlessly, and her skirt hiked up a bit.

"I could do this all day," said Paul.

"What's that?"

"Watch you drive."

"Oh, yeah? Well, just watch this."

Joanne floored the accelerator and they buzzed by cars like they were standing still.

"This is *awesome!*" yelled Joanne over the roar of the wind. She had never experienced raw power in a car like this before. She pushed the car harder.

A half-mile ahead Sonny Jackson, with the Jacksonville Police Department, was cruising along the interstate talking on his two-way radio. He was left speechless in mid-sentence when Joanne passed his cruiser like a rocket.

"Holy shit!" yelled Sonny. "A blonde chick in a red Ferrari just passed me going 105 mph. Gotta go!"

Sonny turned on his lights and began the chase. It was another quarter-mile before Joanne noticed police lights in her rear view mirror.

"Uh oh, I see some police lights," said Joanne as she hit the brakes. Paul craned his neck around, and his heart sank at the sight of a police car catching up to them.

"We're dead," said Paul. "I never even saw him. You've got to use your best charm to get outta this one."

"Don't worry, honey. I haven't gotten a ticket in years. I have this down to a science."

Joanne slowed down and pulled over to the shoulder. She hiked up her skirt as high as it would go and pulled her dress straps off her shoulder to reveal as much cleavage as she could. She straightened her hair up and eyed the policeman getting out of his car from her mirror.

"Does this work every time?" asked Paul.

"Except if he's gay," smiled Joanne.

Sonny walked up to the car slowly.

"Ma'am, do you have any idea how fast you were going?"

Joanne turned and flashed her best smile up at him. Sonny's brain went dead when he caught sight of Joanne's breasts heaving out from her dress. He had a nice clear view of them since the Ferrari was so low to the ground.

"Oh, I'm so sorry officer. This is the first time I've driven a car like this, and I just got carried away. We just left the dealership a few minutes ago. Here, I can show you the paperwork." Joanne leaned over to the glove box to give Sonny a better view. He was glad he had dark sunglasses on because he was getting an eye full.

"I clocked you at 105, and that is an immediate reckless driving citation. May I have your license and registration, please?"

"Here is my license, and the car is registered to my passenger Paul Cousins. We literally just left the dealership. I'll never drive it like that again. I promise," pleaded Joanne.

"I'll be right back, ma'am."

Joanne didn't feel good about this traffic stop.

"I think my luck has run out. He hardly looked at me."

"Oh, he looked at you all right. But maybe he has to give you some kind of ticket for driving that fast."

Sonny returned a few minutes later with a written citation.

"Ma'am, I want you to know that I could have you locked up for driving that fast. I do see that this car was just purchased. I'm going to give you the benefit of the doubt and write you a ticket for 19 mph over the limit. I can't let you go with just a warning."

"Oh, thank you officer. I promise I'll drive the speed limit," said Joanne as she quickly signed the citation.

"You have a choice of going to court or paying the ticket. You can also take an online course to prevent points from going against your license. Have a nice day," said Sonny as he handed her back her copy of the ticket. He got in one good last look at her boobs before he walked back to his cruiser.

"Do you know how lucky you are?" asked Paul. "You need to pay that ticket and count your blessings. The judge could have taken your license for this."

"I know, but I can't believe he still gave me a ticket. My charm must be fading."

"It saved you for sure. He had to give you a ticket for something. He was very lenient with you. Hell, he's probably on the phone now with his buddies talking about the hot babe in the Ferrari he just pulled over."

Sonny got back in his cruiser and called his best police friend.

"Hey, Mark. You won't believe what I just saw. This blonde chick in a red Ferrari passed me at 105 mph, and her skirt was hiked up so high I swear she was showing me her stuff. And her boobs, good god they were beautiful. I couldn't keep my eyes off them!"

Joanne drove home gingerly and pulled into Paul's driveway. It was another beautiful dusk evening.

"Wanna go for a boat ride and cap off another incredible day?" asked Paul.

"Sure, let's go. I've got to forget about my first ticket in years."

Paul took off his shoes and socks and grabbed Joanne's hand. She kicked off her shoes, and they ran barefoot hand in hand down to the dock. Paul always loved the feel of running barefoot on grass. He had it all now. The blonde beauty, the house, the boat, and now the red Ferrari. His dreams had all come to fruition. He was hoping no one came to wake him up.

Chapter 22

Ralph's funeral was set for Saturday at 10 a.m. The only relative Joe could find was an uncle in Virginia. He barely knew Ralph and was not coming to the funeral. Both of Ralph's parents were deceased, and he was an only child. Joe called the police for the results of the autopsy.

"Yeah, this is Joe Martini at the FDA. I'm calling to see if you have the results of the autopsy on Ralph Smedley."

"Let me check, hold on," said the investigating officer. "Yeah, we got them back last night. It appears he died of heart failure."

"Really? It seems so unusual for a man who's 33 years old to die from heart failure."

"Oh, it's happened before. What was a little unusual was the contusion on the back of the deceased's head. It was rather large, but it could have occurred after his heart failed. His head could have hit the floor pretty hard. We have ruled out any foul play at this point."

"Thanks for all your work."

"You're welcome. I am sorry for the death of your co-worker."

"Thank you so much. Goodbye."

Joe had to make all the funeral arrangements himself since there was no family member to do it. He emailed the entire department to let them know that Ralph's service would be a simple graveside burial at the Shady Grove Cemetery. Joe asked the pastor of his church if he would lead a brief ceremony because Ralph was not a member of any local church that Joe could find. He just prayed that some people showed up for the funeral.

Ernie saw the email at work Friday about Ralph's funeral. He checked with his co-workers, and most were not planning on going. Ernie did not want to go by himself, and he knew better than to ask Marlo. She was not speaking to him again. Ernie picked up the phone to call Joanne. His desire not to go to the funeral alone overrode any nervousness he had about calling her.

"Joanne, hi, it's Ernie."

"Hi, Ernie. How are you? You know, I've been meaning to call you. You may have heard that I've moved in with Paul."

"Yeah, I heard."

"It was never planned. It happened so quickly. Paul and I just hit it off at his party. We have the same goals and dreams, and everything just clicked. I certainly never wanted to mislead you. I hope you understand."

"I just want you to be happy. If you are, that's great."

"Yes, I am. Thanks. How are things with you and Marlo?"

"She is still proceeding with the divorce. Nothing has changed there. Listen, I need to ask a favor from you. A friend, uh, co-worker died last week and his funeral is tomorrow at 10 a.m. I don't want to go alone, and I was wondering if you would be kind enough to go with me. I know you didn't know this guy, but it would really mean a lot if you would go with me."

"Tomorrow at 10? Sure, I'll go with you."

"Thanks so much. I'll come pick you up at 9:30."

"See you then. Bye, Ernie."

"Who was that, honey?" asked Paul.

"That was Ernie Zimmerman. Remember the guy at your party that I hung out with some? He just asked me to go to a funeral with him tomorrow."

"Did you know the guy?"

"No, but he worked with Ernie. For some reason he didn't want to go alone. Do you mind if I go?"

"Not at all," said Paul as he took her in his arms. "As long as I get to spend the rest of the day with you. Hey, guess what my most recent Bio-Strength check was."

"How much?"

Paul held up five fingers in one hand and one finger in the other.

"Fifteen thousand? Is that all?" said Joanne. "Hell, I made sixteen thousand."

Paul shifted the order of his hands around and shook his head.

"Oh, you mean fifty one thousand! That's incredible. You're on your way to being a millionaire. I'm so proud of you!" Joanne laid a huge kiss on Paul, and he picked her up and walked her back to the bedroom. Their love-making was the most passionate Paul had ever experienced. They locked their gaze into each other's eyes and became one. Paul felt so connected to her by the power of their locked eyes, and they both fell asleep completely exhausted.

Joe was back at work ordering up a new round of tests on Bio Strength products. He was never satisfied with the first round of tests even though Ralph had done them.

"Make these Bio Strength tests your number-one priority," Joe told the new lab worker.

"I'll get right on them sir. I should have some preliminary results later in the day."

"Call me on my cell when you get them."

Joe was not getting much response from co-workers about attendance at Ralph's funeral. He hated the thought of no one showing up. Ralph was not the most loved person in the building, and Joe knew it.

Ernie showed up on Paul's doorstep at 9:30 a.m. sharp to pick up Joanne. She opened the door with a huge smile and leaned over to hug Ernie.

"Thanks for coming with me," said Ernie as he hugged Joanne back. She was wearing a beautiful long, black dress. He loved the way she smelled, and he soaked up the hug each second it lasted. He knew she would never be with him, but he was pleased that she was so happy with Paul.

"So who is this funeral for?" asked Joanne. "I've never been to one where I had no idea who had died."

"His name was Ralph Smedley," said Ernie as he opened the door for Joanne. "He was in charge of product testing at the FDA."

"I thought you said he was a co-worker of yours," said Joanne slightly confused.

"He was."

"I never knew you worked for the FDA. I never really was sure what you did. What do you do, anyway?"

"I'm an investigator for the FDA. I look into complaints on consumer products."

"Really? That's so cool. Who are you investigating now?"

Ernie hesitated as he glanced quickly at her. He was afraid to tell her the truth, but he had to come clean. He looked back at her for a second.

"You."

"Me? What do you mean me? I haven't made any consumer products that need to be tested. I don't understand," said Joanne with her voice shaking.

"No, but Bio Strength has. In fact, the guy whose funeral we're going to today tested all the Bio Strength products, and each one of them came back positive for high concentrations of steroids. That is why hundreds of people have been complaining about so many adverse side effects from Bio Strength products. I don't know why the company put steroids into their products, but that is cause for an immediate shutdown of Bio Strength. Steroids are not allowed in any products without a prescription."

Joanne sat in stunned silence. She stared straight ahead before erupting at Ernie.

"You're just jealous that Paul and I are together, that's all! Admit it! You can't stand the thought of me with another man, so you concoct this story to get me to leave him. You'll say anything now 'cause your feelings are hurt. Hell, what else have you lied to me about?" Joanne screamed.

"I'm not lying," Ernie shot back. "It's all true. You need to get out of this company now before it implodes. Any product you've got you should get rid of now 'cause it'll be worthless when this gets out."

"I can't believe you're telling me this," shouted Joanne. "Why should I believe you? You're the one that's been lying to me all along," screamed Joanne with tears welling up in her eyes.

"I'm telling you to protect you. I might be envious of you and Paul together, but I would never let that get in the way of the truth about Bio Strength."

"So the company I've poured my life into the past three years is a complete fraud. Is that what you're saying?"

"Basically, yes. I saw the first round of tests come back positive for steroids, and I tried to change the results to protect you believe it or not. But the real truth should be coming out shortly. My boss has ordered another round of tests. He has been after Bio Strength for months, and when he gets what he wants, he moves fast. Real fast. That's why I'm warning you now."

Ernie had pulled up to the cemetery by now, and Joanne was a total wreck. One minute she was on top of the world in every way with the man she loved, and the next minute someone she trusted was trying to sabotage everything. Her mind raced with thoughts of her financial ruin and especially Paul. He had banked everything on Bio Strength continuing on, and now he could lose it all.

"How do I know you're telling me the truth?" said Joanne as they got out of the car. "You've got to show me how you know this to be true. I need to see it with my own eyes."

"Okay. I'll bring you to my work after hours on Monday. We should have the new round of tests back, and you can see for yourself. Fair enough?"

Joanne didn't answer Ernie. She was too emotional to speak. Ernie spotted Joe ahead at a small tent where a minister was standing by a gravesite. There were only two other people besides Joe and the minister at the service for Ralph.

The minister had a small CD player playing background music, and he waited a few more minutes to see if anyone else showed up. At 10:05, he turned off the CD player and began with a prayer. He had never presided over a funeral with only six people including himself before.

"May we pray. Dear Father, we are here to honor the life of Ralph Smedley. We are grateful for his life and for the passion he brought to his work…."

Joanne was still emotional over her conversation with Ernie in the car, and she wiped a tear from her eye and sniffled. Joe noticed Joanne crying and wondered how a beautiful woman like her knew a lab rat like Ralph. Joe suspected that Joanne was the blonde that Ernie had been so worked up over recently. He reached across Ernie to give her a Kleenex. Joanne acknowledged Joe's kindness and honked her nose loud enough to drown out the drone of the minister's prayer.

"How did she know Ralph?" Joe whispered to Ernie.

"I'll tell you later," whispered Ernie.

The minister concluded his opening prayer and looked for help from his small audience.

"Would anyone like to share a few reflections on Ralph's life?" the minister asked. He did not know Ralph, and he was only doing this as a favor to Joe. He had enough funerals to do for his own congregation.

Ernie looked around at everyone else staring at the ground. Since he was responsible for Ralph's death, he felt he owed it to him to say something at his funeral.

Ernie put on his best funeral facade face. "What can I say about Ralph Smedley?" began Ernie. He paused for a second to gather his thoughts. His mind raced as he grappled for words. Joanne started sniffling again, and Ernie turned to console her.

"I know how hard it is. We all miss him so."

"Miss him?" said Joanne. "I didn't even *know* him."

"None of us could really know Ralph," continued Ernie.

"Why are you here anyway?" interrupted Joanne. "You said yourself he was not really a friend of yours. Is there anybody here who was friends with this guy?" said Joanne sarcastically.

"He owed me money," said the man standing beside Joe. Ernie recognized him as one of the security guys that broke through Ralph's lab door. "I figured I might could get some of it back if his family was at the funeral. Are any of you related to Ralph?"

The minister quickly realized he was losing control of the funeral. "Please everyone, let's keep this a reverent occasion. Let's only remember Ralph with pleasant words."

"Okay," said the security guard, "Ralph was a pleasant asshole. Is that better?"

Joe had had enough of this. "Listen everyone. I know Ralph was not a beloved man, but we can do better than this."

"Very well, Joe," said the minister. "Can you tell us some positive remembrances of Ralph?"

"Sure, there was the time that, uh, well, I remember a few years ago…no, that wasn't Ralph. Aw, hell, I can't lie. Ralph was a nasty son of a bitch. He did a hell of a job in the lab, but beyond that, he just didn't like people. There, I managed to say something positive."

"How refreshing to hear such honesty at a funeral," said Joanne. "I'd like to hear more of that these days. Especially from people I thought I trusted," said Joanne as she glared at Ernie.

"I was telling you the truth. You've got to believe me. I only have your best interests here!"

"What is she talking about, Ernie?" said Joe. "Are you sleeping with her? Miss, do you know he's married with two kids?"

"No, I'm not sleeping with him. I'm sleeping with Paul."

"Who's Paul?" asked Joe.

"Paul Cousins, the Bio Strength guy in town," interjected Ernie.

"Does she know anything about Bio Strength?" asked Joe.

"Yeah, I blew my cover with her," said Ernie.

"You what? I'm gonna pretend I didn't hear that," said Joe.

"I know all about the investigation, but I don't believe Ernie," said Joanne.

"This is crazy" said Joe. "Ernie, you and I have to talk."

"I'd like to speak now," said the stranger standing to the side. No one knew who he was, and he hadn't said a word until now. He was a short, Hispanic man in his early forties.

"Please, sir. I've lost all control of this," said the minister. "Please give us a fond memory of Ralph."

"My name is Jose Munoz, and I'd like to tell you about how I knew Ralph."

"Finally," said the minister.

"First, I need the lady here to turn her back please."

Joanne appeared puzzled by the request. "Why do you need me to turn my back?"

"Please, just for a minute. It's all I ask," said Jose.

"Well, okay, if you insist," said Joanne as she begrudgingly turned around.

Jose stepped up beside the hole in the ground where Ralph's coffin was to be lowered. He unzipped his pants and proceeded to urinate into the hole.

"What the hell are you doing!" yelled Joe.

"It sounds like he's peeing in the hole," said Joanne with her back still turned.

"I live beside Ralph, and three years ago he poisoned my dog because he thought it barked too much," said Jose as he continued to pee. "I promised him that I would *peece* on his grave when he died. I am a man of my word, so I am keeping my promise to that *son of a beech*."

Jose calmly zipped his pants up when he finished and walked back to his car.

"I've never presided over a funeral anything remotely like this one," said the minister. "Joe, I'm sorry. You'll have to finish this one on your own." The minister grabbed his CD player and walked quickly back to his car.

Everyone stood around awkwardly and wondered what to do next.

Joe looked at the security guard. "You ready to go?"

"I guess I ain't gettin' no money back."

"No, you ain't," said Joe sarcastically. "The funeral home will bury the casket later."

"Ernie, can we go now?" asked Joanne.

Ernie felt guilty just leaving Ralph's funeral, but there was no funeral left to attend. He glanced at the casket beside the hole in the ground and nodded at Joanne.

"That was the craziest fuckin' funeral I've ever been to," said Joanne. "Pissing on someone's grave, I couldn't believe it."

"He didn't piss on the grave, he pissed in the grave."

"Ernie," said Joe as they walked back to their cars. "You and I and your lady friend have to talk. You got a minute?"

"Sure," said Ernie.

Joe waved goodbye to the security guard as they waited for him to leave. Joe leaned against his car and crossed his arms. Ernie knew this was not a good sign. Whenever Joe crossed his arms, it meant you were in trouble.

"Undercover means undercover. What part of that do you not understand? I know your mistress here is pretty hot, but an undercover investigation is supposed to mean just that!" Joe said angrily.

"I am not his mistress," piped in Joanne. "We're just friends."

"That's not what Ernie told me."

"What did you tell him?" asked Joanne threateningly.

"I never said we were sleeping together. I may have said I would have liked to, but...."

"So you go telling your friends you want me in the sack. Friends don't do that to friends," screamed Joanne.

"You can't tell me you don't use your looks to your advantage. You flaunt your stuff every single day," yelled Ernie.

"Listen you two lovesick birds," began Joe, "I just need to know how much you know about our investigation. By the way, I have not been properly introduced."

"This is Joanne Griggs," said Ernie. "Joanne, this is Joe Martini." Joanne held out her hand for a weak handshake. She didn't like Joe's attitude.

"Again, we're *not* lovers," said Joanne.

"Whatever," said Joe. "Joanne, we both work for the FDA, and your company has been under an investigation for months. Ernie was gathering evidence as part of our case against Bio Strength. What exactly did he tell you?"

"He lied to me and told me that there were steroids in the products and that they were gonna shut us down."

"He didn't lie to you," said Joe.

Ernie and Joanne both gave Joe a blank quizzical stare.

"You know the new test came back yesterday positive for steroids," said Joe.

"No, I didn't know that," said Ernie trying to act surprised.

"You shouldn't be surprised, Ernie, since you knew about the results the first time Ralph did them."

Ernie felt the blood rushing to his head. His game was over.

"I checked out the video on Ralph's laptop of you breaking into his office and tampering with his computer. Now I see why you were delaying the inevitable. Hell, I'd do the same thing if I had a thing going on with a hot chick like Joanne."

"I may have been infatuated with her, but for the last time, we did not have a *thing* going on. Joe, I'm sorry about messing with the results. I guess I'm pretty much fired now, huh."

"Yup. You can come pick up your stuff over the weekend."

Ernie put his head in his hands. "Marlo is going to kill me."

"You shoulda thought of that before you started screwing around."

Joanne had had enough. "We were *not* screwing around!" screamed Joanne as she leaned forward and beat her fists angrily on Joe's chest.

Another funeral was starting in the cemetery, and everyone turned to look at the hysterical blonde in the parking lot screaming and beating on a man.

"Should we call the police?" said one of the guests at the funeral.

"Nah. Just looks like a love triangle going on," said the second guest.

Joe grabbed both of Joanne's arms. "Would you stop hitting me?" he yelled.

Joanne stopped to catch her breath. "Okay, okay. I will." After a pause for a few seconds, Joanne gave Joe a nasty knee in the groin.

"*Ahhhhhhgh*," screamed Joe. He literally saw stars as his knees buckled and he fell to the ground.

"Don't mess with me or I'll do it again," yelled Joanne.

Joe was on all fours on the ground. He hadn't been kicked in the nuts like that since the ninth grade.

"She's a pistol," whimpered Joe to Ernie.

"I know. Just don't mess with her again."

"Don't worry. God, that hurt," said Joe as he grabbed the car to help him stand upright. "I think one of my nuts is still lying on the ground. Anyway, what was I saying? Oh, yeah. We're planning to suspend the operations of Bio Strength very soon, so you better get your affairs in order."

Joanne looked at Ernie in exasperation. "So you were telling me the truth."

"Yes, I was."

"How am I gonna tell Paul?"

"You've got to, Joanne," said Ernie. "He's already bought a house, boat, and a Ferrari. What else does he have planned?"

"We've got the international convention next week in Toronto," said Joanne. "We already have our hotel and plane reservations. Could you wait until after the convention to act? Paul has been looking forward to this convention for months. I'd like for him to enjoy that time in Toronto."

"I can't promise you anything Joanne, particularly after you kneed my nuts into outer space."

"Please," said Joanne sincerely.

"I'll see what I can do," said Joe.

"Ernie, take me home. I've got a lot of thinking to do."

"Sure, so do I. How am I going to explain how I got fired to Marlo?"

"Simple. Just tell her the truth."

"That'll never work. I'll have to think of something better."

Joanne sat in silence on the ride back to Paul's house. Paul was watching television on his new flat screen that he had installed above the fireplace.

"Hi, honey. How was the funeral? I mean, as funerals go."

"Different. There weren't many people there. Ernie is glad I went with him," said Joanne as she plopped down on the couch and curled up on Paul's shoulder.

"Hey, it's beautiful outside. Wanna go for a boat ride?"

"Not today, honey. I've got some Bio Strength stuff to take care of back at my house. I've been neglecting my business too much lately. Can I take a rain check?"

"Yeah, sure. But you've never turned down a boat ride before. Is everything okay?" asked Paul concerned.

"Yeah, everything's fine. I'm just a little behind returning some calls."

"Sure, hey, I've got some great news! You won't believe what is happening next week at the convention."

"What?" said Joanne, afraid of what he was going to say.

"I just found out I'm being honored as the new distributor of the year, and the winner gets to open the convention on stage with Van Halen! The original band with David Lee Roth singing! Can you believe it?! Bio Strength is paying them $200,000 to play for 20 minutes to start the convention. I get to hang out with the band and actually sing with them on stage. How cool is that?"

Joanne knew she couldn't drop a bomb on him now about Bio Strength. She had to let him have his shining moment. Inside she was torn to pieces, but she put her best face forward and managed to smile for him.

"That's fantastic!" said Joanne as she hugged him.

"All my dreams are coming true," said Paul. "It really does work if you just believe. You know that, don't you?"

Joanne hugged Paul even tighter.

"Yes, I do. I still believe," said Joanne as she closed her eyes. "Dreams really do come true."

Chapter 23

Joanne went to her house and immediately took stock of her Bio Strength inventory. She figured she had at least $5,000 in unsold merchandise in her extra bedroom. She put all of it up for sale on eBAY for $1,000. She got bids within a few minutes from people all over the world. Not many people were selling Bio Strength products at discounts like this. She cut up her credit cards and did a quick balance sheet of her assets. She could stay in her house for about another six months with no income coming in. She knew she couldn't replace her Bio Strength income right away. Her latest check was for over $16,000.

Joanne knew Paul would lose everything if Bio Strength shut down. He was counting on his checks going up every month. She knew she could no longer live with him. He would have to sell everything just to be able to eat. Her survival instincts kicked in overdrive-she felt she had to choose between Paul and a roof over her head.

Paul was practicing his speech for the international convention. He was more nervous about meeting Van Halen than his speech. He cranked up the song "Jump" over and over again on his home stereo. He hoped that would be the song they opened with.

Bo Valentine was busy secretly calling several women he knew in Toronto. He desperately wanted to hook up with each of them. Kitty was following him everywhere, and he would have little chance to get away from her in Toronto. He had to time his rendezvous just right.

Melanie Waters and Kim Davis had been planning their revenge for months against Bo. Kitty listened in on their plans through a three-way call days before the convention. She was grateful that Melanie and Kim had shared their past with her about Bo.

"Kitty, we'll pretend we are call girls and come up to the room and say we wanted to do some kinky stuff. We'll blindfold him and lead him into the hallway naked. Then we'll lock the door and let him figure out what to do next," said Melanie.

"I like that," said Kitty, "but he would only be embarrassed for a few minutes. Hell, he likes walking around naked. I think something more publicly embarrassing is better."

"What did you have in mind?" asked Kim.

"Bo is speaking at the convention in front of thousands of people from all over the world. What if we broadcasted through the video screen what Bo has been doing all these years? All three of us could be in it together. We could shatter the image of him as the wholesome, wonderful happily married man. That would completely humiliate him."

"That sounds great," said Melanie. "But how do we get it played? I'm not that good with technology."

"I know someone who is. I've used a private investigator named Rob Thigpen before, and he is a whiz at computers. He could help us make it, and we'll find a way to hack into the system at the convention. It also would not put us in jail like harming him physically would."

Melanie and Kim thought for a moment about Kitty's proposal.

"Okay. I'm in," said Melanie.

"Me, too," said Kim.

"I'll call Rob today, and then I'll get all of us together to record what we want to say on the video."

Joanne spent the remainder of the week before the convention selling off her entire inventory of product for a fraction of her cost. She stopped returning calls from her downline for fear of misleading them into buying and selling more Bio Strength products. Her head was telling her to spill everything about the investigation, the steroids, and the impending bust of Bio Strength, but her heart kept winning out, especially when she saw how excited Paul was about the convention.

Thursday afternoon Paul and Joanne boarded Southwest Airlines from Jacksonville on their way to Toronto for the Bio Strength international convention. Thousands of network marketing distributors from all over the world descended on Toronto for a weekend of motivational speeches all urging them to press on with their dreams.

Paul could not sit still on the entire plane trip. Van Halen was his favorite band in high school, and he had told everyone he knew that he was going to be on stage with them. He made sure he brought a video camera to record his shining moment.

"Can you record me on stage with Van Halen?" asked Paul.

Joanne's guilt was bubbling over, and she almost spilled her guts to Paul right there on the plane. But she saw his excitement, and it once again squelched her thoughts of coming clean.

"Of course I'll record it. This is something you'll treasure the rest of your life." Joanne knew she couldn't take away Paul's time in the spotlight.

"I want you to meet the band, too. Maybe I'll try to get you backstage before we go on. Would you like that?"

"Wow, I'd love to," said Joanne forcing a smile.

Paul leaned over to hug her as the plane began its descent to Toronto. "This is the start of something wonderful. I can feel it. Can't you?"

Paul was not making this easy for Joanne, but at least she didn't have to look him in the eyes when she lied to him again while in an embrace.

"Yes, it is," said Joanne. She forced herself to think she was still doing the right thing.

"Is Carlos staying at our hotel?" Joanne said, trying to change the subject.

"Nah. It was a little too pricey for him. You know what a cheapskate he is. I've got a place for him, you and Mike at the opening ceremony tomorrow in the front row."

"Mike Melito's coming? Is he bringing another bimbo with him? Is he planning anything stupid?"

"I had a long talk with him before we left. He promised me he would be on good behavior. I reminded him that many of our downline will be there watching us. We'll see how long his promise lasts."

Paul and Joanne grabbed a cab from the airport and checked into a five-star hotel near the convention center. Attendants quickly grabbed their luggage and led them into the spacious marble-floored lobby with an elaborate fountain spewing water at least a story high. Carlos had checked into a Comfort Inn three miles away. Luxury hotels were a complete waste of money to him. All he wanted was a quiet room with a clean bed to sleep in.

Paul and Joanne had just checked in when they turned around to see Bo and Kitty walking by. Bo never spoke to other distributors first. He felt it was a sign of respect for others to approach him since he felt he had paid his dues over the years. Most wannabes in network marketing usually approached him first anyway. Paul's success in Bio Strength was too recent in Bo's mind to give him any credibility. Bo liked to see the crusty veterans succeed and not the flash-in-the-pans like Paul.

"Bo Valentine," said Paul as they got closer.

Bo turned his head to face Paul as if he was surprised to see him there.

"Oh, hi, Paul. How's it going?"

"Great! Hey, you remember meeting Joanne at my party, don't you?"

Kitty shot Bo a menacing stare. "What party was that, honey?"

"Oh, that was a Bio Strength meeting Paul had the other weekend that sorta turned into a party. Your house is gorgeous, by the way."

"Thanks. What are you guys up to now?"

"We were just going to grab some lunch," said Bo. "Joanne, this is my wife Kitty."

"Nice to meet you, Kitty." Joanne could tell something was amiss between Bo and Kitty. Kitty stood several feet away from Bo while they were talking.

"We've just checked in and we're hungry, too. Can we join you?" asked Paul.

"Absolutely," interjected Kitty. She was tired of Bo droning on and on about his business, and the thought of having lunch alone with him sickened her. Besides, she was expecting a call from Rob Thigpen to check out the equipment at the convention center with him. She would tell Bo she was going shopping.

"Can we meet you in a few minutes?" asked Paul. "We haven't had a chance to go to our room yet."

"Sure thing. We'll have some drinks waiting for you. What do you like?" asked Bo.

"I like red cabernet, and Joanne likes pinot."

"You got it," said Bo.

"See you in a few minutes," said Paul.

When the elevator doors closed, Joanne let Paul have an earful.

"Why are we having lunch with him? He gives me the creeps. And did you see his wife? She was standing three feet away from him. Something is definitely not right with them."

The luggage attendant stared at the floor, pretending not to listen. He had seen and heard it all in his years carting luggage around. Cheating spouses, arguments, and men calling high-class hookers seemed to be the norm.

"Oh, they've been married a long time. Nobody can keep up that lovey dovey stuff all those years," said Paul.

"Really, so that's what we'll be like in 20 years?" asked Joanne. If she couldn't tell him the truth about Bio Strength, maybe she could start to drive a wedge through their relationship. To her, it was easier than telling the truth.

Paul suddenly realized they were not alone in the elevator. He did not answer Joanne, and he was riding too much of an emotional high to start an argument. The attendant let them into their room and brought in their luggage. He could tell when an argument was starting. Paul tipped him, and he quickly left the room.

"I don't want to eat with that guy. Can you call him and tell him we are too tired or something?" asked Joanne.

"No, I can't. He's a big shot with Bio Strength, and he could be in a position to help us in the future. We're going to have to work with him for years."

"No you won't," mumbled Joanne under her breath.

"What did you say?" asked Paul.

"Oh, nothing. Okay, let's just get it over with. Can we make it a quick lunch? I don't like that guy at all."

"Okay. But remember you can always learn something about the business from someone like Bo. He has years of experience, and if we're going to be doing Bio Strength together, we'll need to call on his expertise in the future. Does that make sense?"

Joanne realized Paul was using one of her lines. She wasn't sure if he was doing it sarcastically or not.

"Yeah, it makes sense. Perfect sense." Joanne had never been filled with so many conflicting emotions in her life. Concealing her sense of dread of the future was eating away at her, and she was not sure if she could hang on much longer.

Bo and Kitty were waiting at a corner table with filled wine glasses waiting for Paul and Joanne.

"Ah, perfect timing," said Bo. "They just brought your wine. Hey, Paul, congratulations on being the new distributor of the year. That's quite an honor."

"Thanks," said Paul as he sat down across from Bo. Joanne was glad she would be sitting across from Kitty. She wanted to get a better read on her, anyway.

"Now you know you'll really be successful if you can make it in the business as long as I have," said Bo.

"Yeah, I hope to be in it as long as you have. Ya know, this business has really been a godsend for me. I was at the end of my rope when Carlos Ackman introduced me to Bio Strength. You don't know what this company has meant to me, both financially and personally," said Paul.

"I know what you mean," said Bo. "Bio Strength has done great things for Kitty and me. We've gotten to travel the world and talk to people. I can't believe I'm getting paid this much to do something I love."

Joanne was watching her as Bo was talking. She looked at her wine glass and the menu the whole time Bo was talking and nervously looked at her watch.

"Where are you from originally?" Joanne asked Kitty. She was trying to engage her since it was obvious Kitty was not comfortable at the table.

"Dallas, Texas. But my father moved around a lot when we were little. Let's see, we lived in Seattle, Sacramento, Denver, and Phoenix." Just then Kitty's cell phone rang, and she excused herself from the table.

"Honey, can you order a Greek salad for me? I've got to get this."

"Sure," said Bo.

"Hello," said Kitty as she headed to the hotel lobby.

"Kitty, it's Rob-you-know who. I want to get a look at *da* layout of *da* audio/video room. Can you meet me at *da* convention center now?"

"Give me about an hour. We just sat down to lunch. I'll call Melanie and Kim to meet us there. They both have checked in at the Comfort Inn a few miles away. They'll be able to meet us, too."

"Good. What time does *da* convention start on Friday."

"Noon."

"Good. I'll see you in an hour."

Kitty called Melanie and Kim to tell them to meet her at the convention center in an hour. She walked quickly back to lunch.

"Some girlfriends have asked me to go shopping with them right after lunch. Is that okay, honey?"

"That's fine with me," said Bo. He was happy to see her go so he could hitch up with one of his girlfriends in Toronto. He had them standing by waiting for his call.

"Paul, how is your website working for you?"

"Great, but I need to update it. I'm getting quite a few hits on it."

"Have you ever looked at mine?"

"I think so."

"Take a look at it sometime. I've got many recorded calls that prospects can listen to anytime. Many of them are interviews with doctors and other health professionals about the success of Bio Strength products. It's a very good third-party endorsement. You know, people are much more apt to believe an outside party than someone seen as having a vested interest. And a doctor speaking about Bio Strength goes a long way towards giving that needed credibility."

Kitty was already starting to zone Bo out again. "Did you order for me yet, honey?"

"Yes, I did, sweetie. We all ordered while you were gone."

"I'll check out your website when I get back," said Paul.

"I used to do tons of three-way calls myself, but it became so time consuming. I was talking to people all over the world in different time zones, and I never knew the result of the call. Did the people sign up? Did they take the next step to research us? Finally, I realized that I could make better use of my time putting recorded calls on my website that people could listen to on their own. Now, I will always speak personally with someone who wants to know about Bio Strength, but I always try to qualify the person first to see if they have looked at my website or gone to a business preview first. They need to be a little farther along in the process before I come in."

Joanne could tell Kitty did not want to be there. Bo was busy talking about how great he was, Kitty was very quiet and interested only in her food, and Joanne was wrestling with her conscience. The conversation at the table was mostly Bo talking about himself.

Kitty finished her salad and stood up to leave.

"It's been wonderful seeing you two. I'm going to go shopping now. I hope you don't mind."

"Oh, please go ahead," said Paul.

"Don't spend too much," said Bo as he leaned over to kiss her. Kitty turned her cheek to him.

"I'll meet you back at the room, honey," said Kitty. "I'll call you when I leave."

"Sounds good. Have fun." Bo couldn't wait to get on his phone and call girlfriend number one.

"I'll pick up the tab for you," said Bo.

"You don't have to do that," said Paul.

"Oh, I insist. It's my way of congratulating you on your new distributor of the year award," said Bo as he handed the waiter his credit card.

"By the way, have you heard about the opening ceremony tomorrow?" asked Paul.

"Yeah, some rock band is supposed to be there."

"Not just any rock band, but Van Halen."

"Van who?"

"Van Halen. You know, the songs "Jump", "Dance the Night Away", "Panama", and "Pretty Woman"…."

Paul was met with an empty stare.

"I'm not up much on the music scene. I'm sure I'll know the songs when I hear 'em." Paul did not bother to tell him he would be on stage with them since Bo didn't even know who they were. The waiter came back with the check and Bo signed the receipt.

"Thank you so much for lunch," said Joanne as they stood up to leave.

"Yes, and thanks for the tips on your website. I'll be sure to look at yours when I get back to Jacksonville," said Paul as he shook Bo's hand.

Bo glanced at his watch.

"Oh, I've got to make a call. I've got a prospect up here, actually. It never stops, you know! I'll see you at the opening ceremony," said Bo as he hustled out of the restaurant. Paul was sure Bo would see him. He would be the guy singing with Van Halen.

Rob Thigpen waited patiently outside the Toronto Convention Center for the ladies to show up. He finally spotted them turning the corner of the building.

"Hi Rob. Thanks so much for helping us with this," said Kitty.

"You're welcome."

"You remember Melanie and Kim?"

"Of course. How could I forget such beautiful ladies after making our little video? Okay, here's *da* plan. I've already been inside and looked around some. We're going to have to tap into *da* audio/video facilities by plugging my laptop into *da* MDF."

"Slow down, Rob," said Kitty. "What the hell is a MDF?"

"Master data facility. Basically it connects lines coming into *da* building with *da* internal network. All I have to do is plug my laptop into *da* MDF, hit video on my laptop, and voila, our show is on. *Der* is one little problem, however."

"What's that?" asked Kim.

"Usually only one person has *da* key to *da* MDF room since its operation is critical. It can be a room offsite, but usually it's a separate locked-up area. I haven't found it yet, so I need your help."

"What does it look like?" asked Melanie.

"You'll see all kinds of computer equipment, lights and cables running everywhere to it, and it will be offstage and out of sight and locked. I haven't seen much in the way of security here today. I suspect *dey* won't get too suspicious seeing two beautiful ladies and another beautiful lady walking around."

"Why didn't you just say three beautiful ladies walking around?" asked Kim.

Rob hesitated before he answered.... "You know I can't say *tree*."

"Oh, sorry," said Kim blushing. "We'll just say we're looking for the restroom."

"Call me if you find it. *Da* place is pretty big, so let's spread out to cover more area. Does everybody have my cell number?"

"Yeah, we do," said Kitty.

"Let's get to work."

Rob, Kitty, Melanie, and Kim entered the arena from different sections. It was a new, beautiful convention center with a capacity of over 10,000. Workers were scurrying around the stage like flies. Speakers were stacked high on both sides of the stage, and the drum set was being set up.

Melanie called Kitty from her cell phone. "Looks like a rock concert is being set up."

"Didn't you hear who's playing tomorrow?"

"No, who?"

"Van Halen is opening up the ceremony, and the new distributor of the year Paul Cousins is going to be on stage with them."

Melanie almost dropped her phone. "You're kidding. You mean the real Van Halen band is going to sing here tomorrow? Oh my *god*! That was my favorite band as a teenager. I was in love with David Lee Roth. Is he going to be here or that other guy?"

"Roth will be here, or so I've been told."

"Awesome!" said Melanie.

"Hey, we've got work to do here. Keep your head on straight. Remember, we're here for a reason."

"Okay, okay. But I'm *soooo* excited."

Rob Thigpen wandered around behind the stage and spotted a bunch of cables exiting the stage and followed them back to a hallway. A security guard spotted Rob and approached him.

"Excuse me sir. Can I help you?"

"Yes, I'm with *da* convention. Can you show me where *da* restroom is?"

"Yes sir, it's right down the hall on your right."

"*Tank* you." Rob walked to the bathroom and pushed open the door. He didn't have to go, so he washed his hands and peered out the door to see if he was being watched. Walking further down the hallway, he spotted a room with a multitude of computers, cables, and blinking lights. Rob walked nonchalantly past the glass pane windows to see a young man in his early 20s inspecting a computer cable.

"Bingo," thought Rob. "This is the MDF." He walked back out to the open floor and called Kitty.

"Kitty, I found *da* MDF. It's down a hallway behind *da* stage."

"Great!"

"Now here is where I need you ladies. Which one of you is *da* best at flirting? I need a cougar to take on a young lion."

"Melanie and Kim can do it."

"We need to get a copy of a key for *da* MDF room. Perhaps you ladies could do your *dhing* and snag his keys for me. Then I'll go to a *locksmid* and have a copy made."

"How are we going to get his keys?" asked Kitty.

"Let's call Melanie and Kim and we'll meet outside where we first met earlier."

"What did you have in mind, Rob?" asked Kim.

"I'd like you two to seduce *da* young man who works in *da* MDF room. I can give you a mickey to slip in his drink. He'll be out for several hours, which gives us enough time to have a copy made and return his keys. How does *dat* sound?"

"Sounds great. I think Mel and I can handle this guy."

"Okay, you two go back and do your *dhing*. Kitty and I will go across the street and have a few drinks until we hear from you. Don't take too long because I have to get a copy made and get it back to you. Here, just slip this powder in his drink when he's not looking. He'll pass out in a few minutes and won't remember a *dhing*."

"Sounds like you've done this before, Rob," said Melanie.

"I've been an investigator for years. Hell, I 'hink I'm going to write a book. I don't have to make any stuff up because it all happened. And don't talk to me about marriage. Some married people do some crazy stuff."

"Bo is probably the biggest hound dog of 'em all," said Kitty. "Okay, you cougars, go get him!"

Melanie and Kim headed down the hallway and spotted the young man Bo told them about coming out of the MDF room.

"Excuse me, but I heard Van Halen is going to perform here. Is that true?"

"Yes, ma'am, it is."

"I'm *sooo* excited," squealed Melanie. "Is there any chance of us getting to meet them backstage before they play?"

"That's not possible, ma'am. Security is going to be pretty tight tomorrow."

"What about tonight? Aren't they going to do a dress rehearsal?"

"Yes, but that's closed to the public."

"Well, I think the two of us could probably get you to change your mind. What's your name?" asked Melanie as she swirled her fingers through his hair."

"Jason."

"The first thing you can do, Jason, is take us to the bar across the street and buy us a drink. Do you think you can get away for a few minutes and do that for us?"

"Sure. One drink won't hurt. But we have to be back soon."

Melanie and Kim walked on either side of him, and Jason walked triumphantly out of the arena with a girl on each arm to the bar across the street.

"You ladies must really like Van Halen," said Jason. "My father really likes them."

"How old are you?" asked Melanie as they took a seat at the bar."

"Twenty-two. I just graduated from college."

"Oh my god, we've got a baby on our hands," said Kim. "We won't tell you how old we are. Let's just say that we're experienced."

"The best way to start this is with some shots of liquor," said Melanie. "You give Kim here some Jack Daniels and she goes wild."

"Then Jack Daniels it is. Bartender, three shots of Jack Daniels with a Coke chaser," said Jason.

Melanie and Kim sat on either side of Jason at the bar. Melanie started rubbing his thigh while the bartender came back with their shots.

"Here's to Van Halen," said Jason as he raised his shot glass. Melanie and Kim clinked their shot glasses to his, and all three downed their shots. Melanie and Kim slammed their shot glasses down quickly. Jason stood up and coughed out one of his lungs.

"Not used to straight Jack Daniels, huh?" asked Melanie as Kim poured the powder Rob had given them into the Coke chaser. Jason finally stopped coughing and reached for the Coke chaser downing most of it.

"You ladies need a chaser?" asked Jason with tears still in his eyes.

"Nah, we're used to it," said Kim. "So tell me, what do you do there at the convention center?"

"I run the audio visual equipment from the control room."

"Really," said Melanie. "So you have your own little private room to work out of, huh? Does it have a lock?"

"Yes, it does, but there is a window. It's not a good place for privacy, if that's what you mean."

"That's exactly what I mean. If the three of us were to go there, you'd be the only one with a key, right?" asked Melanie.

"Right."

"So no one else could get in." said Kim.

"That's true, but people could still see in," said Jason.

"That's the thrill of it. It's the possibility of getting caught that is so exciting."

"I guess you're right. Hey, is it getting a little hot in here? I'm feeling a little woozy."

"What's the matter, honey? Was that shot of whiskey too much for you all at once?"

"No, I'm just…not feeling real well all of a sudden. I feel like I could go to sleep." Jason tried to stand from his barstool and fell in a heap on the floor.

"Kim," whispered Melanie, "Look in his pockets for a key."

Melanie reached into his right front pocket and found nothing. She stuck her hand in his left pocket and pulled out a single unmarked key.

"This has to be it. There are no other keys," said Kim.

"I'll call Rob and give this to him," said Melanie. "In the meantime, you can probably lay him down on that bench over there until he comes to."

The bartender leaned over to look at Jason. "That's the most pitiful thing I've ever seen. One shot and he hits the floor. What a lightweight," laughed the bartender.

"Can we set him over here on this bench for a little while?" asked Kim.

"Sure. Is he gonna be okay?"

"Yeah, I think he just needs to rest a little. Can you help us put him over there?" asked Kim.

"Of course." The bartender helped Melanie and Kim pick up the unconscious Jason and set him on a bench near the restrooms.

"Thank you," said Kim to the bartender. "I'll sit with him for a little while until he comes to."

"I'll call you in a little bit," said Melanie as she turned to leave. "You take care of our little Jason."

"I will," said Kim as she sat down on the bench and put Jason's head in her lap. She gently ran her fingers through his hair. He was knocked out completely from whatever Rob gave them to put in his drink. "Poor kid," thought Kim. "He coulda had a good time tonight."

Melanie called Rob as soon as she walked out of the bar.

"I think we've got the key. Where are you?"

"Right behind you," said Rob.

"What do you mean right behind me?"

Rob reached out and tapped Melanie on the shoulder as she turned around.

"You scared me! I didn't expect you to be breathing down my neck."

"I saw ya'll walking arm in arm with him into *da* bar, and I've been waiting out here for you. You gals are fast workers."

"Well, you know us cougars. We pounce on our prey. Here's the key."

"Good work. Why don't you go back into *da* bar and have a drink while I go get *da* spare made?"

"Okay. You don't have to hurry. I think the kid will be out for quite a while."

"I'll be back with *da* key in twenty minutes. I've already looked up *da* closest *locksmid*." Rob hailed a cab and hopped in while Melanie went back into the bar to check on Kim and Jason.

"How's he doin'?"

"Purring like a kitten. He looks so peaceful."

"How 'bout a beer while we wait for Rob?"

"Sure," said Kim. "Jason isn't going anywhere."

Thirty minutes later Rob came back from the locksmith. He handed the key back to Kim and she discreetly put it back into Jason's pocket.

"Now that we have the key, how are we going to get into the room tomorrow without being noticed?" asked Melanie.

"I haven't figured *dat* out yet," said Rob. "I figured you ladies could use your cougar skills again."

"Jason won't remember a thing, but we'll make him think we're coming back for more," laughed Kim.

Meanwhile Bo had called girlfriend number one as soon as Kitty left. He had arranged to meet her at the Park Hyatt Hotel about fifteen minutes from the convention center. Bo hadn't seen this girlfriend in several years, but he remembered she was very attractive. Bo was psyched to finally get to spread his wings without his nosy wife around.

Mike Melito had checked into the Park Hyatt late in the afternoon and headed to the bar in the hotel restaurant. He took a corner seat at the bar and struck up a conversation with the bartender about the Toronto Blue Jays. A few minutes later an attractive brunette sat two seats down from Mike. She was by herself and wore a short, tight, white skirt and a maroon strapless halter top. Before she could get the bartender's attention, Mike introduced himself.

"Hi, I'm Mike Melito. Whatcha drinkin'?"

"A seabreeze," she said with a smile.

"Phil, could you get this beautiful lady a seabreeze please?"

"Sure thing, Mike."

"Hi, I'm Melody Redd." She loved the way Mike effortlessly and smoothly introduced himself and ordered her drink for her.

"Are you from here or visiting?" asked Mike.

"I'm visiting from Chicago."

"What a great city. Do you live near the Magnificent Mile shopping district?"

"Yes, I do. I love shopping there."

"Yeah, so do I. Are you here on business or pleasure?"

"Business and pleasure. I'm here for the Bio Strength international convention."

"You're kidding. So am I. I came from Jacksonville, Florida. How long have you been in the business?"

"About four years now. I love the products."

"I do, too. They got rid of my shoulder pain right away. It's amazing. I jumped right on board after that and have almost equaled my earnings from my restaurant. I'll sell the restaurant in another year or so and live off Bio Strength."

"It's funny that you own a restaurant. My father owned an Italian Restaurant in Chicago. I lived in it as a kid."

The bartender watched in amazement as Mike schmoozed his way with her. He had seen thousands of lounge lizards in his day, but none was as suave and silky smooth as Mike Melito.

"So are you meeting someone tonight?" asked Mike. He was hoping the answer was no, but he figured she was too hot to be spending the night alone.

"As a matter of fact, I am. I'm meeting an old friend. Oh, there he is right now."

Mike turned around to see Bo Valentine walking towards them.

"You're not meeting Bo Valentine, are ya?"

"Yes, I am."

"Did you know he's married and his wife is here in town with him?"

"He told me he was separated. So he is still married?"

"Oh, yeah. I better shut up now," said Mike as Bo came over to hug Melody.

"Melody, you look fantastic," said Bo. "How long has it been-two or three years?"

Melody got off her barstool and faced Bo. "You lying son of a bitch," said Melody as she slapped him hard across the face.

"What the hell was that for?" asked Bo stunned.

"Oh, this drink is from your wife." Melody picked up her seabreeze and sloshed the contents into Bo's face. "My friend Mike here told me you were still married, you lying scum bag," said Melody as she stormed out of the bar.

Bo stood there beside Mike dripping wet and stinging from her vicious slap. He wiped his eyes clear and squinted to see who it was who had ratted him out.

"Melito? What the hell are you doing here?"

"Bio Strength asked me to do a survey on how many of their top producers screw around on their wives. And guess what? Your name appeared first. Isn't that funny?"

"This is none of your business," yelled Bo.

"It sure is my business. Melody is a friend of mine, and she deserves a lot better than you."

"How long have you known her?"

"Oh, about 10 minutes, but I plan on getting to know her a *lot* better," said Mike mockingly.

"So that's why you snitched on me. I always heard you were an asshole," said Bo as he stuck his pointed finger into Mike's chest on the word *asshole*.

Bo had done the one thing that set Mike off more than anything. He absolutely hated anyone sticking a pointed finger into his chest. To Mike it was an act of war. The next second or two was pure instinct taking over Mike. He threw a fierce punch directly into Bo's left eye. Bo had no time to react, and the punch sent him reeling against the table behind him.

"Come on, Bo. Wanna fight for your woman? I'm gonna make some sweet music with Melody tonight," said Mike as he danced around with his arms up ready for a fight. Bo held his hand over his eye. It stung like hell, and he knew he was going to have a shiner. The bartender held his breath hoping the inevitable fight wouldn't destroy his bar.

Bo felt like he could take Mike down, but he remembered he was going to be speaking in front of a huge audience the next day. Any more bruises or scrapes would be hard to explain away as just a clumsy fall. Bo turned around, walked out of the hotel and hailed a cab back to his hotel. Mike stopped his Ali dance moves and thrust his arms in the air.

"Yes, I *am* the greatest!" He shadow boxed a few more times and sat back down at the bar.

"Is this a typical day for you, Mike?" asked the bartender.

"Not really. I haven't gotten the girl yet, but I suspect she will be arriving shortly."

Just as Mike predicted, Melody came back to the bar to see him.

"I watched you from the lobby, and I've never seen Bo turn and run like that."

"I like to fight for what I believe in. You seemed like the right person to fight for. Can I interest you in front row seats at the convention tomorrow?"

"Really? You're in the front row?"

"Yeah. It'll be a great view of Van Halen when they open up the convention. My good friend and sponsor Paul Cousins is going to be onstage with the band."

"Wow, am I glad I met you. That sounds like an offer too good to refuse."

Meanwhile Paul and Joanne were eating dinner before Van Halen's sound check. Paul was giddy with excitement over his chance to meet the band.

"What time does the rehearsal start?" asked Joanne.

"8:00," said Paul.

"What do we wear?" asked Joanne.

"Hell, I don't know. I really don't think the band cares."

"Well, I do. I want to make a good impression on David Lee Roth. Who knows if I'll ever get to meet him again."

"I'm just a little nervous. We should leave in a little bit to get to the convention center. I don't want to be late."

Paul and Joanne left their room at 7:30 to head to the convention center. At 7:40 they walked into the arena to find a few workers milling around, but it was mostly quiet on the set.

"We must be early," said Paul. He approached a man carrying a stack of cables beside the stage.

"Excuse me, what time does Van Halen come out to rehearse?"

"You just missed them."

"What do you mean?"

"They decided to come out early. All they needed was one take. Those guys are seasoned veterans."

Paul was dumbfounded. "But I'm supposed to be on stage with them tomorrow. I thought we were going to do a take or two together."

"Nobody told us you were supposed to be here. Besides, we had another problem. Nobody could find the audio/video guy to run the video on the big screen during the song. He's the only guy with a key to the MDF, so we just went on without him. We called him dozens of times, but he never answered. Kinda strange."

Paul sat down in a chair and put his head in his hands. Joanne could see the energy draining from his body.

"Honey, it's okay. You've still got tomorrow. Don't worry."

"I know. But I was so looking forward to this. I can't believe I missed it."

"That's rock and roll," said Joanne.

At 11:15 p.m. Jason was still fast asleep on the bench at the bar. The wait staff had taken turns completely covering his face with whipped cream, and they were waiting for him to wake up. One of the waitresses couldn't wait any longer, and she shook Jason.

"Hey, are you all right? Wake up. Hey, it's time to get up, come on."

Jason mumbled something and reached up to rub his face. His hands were completely lathered in whipped cream.

"What the…" said Jason as he rolled off the bench and hit the floor.

"*Oowww*," yelled Jason. "Where am I? What time is it?"

The wait staff started laughing at the whipped cream covered young man.

"It's 11:20, and you're in the best bar in all of Toronto."

"11:20?!" Jason pulled out his cell phone to check his voicemail. His phone slipped out of his fingers like a bar of soap. He could make out that he had over 20 voicemails.

"I'm in big trouble," thought Jason as he ran out the door. People on the street gawked at the whipped cream-faced drunk running out of a bar. He grabbed his shirt tail and wiped his face as best as he could. He could not believe he had passed out after only one drink. Then he remembered talking to some ladies at the bar, and after that everything was blank. He ran across the street and into the convention center. The doors were locked, and he really started to panic. He called his boss from his cell.

"Hey, John, I know it's late, but I had something really strange happen…."

"Yeah, I can't wait to hear this one. We tried calling you dozens of times tonight for the dress rehearsal, but you wouldn't pick up. You're the only one with a key to the MDF, so we had to go ahead without you. Van Halen wanted to get going early, and we tried to call you. They just did one take and called it a night.

We just left the video portion out of the dress rehearsal. I'm hoping you can wake up in time to work tomorrow," said John sarcastically.

"Oh, man, I don't know what happened. Some ladies bought me a drink, and then I remember nothing."

"That's a good one. Can't you be a little more original? Listen, if you don't show up tomorrow, don't worry about ever working for me again."

"Got it," said Jason as he swallowed hard. He knew he had to be the first one at the convention center tomorrow.

Paul got ready for bed early. Tomorrow was going to be the biggest day of his life.

"Do you have a spare battery for the video camera?" asked Paul.

"Yes, honey. Don't worry. I'm taking care of everything."

"I just want to be able to remember tomorrow forever."

Joanne bit her lip one last time. There was no turning back now. It killed her to watch Paul get so excited as she knew it would be a fleeting moment before the inevitable collapse of Bio Strength. All his hopes and dreams would come crashing down like a giant wave breaking on the shore. She steeled her nerves and reminded herself for the thousandth time that she was doing the right thing. The only thing she was certain of was that her life would be forever changed after tomorrow.

"I can't wait until tomorrow," said Paul sitting on the edge of his bed. "I love you so much."

Joanne sat on the edge of the bed and hugged Paul. She could feel the sincerity in his voice, and it cut her like a knife. "I love you, too."

Chapter 24

Thousands of eager Bio Strength distributors from around the world descended on the Toronto convention center hours before the official convention kick-off. The exhibition hall next door was filled with displays of Bio Strength products and industry experts touting the benefits of the lotions, sunscreens and nutritional drinks. Doctors stood in their white doctor garb answering questions, including Dr. Roy Garfinkel. Several people were surrounding him, hanging on his every word. There were thousands of new distributors who had just signed up with eager expectations of getting rich.

Carlos milled around the hall taking in all the excitement. He caught sight of Paul and Joanne entering the exhibition hall. Carlos weaved through the crowd to Paul.

"Hey, Paul. Are you ready for the big time? How do you feel?"

"I feel great. I just wish I hadn't missed the dress rehearsal last night."

"You missed it? You're kidding. How did that happen?"

"It doesn't matter now," said Joanne. "He's ready to rock."

"What song are they gonna play?" asked Carlos.

"I don't know. I guess I'll find out backstage. Man, there are a ton of people here."

"Yeah, there are a lot of new people here taking in their first big convention. Most of them just like getting out of the house and going on a trip. They probably won't be in the business in a couple of years. Then there are some distributors who pay big bucks to pay the way for their prospects to come look at the "big picture." I never did that sort of prospecting. It can work, but it just costs too damn much for me."

"Everything costs too much for you, Carlos," said Paul.

"You're right about that. Hey, don't you think you should be going back to meet the band?"

"Yeah, I guess so. I'm nervous as hell. What do I do onstage?"

"Just be yourself," said Carlos.

"I had a feeling you were going to say that. Okay, are you ready, Joanne?"

"Let's do it," said Joanne.

"Break a leg," smiled Carlos.

"Thanks," said Paul nervously.

Paul led Joanne towards the stage. He showed his credentials to security, and he kissed Joanne goodbye before heading backstage.

"Good luck, honey."

"This is it. I can't believe it," said Paul.

"Go for it. I'll get it all on video. Have fun."

Joanne turned around to see the convention center filling up early. It was over an hour before the start, but people wanted to get a good view of Van Halen. The seats on the floor were all reserved and were held for high-ranking distributors and their families and guests. Paul had six seats reserved on the front row.

Rob, Melanie, Kitty, and Kim were hatching their plan outside the hallway leading to the MDF room. Rob saw Jason hard at work in the control room both times he walked past.

"Okay, here's *da* plan," said Rob with all three ladies listening intently on either side of him. "We're just going to have to use some more of your charms to get him out here when Bo starts speaking. If you can get him into *da* men's restroom, I'll blindfold him and tie him up. *Dat* will give me enough time to get in and play our little video. How does *dat* sound?"

"Is that all you got?" asked Kitty. "I mean, I'm paying you good money to come up here, and your plan is for us to do all the work."

"You got any better ideas?" asked Rob.

"Why don't you go in there and knock him out or something? That's what they would do on the show *24*."

"This ain't TV, Kitty, and I don't want to be charged *wid* assault."

265

"Oh, so kidnapping is better than assault."

"Yes, especially since he'll never see my face. I'll blindfold him and tie him up. Someone will eventually come find him. And besides, you ladies are much prettier *dhan* me. He'd never come outta *dat* room for me."

"We'll try it," said Kim.

"Remember, we don't make our move until Bo gets up to speak," said Rob.

The convention center was a complete sellout, and it was just two minutes before the start of the show. Paul saw David Lee Roth walk up back stage with the rest of the band. His jeans and black tank top proved he was still in great shape. Paul took a deep breath and went to introduce himself.

"Hi, I'm Paul Cousins, and I'm the guy that's gonna come with you on stage. What do you want me to do?" asked Paul nervously.

"Man, just have fun," said David. "It's just rock n' roll."

"What song are you gonna play?"

"Jump." Oh, yeah. That reminds me. We were gonna have you enter through a trap door under the stage after the song starts, but you missed the rehearsal for it. Do you still wanna try it? It's really cool. Just stand up straight, and they'll tell you when you're goin' up. Jagger used to do it with the Stones. It's quite a bold entrance."

"Hell yeah, I'll do it," said Paul.

"Let me get the stage manager and tell him," said David. He motioned for a man to come over and talk to them.

"Yes, David?" said the stage manager.

"Paul wants to enter through the trap door. Do we still have time to show him?"

"If we hurry. Follow me, Paul."

The manager led Paul underneath the stage through a maze of cables and supports. A small light illuminated where the trap door was.

"Jimmy, can you lower the trap door for us? Our guest wants to try it," said the manager through a two-way radio."

"Sure thing."

The trap door measured three feet by three feet and was slowly lowered to the floor of the sub-stage. Light trickled in through the opening above revealing the small section of hardwood platform that was to become Paul's launching pad.

"Just stand on this, keep your arms to your side, and watch for my count. You'll enter about a minute into the song. Okay?" said the stage manager.

"Okay," said Paul nervously. He felt like a kid going on his first roller coaster ride.

"We've got 30 seconds until the start. Just keep your eyes on me for the count, and bend your knees when you land, for god's sake."

Joe Martini stood at the back of the arena with two high-ranking FDA officials and four federal agents. Joe was going to make this the most spectacular bust of his career. He would honor Joanne's request for Paul to have his thrills, but then he would make his move.

Kitty, Melanie, and Kim went through their plans to hijack Jason from the control room one more time. They had prime seats, front row center, to see Bo's reaction when the video aired.

Carlos sat in the front row on stage right beside Joanne. He turned and looked at her with a huge grin. She knew how proud Carlos was of Paul. Mike Melito sat on the other side of Carlos with his arm around Melody Redd, the woman he had just met when he punched Bo. Melody was as happy as a sixteen-year-old on her first date.

The convention center lights turned off, and the crowd roared in anticipation. The atmosphere was just like a rock concert from the 80s.

"Ladies and gentlemen," began the master of ceremonies, "Welcome to the Bio Strength international convention. We are thrilled to have a legendary rock band open our show for us. Everybody, give it up for *Van Halen*!"

The opening chords for "Jump" filled the arena, and the entire crowd of 10,000 rose to their feet at the sound of the instantly recognizable hit song from the 80s.

David Lee Roth opened his arms up to the crowd and embraced the pulsing energy he received from them. Paul stood on the sub-stage platform and watched the stage manager intently for his cue.

"I get *up*, and nothing gets me down," sang David Lee Roth in the first line. Mike and Melody rushed from their seats to the security fence in front of the stage. The stage manager counted down as Paul watched…three, two, one….

The platform blasted up through the opening, and in an instant Paul was airborne and flying five feet above the stage. His stomach rose into his throat as he emerged from darkness into the lights. David Lee Roth spotted Paul erupting from the hole in the stage, and he sang the words, "You might as well….*Jump!*"

Paul started his free fall back to the stage and remembered to bend his knees on impact. He prayed he wouldn't fall flat on his face. Joanne had no idea Paul would be making his entrance this way. Her camera was focused on David Lee Roth, and she spotted someone shooting up from the stage like a rocket. It happened so quickly that she didn't recognize that it was Paul.

Paul landed perfectly on his two feet and seamlessly joined in with the band. He mouthed the words, "You might as well….*Jump!*" Paul strutted around on stage as the crowd went wild seeing one of their own jamming with Van Halen.

Carlos stood with his mouth wide open watching the spectacle in front of him. Paul was having the time of his life dancing and high-fiving David Lee Roth. Eddie Van Halen broke into a searing guitar solo, and Paul fell to his knees beside him and played a vicious air guitar solo. The crowd was going bonkers and jumped in the air in sync whenever David Lee Roth sang the word *Jump*.

As the song reached its climax during a keyboard solo, David Lee Roth put his mouth up to Paul's ear to instruct him what to do next.

"I'll climb these speakers here, and you climb the speakers over there. Look for my lead, and we'll jump down to the stage together."

Paul nodded his head and headed to the speaker stack. He looked out at the audience waving their hands and screaming, and he realized this was not a dream. He saw Joanne filming with her video camera and Carlos smiling from ear to ear. He stood tall and proud as if he had just climbed Mt. Everest. David Lee Roth gave the signal, and they leapt in the air and landed on the stage simultaneously. Huge pyrotechnic flashes exploded on their impact, and billows of white smoke filled the air. A large net above the stage released a huge cache of fake dollar bills that rained down upon the stage. David Lee Roth gave the microphone to Paul to sing the last "you might as well....*Jump*!" He high-fived Paul again as the song ended, and the rest of the band joined Roth and Paul at the front of the stage for a curtain call bow. Paul waved and exited the stage with the band.

"That was fucking *awesome*!" screamed Paul to Roth backstage.

"Man, that was like you've done this a thousand times. It was perfect," said David Lee Roth.

"I've done it in my mind a thousand times before," said Paul.

The crowd was going absolutely nuts and stood clamoring for more music. Carlos had been to dozens of conventions over the years, but the opening for this one was the best he had seen by far.

"That was fantastic. Let's thank Van Halen again for starting our convention with a bang," said the master of ceremonies who had walked on stage to a scattering of boos.

"I'm David Taylor, director of communications for Bio Strength. I know you want to hear more from the band, and we'll have them out again later. The person on stage with the band was our distributor of the year, Paul Cousins. Can we bring him out again?"

The crowd gave Paul a standing ovation as he came back on stage and waved.

"Great job, Paul. Congratulations!" said David. "I'd like to bring up our first speaker who has had tremendous success with Bio Strength. He is a Royal Diamond distributor, and he is going to tell us what he has learned along the way in his voyage with Bio Strength. Let's hear it for Bo Valentine!"

Kitty was completely surprised that Bo was speaking so soon. She motioned for Melanie and Kim to follow her, and they quickly left their seats to head towards the control room. Rob Thigpen had been wandering around waiting while carrying his laptop. Convention center security let him bring it in without a carrying case.

Kitty, Melanie, and Kim approached the control room while Rob waited in the bathroom. Jason was alone in the room and hard at work when he spotted someone waving at him from the window. He turned around to see all three ladies smiling and pursing their lips at him. Kim bent over to make sure he got an eyeful of her cleavage.

Jason walked over to the door and stuck his head out. "I'm a little busy right now, ladies. Can you come back later?"

"We know you're a busy boy with such an important job, but you were so good to us yesterday that we just had to come back for more," said Melanie.

"You can come back later, but I'm busy now. Hey, what the hell happened yesterday? I was having a few drinks, and the next thing I knew I was on a bench."

"Oh, you don't remember? Well, we'll just have to give you a taste of what's coming to you later," said Kitty as she grabbed his wrists and pulled him into the hallway. She pulled Jason close into her and laid a huge kiss on him as Melanie and Kim ran their fingers through his hair.

"Just come in the bathroom here for just a minute," breathed Kitty heavily into his ear. "All we need is a minute," said Kim as they pushed him towards the bathroom. Jason was helpless to resist the three of them pushing him into the bathroom.

"You ladies promise not to get me in trouble this time? 'Cause my boss was real mad at me yesterday…."

Rob was waiting behind the door and grabbed him from behind. He cuffed and blindfolded Jason in an instant.

"What the hell is going on?" yelled Jason. "Is this your idea of something kinky?"

"That's enough talking now, Jason," said Kitty as Rob tied a handkerchief through his mouth and around the back of his head. Rob secured Jason to the pole on the bathroom stall.

"We'll be right back, Jason. Don't you go anywhere," said Kitty as they left the bathroom. Jason tried screaming and jerking at the cuffs to no avail. The three of them calmly walked back to their seats. Kitty dreaded the thought of listening to Bo drone on and on, but she knew his speech would be cut short now. She couldn't help but notice that it looked like Bo had the beginnings of a black eye. He told her he fell the day before, but it looked exactly like someone had slugged him. He piled on tons of makeup to try to cover it up.

"I am forever grateful to Bio Strength CEO Steve Hudgins for inspiring me to reach my dreams," continued Bo. He motioned to the Bio Strength CEO who was sitting in the front row.

Rob used the spare key he had made to enter the control room. He connected his laptop to the control room computer and hit play on his laptop. No one had walked by the control room yet.

Bo was in mid-sentence when he heard a hush go up from the crowd. The huge screen behind him blinked, and the image of his wife Kitty appeared. She looked beautiful in a lace fringed navy blue dress.

"Hello, everyone," said Kitty on the screen. "I'm Kitty Valentine, Bo Valentine's wife." Bo turned around to see a 20-foot image of Kitty on the screen. He flashed a nervous smile as he turned around and gave her a weak wave. She waved back with only her fingers and a cutesy pie smile.

The head of the convention center security was baffled. He couldn't unplug the projector since it was so high in the air. He called Jason from his two-way radio.

"Jason, what the hell is going on?" he screamed. There was no answer. Jason was struggling in the bathroom to free himself. His handcuffs were made of hard plastic which enabled Rob to sneak them in past the metal detectors.

"You're probably wondering what I'm doing here on the big screen at the Bio Strength convention. Bo is most likely standing there on the stage, and I wanted to tell you about my husband of 25 years. You probably think of me as the supportive wife from all the articles and pictures of us over the years. Actually, all of that is a load of crap. Bo has been screwing around on me for years, and here are two of my friends who he screwed around with. I'd like to introduce you to Melanie Waters and Kim Davis." Melanie and Kim smiled as they watched their image on the screen.

Bo felt his chest tighten, and he started perspiring profusely. There was nowhere to hide, so he just had to stand there and take it. A steady rumble of voices could be heard throughout the convention center as people tried to determine if this was real or some practical joke.

"But that's not all I want to tell you. You see, for months the FDA has been investigating numerous complaints about side effects from Bio Strength products. I have it from a reliable source that Bio Strength is going to be shut down due to illegal steroids being detected in them. All of you need to find some other way to make a living. Especially you, Bo. Oh, by the way, I'm divorcing you today."

A man in a dark suit walked on stage and served Bo his divorce papers. Bo's face turned white as he briskly walked off stage. Rob Thigpen felt the message had gone through, so he unplugged his laptop and bolted out of the control room. The screen suddenly went blank and the crowd booed loudly.

Joe Martini stood stunned as he heard the results of his investigation being revealed.

"How the hell did she get that information," Joe said angrily to his assistant. "Okay, it's show time," he said on his radio to his cohorts as he walked up on stage and grabbed the microphone from the stand.

"Hello, I'm Joe Martini with the FDA. This is an official notice that all operations of Bio Strength are being suspended immediately. Product testing revealed steroids in all of your products. A number of Bio Strength representatives are being brought in for questioning. Cease any and all sales of these products. Thank you."

Two burly federal agents handcuffed CEO Stephen Hudgins in the front row. Mike Melito could not believe what he was seeing.

"Is this true?" Mike yelled to Stephen Hudgins as he was being escorted out.

Carlos put his head in his hands. He had been a part of dozens of network marketing companies that went under, but most went out with a slow whimper over years of declining sales. He never expected an atom bomb to be dropped on Bio Strength.

Paul came out from backstage to see what all the commotion was about. He saw two men in suits escorting out the CEO, and two others were handcuffing Bo Valentine.
He ran over to Joanne who was now crying.

"What the hell is going on?" asked Paul.

"They're busting the company. They said there are steroids in the products."

"Who is busting us?"

"The FDA."

Joanne knew she had to come clean. Her conscience was killing her.

"That man told me last week that he was gonna close down the company," said Joanne pointing to Joe Martini who was escorting Bo out of the center.

Paul was in shock. He didn't know what to say. He had never been the victim of complete betrayal like this before.

"You *knew* about this and didn't tell me? How could you do that to me!" screamed Paul.

"I didn't find out until a week ago, and you were so excited about today that I just couldn't take this away from you. Here, I've got you and Van Halen all on this disc. Honey, you were incredible. You'll have this day for the rest of your life. If I had told you, you never would have had this experience. Isn't that what life is all about…experiencing life in each moment to its fullest? Here, you take it," said Joanne as she handed him the video camera.

"You let me buy all that stuff when you knew the company was going down? I don't know what to believe now."

Carlos walked up behind Paul and placed his hand on his shoulder. Paul turned around and looked straight into Carlos's eyes. Carlos could feel Paul's pain. He had been with Paul from the beginning, and he knew how much Bio Strength meant to him.

"Carlos, let's go buddy. I know I can trust you."

"Paul, please don't leave," pleaded Joanne. "You know I didn't want to hurt you…."

"You can fly back alone," he said to Joanne. "I'm taking an early flight back to Jacksonville. I really did believe all that stuff about dreams coming true. Financial freedom, work your Plan B, and all that network marketing shit. What a load of crap that is. I bought it, and look what happened to me! I'm gonna lose everything!" yelled Paul.

"But you've still got your girl," said Joanne.

"Not anymore," said Paul as he turned to Carlos. They walked away with Paul putting his arm around Carlos's shoulder.

Joanne collapsed on her chair and cried harder than she ever had in her life. Paul was the one who she had let get close, and now he was walking away because she wanted him to fulfill his dreams. Dr. Garfinkel saw her crying and came over to console her.

"Joanne, I'm so sorry. I never suspected there were steroids in Bio Strength. My patients loved the stuff. I'm going to miss that monthly check just like you."

Joanne looked up with mascara running down her face. "It's not the money I'm going to miss. It's Paul," said Joanne as she burst into tears again and wrapped her arms around him. Dr. Garfinkel was not expecting a hug from her. She had always been a cold, calculating business person, but now he just saw her as a woman who needed a friend's shoulder to cry on. He held her and let her cry until there were no more tears left.

The convention center was almost empty, and Jason's boss walked down to the control room to look for him. He was curious as to why he had never answered his radio. The control room was open, but no one was inside. He walked down the hall and heard a muffled voice and banging from inside the bathroom. He opened the door up to see Jason handcuffed to the stall and a cloth tied inside his mouth and around his head.

"What in the world happened to you?" he asked as he pulled the cloth from Jason's mouth.

"Three ladies kidnapped me and tied me up in here," said Jason out of breath.

"Three ladies, huh? Who were they?"

"The same ladies that bought me a drink last night when I passed out."

"Really? What are their names?" asked his boss.

"Uh, I don't remember. I don't think they ever told me their names."

"So these three mysterious ladies kidnapped you, tied you up and then just left? Did they rob you?"

"Maybe they did. Hey, get these handcuffs off and I'll check my wallet."

His boss retrieved some wire cutters and easily clipped the hard plastic handcuffs. Jason reached back for his wallet and found it intact with all his cash.

"There goes the robbery theory," said his boss. "Personally, I think you're into some pretty kinky stuff. Now, I don't mind that if it doesn't affect your work, but you weren't around when we needed you two days in a row. Did you know someone hacked into our system during the convention and played an embarrassing video?"

"How could that have happened?" asked Jason. "I'm the only one with a key."

"Well, maybe while you were getting your rocks off, somebody went in there. Did you think of that? Never mind, you're fired."

Rob, Kitty, Melanie, and Kim all met for drinks across the street from the convention center.

"Here's a toast to the coolest cougars I ever worked with," said Rob raising his glass to the three ladies. By the way, you never told me who your contact was in the FDA."

"Let's just say he's no longer working there," said Kitty. "I promised him I wouldn't reveal his name. Wow, that look on Bo's face was priceless. I feel such a weight lifted off my shoulder getting rid of that man."

"I do feel a little bad about leaving Jason like that in the bathroom," said Kim.

"Poor kid," said Melanie. "He'll probably never trust an older woman again."

Chapter 25

Carlos and Paul took an early flight back from Toronto and sat by Paul's pool the next day. Carlos reviewed Paul's desperate financial situation over a couple of beers.

"How much have you saved towards your estimated taxes?" asked Carlos.

"Nothing yet. I was counting on using my future Bio Strength paychecks to take care of that."

"That was dumb. You've always gotta put away a third of your check for taxes when you're self-employed."

"I never expected Bio Strength to be shut down and my income to go from $51,000 a month to zero the next."

"Ya know ya gotta sell this house."

"I was afraid you were going to say that."

"Listen, all great business people have financial problems more than once in their lifetime. If ya built up a business once, you can build another one."

"Don't you dare talk to me about network marketing again."

"Look, I've got four other checks comin' in from other companies I've been involved with for years. Hell, I ain't gettin' rich, but at least I'm makin' a living. Let's take care of first things first. Let's sell this house."

"I guess you're right. I better do it sooner than later." Paul took a deep breath and picked up the phone to call Betty Tisdale.

"Betty, hi. It's Paul Cousins."

"Are you in jail? Every time I see you there are cops involved."

"No, I'm not in jail. I need you to sell my house for me."

"So soon? Oh, my. What do you want to ask for it?"

"The same price I paid for it. Eight ninety nine."

"Are you sure? After commissions you will have a loss on the sale."

"I'm sure. I need to sell it."

"Are you in some kind of legal trouble? Cops always seem to follow you around."

"No. Just IRS trouble."

"Oh, I'm sorry. I've got quite a few clients with tax problems. I'll do my best to sell it for you. The market has not changed much since you bought it. Most sales have a bank involved in some fashion. I'll come take a picture of it today, and it will be in the MLS this afternoon."

"Thanks, Betty."

"This is the right decision, Paul," said Carlos. "There is no way you can afford the Ferrari or the boat. You're gonna need every penny to pay the tax man."

"Where am I going to live? I've got no income coming in. What place will rent to me if I can't show an income?"

"Come stay with me. You can stay for six months max. I made the mistake of letting a cousin live with me once rent-free with no expectations on when he had to move. I finally had to throw him out. That was no fun. So remember, six months tops. I wanna remain friends with you, and if you stay too long, you'll get too comfortable. That's where the tough love comes in."

Paul looked down at his feet. He was touched that Carlos would let him move in, and humbled that he had no place to go.

"Okay. Six months max. Thanks, buddy."

"Hey, maybe Joanne will let you move in with her later."

"No way. I'm through with her. She lied to me."

"She didn't lie to you. She let you have your day in the sun. She did that because she loves ya. I bet you two kiss and make up."

"I don't want to see her. Besides, I'm on my way to having nothing again. She likes successful men, and I won't be one. Hell, I saw a homeless guy today and was jealous. He may have nothing, but I'm gonna have less than nothing real soon with all my tax debt."

"I'm just sayin', don't count her out yet."

The doorbell rang, and Paul walked around the side of the house to see who it was.

"Ernie. Hey, come on back to the pool. Carlos and I were just having a beer. How ya been?"

"Well, if you don't count the fact that my wife has filed for divorce, I got no place to live, and I was fired from my job, then everything's just rosy."

"I thought she was gonna let you stay in the house."

"She changed her mind when she found out I was fired. I lied to her and told her I was downsized. It didn't take her long to find out the truth. Then she threw me out."

"Hey, I'm gonna be homeless soon, too. My friend Carlos is letting me move in with him. I'm sure he wouldn't mind you crashing there for a little while."

"Really? That's so nice of him. See, my day has gotten better already," said Ernie as they walked to the pool.

"Hey, Carlos. I told Ernie here that I didn't think you'd mind if he crashed at your place for a little while. His wife just kicked him out, and he needs some help."

"You're kiddin', right?" asked Carlos.

"No, I'm serious. You don't mind do you?"

"Why don't you just put an ad in the paper and invite the whole damn town to come stay with me? I suppose he's got a dog, too."

"No, I don't have a dog," said Ernie. "Listen, I know it's an imposition. I can find a place somewhere."

"Oh, it's okay," said Carlos. He was mad at Paul for inviting Ernie without asking him, but the soft spot in his heart won over. "But six months is the max. That's my rule. After that your ass is out on the street."

"This is gonna be great. Three bachelors under one roof. It'll be just like college days," said Paul.

"Now I ain't no big party guy. And you can forget me helpin' you move. The last time I helped you I almost got shot during a bank robbery. I don't know why the hell I'm doin' this. I know. You guys get to do all the cookin' and cleanin'. I don't do a damn thing."

Ernie and Paul looked at each other for a second and turned to Carlos and simultaneously said, "Deal."

The next week Paul sold both his boat and his Ferrari back to the dealerships and took a killing on them. Carlos figured he would owe at least $110,000 in estimated taxes. His old Camry was still for sale in the used car lot. His car salesman Bubba Jones felt sorry for Paul and let him have it back for the trade-in price of $2,500.

"When you git rich again, come see me Mr. Cousins. We'll put you in a brand new Ferrari this time," said Bubba.

"I think I'm through with dreaming," said Paul dejectedly. "I'm just happy to have a roof over my head."

"Man, I'll never forget you and your lady comin' in that day. She was one fine lookin' woman. And that test drive, good Lord you scared the shit outta me."

"Sorry about that. Hey, thanks for everything," said Paul as he pulled away in his Camry.

Bubba stood in front of the dealership and waved goodbye. He pulled up his pants over his beer gut, scratched his rear end, and walked back inside.

Paul had sold most of his furniture on eBAY. He had one chair in his family room and the bed in his bedroom left. He was sitting in his pajamas watching television when his cell phone rang.

"Paul, it's Betty Tisdale. I've got an offer on your house."

"How much?"

"Eight forty-nine. It has no contingencies, though. I think it's a strong offer and you should take it. They are a married couple with two kids and are qualified."

"How soon do they want to close?"

"As soon as possible. Can you move out in two weeks?"

"Hell, I could move out tomorrow. There ain't nothing left in here except a chair and a bed."

"I'll bring over the contract for you to sign today. How's one 1:00?"

"I'll be here. I've got nothing else to do."

Paul realized he needed some money coming in, and he knew the job market was pretty tight. It could take months to find a good paying job, and he needed something now. He looked in the classifieds under food service and found a number of advertisements for help wanted. One classified in particular caught Paul's eye.

"Local sub shop looking for energetic, creative soul to help with advertising. Call 287-9690."

Paul picked up his cell and called the number. He loved sub sandwiches, and if he could succeed at network marketing he could certainly sell advertising. He set up an appointment with a manager named Danny that afternoon.

Paul walked into Larry's Giant Sub Shop for his interview wearing his best dark suit and black Italian leather shoes. It was 3:00, and the place was empty except for two teenage workers cleaning up from lunch.

"Excuse me, I'm looking for Danny."

"He's in the office right there," one of the teenagers said pointing to the back.

Paul walked through the kitchen into a tiny office in the back. Danny was staring intently into a computer and was oblivious to Paul's presence. Paul figured Danny was 22 years old, tops.

"Hi, I'm Paul Cousins, and I spoke to you today about the advertising job."

Danny looked up and did a double take at Paul's appearance. He was not used to gray-haired older men in expensive suits walking into his office.

"Here, fill out this application, and when you're done I'll tell you about the job."

Paul filled out the form and lied about the income he made at Bio Strength. He knew putting down an income of $350,000 for the year would not go over well. Of course, his income now was zero. Paul handed the application back to Danny, and he perused it for a moment.

"What in the world is Bio Strength?" asked Danny.

"They are, I mean were a leader in health-related products. They have recently gone out of business."

"I've never heard of them. You were earning $50,000 a year with them. Not bad."

"Yeah, I'm not earning anything now, so I really need a job. And I'm a pretty good salesman."

"Okay, here's the job. We need someone to help bring more customers in for lunch. The hours are 11a.m. to 1 p.m. Monday through Friday."

"That's it?" asked Paul.

"Yup. You're the first person to respond to the ad, so you get the job."

"Fantastic!" said Paul excitedly. When can I start?"

"Tomorrow. Here's what you're gonna need." Danny turned around to a locker and opened it up. He pulled out a large black gorilla head and gorilla suit.

"It gets pretty damn hot in there, so you'll need a five-minute break every 30 minutes. You have to go around back to take it off. We can't have you coming out of character out by the street."

"You want me to be a gorilla?"

"That's right. What did you think the job was?"

"I thought I'd be promoting your restaurant, but I didn't think I'd be wearing a damn gorilla outfit."

"Hey, it's more fun than you think. Just drink lots of water before you come. Come around 10:30 tomorrow and I'll help you get the outfit on. By the way, the pay is $30 a day. It's an easy $150 per week."

Paul left wondering what in the hell he had agreed to. He'd have to find several more jobs to scrape by, but at least he had a start. He had driven by many people over the years holding advertising signs hawking places like restaurants, furniture stores, golf shops and home builders. He remembered feeling sorry for these people standing by the road waving at motorists, and he could never imagine making a fool of himself out in the heat. Paul wondered how low you have to stoop to stand by the road with a sign and wave at people. Now he was going to be one of them in a gorilla outfit.

Paul drank six glasses of water in the morning before showing up at 10:30. He was too embarrassed to tell Carlos what he was doing. Maybe he would tell him after he moved in with him in a couple of weeks. Danny helped Paul into the gorilla suit, and handed him a sign that said "*You'll go APE over Larry's Giant Subs.*"

"Stand on the sidewalk and wave at people," said Danny. "Our research has shown that an effective street advertising person can increase business by 30 percent on any given day. Your job is just to get people to notice you. Do that any way you can, short of running in front of their car."

Paul took the sign and trudged towards his station on the sidewalk. It was already stuffy in the suit, but fortunately several large oak trees with overhanging branches covered with Spanish moss provided shade. He had never felt so self-conscious in his life. Then he remembered that no one would know who he was. He started by waving politely as cars whizzed by. He got a few stares, but after a few minutes he got bored and decided to ham it up a bit. He had seen some pretty outrageous acting street advertiser kids dancing to their iPod music before. If acting is what they wanted, then that is what they were going to get.

Paul beat his chest like a gorilla and jumped up and down. He stuck the sign in the ground so he could act out his part better. He knew he was supposed to hold the sign, but who was going to turn him in? The sign police? Paul started to get a few smiles and waves from passing motorists. Most people just drove by without reacting, but Paul got immense satisfaction from making people smile. He would wave and point to Larry's Subs, and he started doing forward rolls on the grass and hopping around like a complete lunatic. Paul got completely into character and started having serious fun with it.

After 30 minutes, Paul was drenching wet, and the suit began to smell like dirty gym socks. He also had to pee really badly, and he walked quickly to the back of the store and removed his gorilla head. His hair was sopping wet, and he stepped in the back door of the restaurant to splash cold water on his face. Getting in and out of the outfit was harder than he thought, and he fell and knocked the bathroom trash can over while standing on one leg to undress. Air conditioning never felt so good. He put his suit back on and poured some of the jug of ice water he had brought with him down the front of his suit. He put his head back on and returned to gorilla duty.

The next two half-hour stints were much busier than the first due to the lunch hour crowd looking for a place to eat. Paul was having a ball monkeying around and waving and pointing to Larry's Giant Subs. He was so hot he wasn't sure he could make the last 30 minute session. He burst open the rear door of the restaurant and headed straight for the bathroom. He thought he must have lost five pounds in less than two hours. He had one more session to go. Paul decided to calmly wave to people the last session. He was so spent, and he didn't want to completely burn out in his first day. He was hot, thirsty, and smelly, and after downing the last of his water he took it easy the last 30 minutes. Paul walked back to the restaurant and walked in the front with his full gorilla suit on. All the customers applauded when he walked in. Paul forgot he was supposed to come in the back entrance, and Danny came over to greet him.

"Man, you were awesome," said Danny. "The customers loved it, and we were up 25 tickets over last Monday. Every person asked who the new gorilla was."

"Do I have to wear this every time?" asked Paul. "I don't think I can get this smell off of me."

"We air the suit out with a fan. No, you don't have to wear it every day, but you sure had good results. Will you be back tomorrow?"

"Sure. I just hope it's a little cooler."

Paul spent the next two weeks getting more creative with his antics. He brought a golf club and swung and pointed it in the direction of the restaurant. One day he brought a ladder and hung from a low lying branch. He brought bananas and ate them under a polka-dot umbrella. Carlos drove by one day to check out his new gorilla job. He smiled and waved at him as he drove by, and Paul beat his chest and roared like a real gorilla. Paul had even looked at videos of gorillas in captivity to try to mimic them. The weather cooled off into the upper 70s, so it made wearing the gorilla suit a little more bearable. On Friday of his second week he scheduled the closing on his house at Burton & Burton for 2 p.m. That would give him just enough time to do his gorilla gig and go home to shower off his gorilla funk.

Paul kept his cell nearby in case the Burton law firm had any questions for the closing. His phone rang during the busy lunch hour at 12:30, and he could see that it was the law firm calling him.

"Hello," said Paul through his gorilla head.

"Mr. Cousins, this is the Burton law firm. We had you down for a noon closing today. Are you on your way?"

"Noon? I thought it was at two."

"No, but we can still squeeze you in if you can get here in the next few minutes."

"Okay, I'll be right there." Paul panicked and walked over to pick up his chair, golf club and sign. A policeman seemed to come from nowhere and approach Paul.

"Excuse me sir, but you're supposed to be holding your sign. You are in violation of the local sign ordinance."

Paul couldn't believe it. There really was such a thing as the sign police.

"I promise I'll hold it next time. I'm sorry, but I have some business to attend to."

"I'm sorry, too, because I'm going to have to arrest you," said the officer as he handcuffed Paul. Passing motorists got to see the first-ever arrest of a gorilla.

"What the hell…you're kidding me. You can't arrest me for not holding a sign. That's ridiculous!"

"There have been numerous warnings to your restaurant. I suppose they never told you," said the officer as he opened his squad car door for Paul to get in.

"Listen, officer. I promise I'll hold the sign from now on. Who complained about a dancing gorilla not holding a sign? Oh, I know. It must have been other restaurants close by who didn't like it that I was stealing their business. That's it, isn't it?"

"It doesn't matter who complained, but I didn't write the law. I just enforce them."

"I know you're just doing your job, but could you do me a huge favor? I'm late for the closing on my house, and I need to sell it right away. You see, I'm in a little trouble with the IRS."

"I see. You're the gorilla who didn't pay his taxes. Priceless."

"I was wondering if you could take me to my attorney's office first and then take me to the police station. You can follow me in there if you want. This is very important to me."

"Where is your attorney located?"

"Burton & Burton on San Jose Blvd."

"Oh, I know where they are. Okay, you don't look like a gorilla that would run away."

"Could you also uncuff me so I can take this gorilla head off? It gets pretty damn hot in here."

"Sorry, sir. I can't uncuff you until you get to the station. Police regulations."

"How am I supposed to sign all those papers with handcuffs on? And I don't think it's legal for a gorilla to sell a house."

"Where there's a will there's a way," said the officer as they pulled into the parking lot of Burton & Burton.

Betty Tisdale checked her watch for the tenth time in the Burton Law firm office with Mr. Burton and Carlos present. Carlos had introduced himself as Paul's financial advisor and asked to be present at the closing. Betty got up to look out the window for Paul to arrive. She saw a police car pulling into the lot, and Betty's jaw dropped when she saw the officer get out and let a handcuffed gorilla out of the back seat.

"I think Mr. Cousins is here," said Betty.

"Good," said Mr. Burton still sitting at his desk. "We'll make it just in time."

The officer led Paul up the stairs and into the waiting room of Burton & Burton. The same receptionist was working away at her computer when they entered. She asked "May I help you," without looking up from her computer. The officer escorted Paul from behind as they approached the receptionist.

"Yes, I'm here for my closing," said Paul from behind his gorilla head.

"Name please."

"Paul Cousins."

"Whoa, who are you?" exclaimed the receptionist as she glanced up to see a policeman standing behind a handcuffed gorilla. "Is this some kind of joke?"

"No ma'am," said the officer. I have him under arrest and need to escort him to the police station after his closing. I can't uncuff him until we are there."

"I'll be right back," said the receptionist as she ran back to Mr. Burton's office.

"Mr. Burton. You won't believe who…what just walked in."

"Is it Mr. Cousins painted green this time?" asked Mr. Burton.

"No, let me go get them."

"Who is *them*?" Mr. Burton asked as the receptionist went back to the lobby. She escorted Paul in full gorilla gear into the closing room handcuffed, with an officer right behind.

Carlos burst out laughing when Paul walked in.

"Mr. Cousins," said Mr. Burton, "you certainly make my job interesting. This will be my first closing ever for a gorilla with a police escort. And a handcuffed one at that."

"What the hell are you doing here?" Paul said to Carlos.

"Paul, this is priceless. First you show up in blue paint, but this one takes the cake," said Carlos as he laughed hysterically.

"It's not funny," said Paul. "And could someone please take my gorilla head off? I'm about to burn up in here."

Carlos got up and walked over to Paul and removed his head. He smiled at Paul and said, "Happy April Fools, Paul."

Paul stood stunned without uttering a word for a few seconds.

"You mean this is a set-up?"

"Yeah, I set it all up. My friend Bill Simmons here with the police department agreed to go in on this," said Carlos as Bill uncuffed Paul's hands. I also called Mr. Burton and pretended to be you and moved your closing time up. They had no clue."

"So I'm not under arrest?"

"No sir," said Officer Simmons, "but you *are* supposed to hold your sign. Carlos, I've got to get back to work. Good seeing you, buddy."

"Thanks for pitchin' in here. Nice job. Now go get some real criminals," said Carlos.

"I'm gonna kill you," said an exasperated Paul.

"Oh, yeah? Then where are you gonna live after you sign these papers? Hell, I thought we could all use a laugh after what we've been through."

"I don't like being arrested," said Paul angrily.

"I would have thought you were used to it by now?" interjected Betty. "Let's see, I've met you three times, and each time has had the police involved. Those aren't very good odds, are they Mr. Cousins?"

"No, but…oh, never mind. Let's get these papers signed. Would ya'll mind if I take off the rest of my gorilla suit?"

"As long as you're not naked underneath," said Betty.

"Yeah, I've got clothes on," said Paul as he pulled his gorilla body off. Sweat was pouring from his whole body, and the sweaty smell of gorilla funk permeated the office.

"Good god, you stink," said Carlos.

"Stop complaining." Paul signed his name a hundred times on all the documents and reached out to shake Mr. Burton's hand.

"It's always a pleasure doing a closing for you, Mr. Cousins. I can't wait to see what you bring to the table next time."

"I'm not sure there's gonna be a next time," said Paul.

"Why, are you going to jail or something?" asked Betty.

"Maybe, I may kill someone when we get home," said Paul glaring at Carlos.

"Lighten up, man. I've got a whole new plan for us," said Carlos.

"Now this I can't wait to hear," said Paul sarcastically. "Let's go home."

"You mean to *my* home."

Paul carried his gorilla suit under his arms and threw it in the back of Carlos's pickup truck. The reality of being homeless finally hit Paul. He had to rely on someone else for shelter for the first time since he was a teenager. On the way to Carlos's house, Paul reflected on the roller coaster he had been on the last 18 months.

"Carlos, I had it all. I had the dream life, and it disappeared in a matter of days. I have less now than when I started with Bio Strength. I'm beginning to wish I had never even tried."

"Don't be a fool," began Carlos. "You had a blast, man. You got to jam with Van Halen. How many people can say that? And look at the wonderful people you met. Look at the lessons you learned from your mistakes. You had a dream Paul, and you made it happen. If you did it once, I know you can do it again."

Carlos was enjoying having his two new roommates Ernie and Paul since they did all the cooking and cleaning. Ernie was still unemployed, and Paul had moved on from his job as a street gorilla. He found a job as a bagboy at a local supermarket, and his boss was 18 years old. Paul just had to suck it up and realize that no honest work is demeaning. It paid very little, but it was a job.

"The job market sucks right now," complained Ernie as he and Paul cleaned up after dinner. "Nobody is hiring."

"The grocery store is," said Paul. "As long as you don't mind bagging groceries and having an acne-faced teenager for a boss."

"Did you guys hear about the charges brought against Bo Valentine and the CEO of Bio Strength?" asked Carlos.

"No, what happened?"

"Both of them are facing federal charges of fraud. And that's on top of huge fines from the FDA for putting steroids in the products."

"Do you think Bo knew about the steroids?" asked Paul.

"Hell, yeah. He had to know. He was too high up not to know. But he's already professing his innocence. His wife is divorcing him. She better hurry because that dude is already trying to hide money I bet."

"He was so full of it," said Paul. "I hope he goes to jail for a *loooong* time."

"He deserves to," said Carlos. "Not everybody in network marketin' is a crook. I've still got checks comin' in from four companies I've been in for years. They are all good, legitimate companies."

"You're the exception to the rule," said Ernie. "Most people don't last as long as you have in the business. What is your secret, anyway?"

"Ain't no secret to it. I just tried to find people who were bored. You can't go around blabbin' about your new business to every person you meet. You'll really piss off your friends and family doin' that. I learned that the hard way."

"Well, I'm done with network marketing," said Paul.

"Paul, you just got with the wrong company. What if there hadn't been steroids in Bio Strength? Would you still be in that mansion with all those toys?"

"Probably, yeah," said Paul.

"So, network marketing can work, right?"

"Yeah, but I lost my shirt."

"You also lived like there was no tomorrow, but I won't beat that dead horse again."

"I know, I know. I spent too much too fast."

"Guys, I know you both are not hip on network marketin'right now, but look at me. I'm still goin'at it after 20 years. I'm gettin' paid on other people's sales that I've never met and never will. Without some kind of residual income, you'll be tied to a paycheck the rest of your life. People that create things can earn money for years. That's what insurance guys do. They get paid renewal commissions every time customers make a payment. And Paul, you'll never pay off your tax debts dressin' like a gorilla or baggin' groceries."

"Uh oh, here it comes, Ernie."

"Guys, I've come across the most unique sellin' plan I've ever seen. I've been in this business over 20 years, and this one could replace all the income I'm making with four different companies now. This one truly is a ground-floor opportunity. I hate using that cliché, but it really is."

"The suspense is killing us," said Paul. "What is it?"

"It's called Number One."

"Never heard of it," said Ernie.

"Me, neither," said Paul.

"That's good. That just means it's a new well-kept secret. It won't be for long. Their goal is to be the number one network marketin' company in the world. And here's the best thing about 'em. Get this….they don't sell any products themselves."

"What do they sell then?" asked Paul.

"Memberships. You buy a lifetime membership and you get discounts on all sortsa things. It's kinda like combinin' Costco and network marketin'. They've got agreements for special pricin' with all kindsa retailers. You get great deals on things like cruises, hotels, and electronics. It's really a one stop shop. You pay your one-time membership fee of $1,999, and you get access to discounts that the ordinary person would never get. The biggest savins' is with a national builder. If you sign a contract for them to build your home, you save 20 percent on materials. That's huge."

"Have you signed up yet?" asked Paul.

"Two weeks ago. I didn't wanna tell you guys about it until I had a chance to try it out myself. I've already got four people signed up, and I've made my money back already. You get paid $1,000 for each new distributor who signs up, so I've already made two thousand dollars profit in my first two weeks. And I haven't even bought anything yet."

"Are there any requirements that you buy a certain amount each month?" asked Ernie.

"Nope. I couldn't believe that either. Most companies require a certain amount of volume to qualify for your paycheck. Number One has no monthly requirements. I'm telling ya, this is the one I've been waitin' for all these years. Two grand cleared in two weeks is unheard of in this business. And the savins' is gravy. You'll be savin' money on things you'd be buyin' anyway. If you guys sign up, I promise you you'll make all your money back in a month or less. I'll see to that."

"There's only one problem, Carlos," said Paul.

"What's that?"

"I don't have $2,000."

"I don't either," said Ernie. "Marlo would kill me if I did this. It sounds good, believe me. But I don't have that kind of money to burn."

"I figured you guys would say that, so here's what I'm gonna do for you. If you each give me $200, I'll pay the rest of your membership. Then you can pay me back the other $1,800 after you make your first two sign-ups. All you gotta do to break even is sign up two people. Hell, even Ernie could do that."

"Thanks, Carlos."

"Oh, you know what I mean. This is so simple anyone can do it," said Carlos.

"Are you paying for other peoples' memberships like you're doing with us?"

"Hell, no. I really thought hard about this, and I'll never offer to pay for someone's fee again. And don't ya'll do it, either. I just am so certain this will work for ya'll. You really need the money more than I do. I felt that I'd be doin' you an injustice if I didn't tell you about it."

"Why don't they offer a payment plan like two easy payments of $99 and one hard-as-shit payment of $1,800?" asked Paul.

"Good question. They figured out that most people would put it on their credit card anyway. I guess they didn't want the hassle of keeping track of who paid what."

"So the emphasis is really on recruiting and not the savings," asked Paul.

"Right. But most people will save money in the long run even if they never recruit a soul," said Carlos. "So what do ya say?"

Ernie and Paul looked at each other waiting for the other to make a move.

"I can't believe I'm doing this, but it's only because I trust you, Carlos," said Paul.

"Okay, I've got 200 to spare," said Ernie. "But I better sign two people up. I don't want to end up owing you money."

"Congratulations, gentlemen. Let me get some beers to celebrate. Why don't we go for a little walk and strategize some. It's beautiful outside."

Just then the doorbell rang, and Carlos peered through his peep hole and saw no one. "Must be some kids playin' ding n' ditch again he thought," as he opened the door.

Standing on the front stoop with a huge grin on her face was none other than Miss Ellie.

"Miss Ellie! Boy, are we glad to see you. We've got some ol' friends of yours here," said Carlos.

"Lordy, is that Paul? Goodness gracious, come give this little old lady a hug. I *sho'* have missed you," she said as Paul gave her a hug.

"You look fantastic today," said Paul. "Is that a new dress?"

"Uh-huh. I just came from church. I been so worried 'bout you since Bio Strength closed. I don't care if they had steroids in 'em, that stuff really helped me."

"I know. But Carlos just told us about a new opportunity that should be even better than Bio Strength."

"You mean 'bout Number One?"

"Yes! How did you hear about them?"

"Carlos tol' me 'bout 'em. I got me a good little tax refund and some rainy day money, and I'm all in."

"That's fantastic," said Paul. "It's gonna be great to work with you again. You were always an inspiration."

"She's also gonna be your upline," said Carlos. "I'm gonna sign both of you up under her. Meet your new upline, gentlemen, Miss Ellie Washington."

Miss Ellie stood proudly with a smug grin on her face. "Don't you worry, boys. I'm gonna treat ya'll just fine."

"Well, this calls for another beer. Miss Ellie, can I get you one?" asked Paul smiling.

"Heck, yeah. It might be Sunday, but one beer never hurt nobody."

Paul, Ernie, and Carlos, and Ellie walked down Carlos's shady tree-lined street on a beautiful Florida afternoon. Paul kick started his imagination again. He was already visualizing his next mansion. This time it was on the ocean.

"You know Paul, you've got a natural market of your former Bio Strength downline," said Carlos. "I'll bet you can get most of them to follow you."

"I didn't think about that," said Paul excitedly.

"It's a standard method in network marketin'. When one company busts, just take your downline with you. They all believe in you, so you have a captive audience."

"Here's to our new partnership," said Paul raising his beer to Ellie, Ernie and Carlos. The four of them clinked their bottles together in unison.

"We're gonna make it big again," said Paul. "I can just feel it."

About the Author

Dan Sizemore graduated from Virginia Tech in 1982 with a degree in Political Science. He attended The National Center for Paralegal Training in Atlanta, GA and upon graduation became a legal assistant with the Allen & Allen law firm in Richmond, Va. He then began a new career in insurance sales and started his own Nationwide Insurance Agency in Richmond. It was during his insurance career that he became exposed to the bewildering world of network marketing. Dan dove head first into network marketing with little idea of exactly what he was jumping into. After three years and many thousands of dollars spent, he finally saw the light and hung it up.

But alas! Dan figured there had to be literally millions of others who had similar experiences with network marketing. He set out to write a story that tells what it is like to be a network marketer, and The Money Maker was born.

If you have an interesting personal story about your experiences in network marketing, Dan would love to hear from you. Contact him at www.dansizemore.com or dansizemore@comcast.net.

Dan currently resides in Jacksonville, Florida with his wife and two daughters.

www.ingramcontent.com/pod-product-compliance
Lightning Source LLC
LaVergne TN
LVHW051622080426
835511LV00016B/2123